John De Soyres

Montanism and the Primitive Church

a study in the ecclesiastical history of the second century

John De Soyres

Montanism and the Primitive Church
a study in the ecclesiastical history of the second century

ISBN/EAN: 9783337262815

Printed in Europe, USA, Canada, Australia, Japan

Cover: Foto ©Lupo / pixelio.de

More available books at **www.hansebooks.com**

MONTANISM

AND

THE PRIMITIVE CHURCH

A STUDY IN THE ECCLESIASTICAL HISTORY
OF THE SECOND CENTURY.

THE HULSEAN PRIZE ESSAY, 1877.

BY

JOHN DE SOYRES,
OF GONVILLE AND CAIUS COLLEGE, CAMBRIDGE.

"Ubi Spiritus Dei, illic Ecclesia."
    IRENAEUS (*adv. Haer.* IV. 31. 3).

CAMBRIDGE:
DEIGHTON, BELL, AND CO.
LONDON: GEORGE BELL AND SONS.
1878

Cambridge:
PRINTED BY C. J. CLAY, M.A.
AT THE UNIVERSITY PRESS.

DEDICATED TO

ARCHDEACON ALLEN,

WITH THE WARMEST FEELINGS OF AFFECTION
AND RESPECT.

"Δεῖ γὰρ καὶ αἱρέσεις ἐν ὑμῖν εἶναι, ἵνα οἱ δόκιμοι φανεροὶ γένωνται ἐν ὑμῖν."
1 Cor. xi. 19.

"Now, because Faith is not only a precept of doctrines, but of manners and holy life, whatsoever is either opposite to an article of creed, or teaches ill life, That Is Heresy: but all those propositions which are extrinsical to these two considerations, be they true or be they false, make not heresy, nor the man a heretic."
TAYLOR, *Liberty of Prophesying.*

"Heresy and Schism, as they are in common use, are two theological Μορμώς, or scarecrows, which they who uphold a party in religion use to fright away such as, making enquiry into it, are ready to relinquish and oppose, if it appear either erroneous or suspicious. But howsoever in the common manage, heresy and schism are but ridiculous terms, yet the things in themselves are of very considerable moment; the one offending against truth, the other against charity; and therefore both deadly, where they are not by imputation only, but in deed."
THE 'EVER-MEMORABLE' JOHN HALES OF ETON.

"Quodsi mihi fortasse contingat, ut aliter sentiam quàm plerique ....sentiendum judicent, veniam mihi dari postulo, qui sine pruritu lacessendi Patres, (quos alioquin merito magnifacio,) sine insano studio pravorum hominum errores excusandi, cum tanto temporum intervallo a Montanistis remotus sim, ut nullo commodo meo ad eorum partes tuendas adducar, sine libidine novum aliquid comminiscendi, ex eoque gloriam aucupandi, nihil aliud quæro, quam indagare verum."
WERNSDORF, *de Montanistis.*

TABLE OF CONTENTS.

INTRODUCTION. Materials and arrangement. List of authorities consulted 1

BOOK I.

ERRATA.

Page 19, line 22, *for* "1834" *read* "1832."
,, 82, ,, 13, *for* "M. Aurelius" *read* "Severus."
,, 105. *Dele* Note.

BOOK II.
The Tenets of Montanism.

Section 1. General remarks on the evidence 55
,, 2. The character of the new revelation 58
,, 3. Tertullian's views on the Trinity, and the charge of Sabellianism : 68
      a. Monarchianism and Subordinationism.
      b. The Montanistic Trinity.
,, 4. The Montanistic Eschatology 77
,, 5. Asceticism 79
,, 6. Marriage 83
,, 7. Penance 86
,, 8. The Church 91
,, 9. Sacraments and ritual 96
,, 10. Historical position of Montanism . . . 102
,, 11. Montanism and Gnosticism 104
,, 12. Summary 107

TABLE OF CONTENTS.

INTRODUCTION. Materials and arrangement. List of authorities consulted 1

BOOK I.
History of Montanus and his followers.

Section 1. The chronology of the party 25
,, 2. Names and nicknames 29
,, 3. Montanus 31
,, 4. The prophetesses and the disciples . . 34
,, 5. Progress of the opinions in Asia Minor . . 36
,, 6. ,, ,, Rome . . . 37
,, 7. ,, ,, Africa. . . 44
,, 8. Tertullian 45
,, 9. The assailants of Montanism . . . 47
,, 10. Decisions of Councils 51
,, 11. Decline and gradual extinction of the party . 53

BOOK II.
The Tenets of Montanism.

Section 1. General remarks on the evidence . . . 55
,, 2. The character of the new revelation . . . 58
,, 3. Tertullian's views on the Trinity, and the charge of Sabellianism : 68
    a. Monarchianism and Subordinationism.
    b. The Montanistic Trinity.
,, 4. The Montanistic Eschatology 77
,, 5. Asceticism 79
,, 6. Marriage 83
,, 7. Penance . 86
,, 8. The Church . . . 91
,, 9. Sacraments and ritual . . 96
,, 10. Historical position of Montanism . 102
,, 11. Montanism and Gnosticism . 104
,, 12. Summary . . 107

BOOK III.

The Influence of Montanism upon the Church.

		PAGE
Section 1.	Revolution and reaction	110
,, 2.	Points of cohesion	112
,, 3.	Reasons for rejection	113
,, 4.	Extent of influence	116
,, 5.	Later manifestations	118
,, 6.	Conclusion	130

Appendix A.	Kestner's *Agape*	134
Appendix B.	Perpetua and Felicitas	138
Appendix C.	Jane Lead, Petersen, &c.	142
Appendix D.	Swedenborg	153
Appendix E.	Chronological Tables (A.D. 130—250)	158

INTRODUCTION.

IF it has been said with truth that a perfect historian of secular events will never be found, how much less hope can we entertain that the vast field of ecclesiastical history will ever find a really successful explorer! If historians of Greece and Rome cannot banish the political prejudices of modern times while busied with the past, is it to be wondered at that those who examine the religious questions which agitated the early Church, perceive in them the mirror of later controversies, and deal with them in a congenial spirit? It would seem that the two essentials, knowledge and impartiality, are rarely to be found together unimpaired. The mature scholar has acquired deep convictions as well as profound acquaintance with his subject, and all his conscientious striving after a perfect objectivity of treatment fails to attain success. The beginner, possessed indeed of all the impartiality which ignorance can grant, finds himself compelled to attain first, by long and painful industry, a knowledge of the instruments of research, before he can profit by them,—or is driven to the easy and worthless dependence on interested advocates and second-hand erudition[1]. It is acknowledged on all hands that it needs half a lifetime to acquire a sufficient knowledge of patristic language, rhetoric, and logic, without

[1] Baur, in his fierce onslaught upon Thiersch (*Der Kritiker u. der Fanatiker*, 1846), contemptuously notes that the latter had only bestowed eight years on the study of Irenæus!

which the student is at the mercy of all the arbitrary (and contradictory) catenas which can be manufactured to prove anything and everything. Accordingly the prospect that a tyro in the great science of theology could do more than gather together and coördinate the researches of previous explorers is small indeed, and the writer of the present essay aims only at amassing some " Materials for a Critical History of Montanism," and will find his hopes fully gratified should he succeed in the attempt. It might seem, at first sight, as if the subject was of a character to limit the number and character of the obstacles. The history of a heresy which only emerged into notice for less than a century, which concerned practical rather than theological or metaphysical questions, and which is treated of by but few out of the great army of ecclesiastical writers,—ought not to involve very excessive difficulty or research. But almost the next glance, and certainly the first examination, reveal the falsity of such a supposition. It is found that the chronology of the period has been, ever since history was written, the subject of the most contradictory hypotheses; that the statements of the witnesses are of the most partial and conflicting character; and that the questions as to the origin of the heresy, and its ultimate influence upon the Christian Church, involve a consideration of many important ecclesiastical controversies. And when the student has worked through his materials, and has studied not merely the text but the context of his subject, his difficulty is enhanced a hundredfold by the conviction which is forced irresistibly upon his mind. It flashes upon him, namely, that the religious upheaval known as Montanism is no isolated phenomenon, no product of one man's invention, but the first of a vast series of manifestations, which, fraught with good and with evil, have been permitted by Providence to break forth in the Christian Church. He sees the same forces at work, the same reaction, the same results, in the Cathari and Waldenses of the Middle Ages; the Fraticelli and the " Homines Intelligentiæ;" in the Anabaptist sects of the Reformation; in the marvellous speculations of Jacob Boehme; in the wonderful spiritual revivals of the 17th century, Fox and the Quakers in England, Saint Cyran and Labadie in France and Holland, the Alombrados in Spain, Molinos in Italy, Spener and Petersen in Germany. He recognises a deep truth in Bossuet's taunt against his great adversary, "that the new Priscilla had found a new Montanus," for he feels that the same influences directed Madame Guyon and the Archbishop of Cambrai in their ill-fated endeavour to revive the expiring embers of spiritual religion. In the next century, he sees the same forces at work in the great Pietist movement in Germany, while its abuses are shewn in the follies of the Illuminaten-Orden. Swedenborg with his vast theosophic system simply gives form and definition to the revelations of the Phrygian prophets sixteen centuries before[1]. Edward Irving in more recent times completes the list of parallels with his prophets, his unknown tongues, and his passionate revolt against the formalism of a callous age.

Such a historical vista is indeed calculated to appal the writer, and to cause him to shrink from the task before him. It would need the imagination and the receptive faculty of a Coleridge, added to the acumen of a Thirlwall, to do the barest justice to this enormous and as yet uncultivated field. But the purposes of the following essay do not require the prosecution of so hopeless a quest. It is enough to have recognised the true horizon, and to take one's observations by the real luminaries: as for the rest, an analysis of one link in a great chain will be the best help for a later comprehension of its extent and its agency.

Before proceeding to enumerate and classify the historical materials at our disposal, it is necessary to state the reasons which have induced me to depart from

[1] As to the points of contact between Montanism and Swedenborgianism, see Appendix D.

the ordinary methods of arrangement. Ever since history has been regarded and dealt with as a science, the chaotic plan which once obtained of mingling together, in one perplexing heap, external and internal narrative, the statements of fact and the analysis of opinion, has been completely abandoned. But it is at least an open question whether the methods which the new historical schools have adopted, have not almost equally serious defects. Instead of working steadily *from* the solid facts of history, there is a marked tendency to reverse the process, and to employ these facts merely as the buttresses for a previously constructed theory. Now it may be very allowable for the astronomer or the physiologist to elaborate a theory from an ingenious conjecture, and then to submit it to repeated tests of the telescope or microscope; but the system when applied to historical research is by no means so advantageous. There is an elasticity in historical facts, especially (of course) when one is dealing with ancient history, which enables even the most conscientious writer to shape them to his purpose. Möhler finds the Papacy in the records of the Primitive Church; Bishop Browne the Anglican system; somebody else, with equal candour and learning, Presbyterianism. I do not say that differences would cease if a more strictly inductive method were adopted, but I feel convinced that some theories would never have been committed to print. The two most recent writers on Montanism, Schwegler and Ritschl, not only practise this dangerous method, but take credit for so doing[1]. In the first case, we may venture without presumption to conjecture that, had Dr Schwegler reversed

---

[1] Schwegler puts the history into the last (third) book of his essay, "weil zwar die beiden ersten Haupttheile ohne den dritten verständlich und zusammenhängend sind, der dritte aber nicht ohne die Voraussetzung der zwei andern" (p. 13). Ritschl prefaces his account, also placed last, with the words :—"Es ist nur der Zweck, die zerstreuten und spärlichen Notizen über die Geschichte des Montanismus in der Kirche zu sammeln, um die vorausgehende Darstellung zu bestätigen" (p. 525).

his plan, he might neither have abolished the personality of Montanus, nor have concocted the extraordinary theory of the Ebionitic origin of Montanism, which provoked a criticism from the patriarch of the Tübingen school himself[1].

The present writer wishes to observe a more humble and prudent method. It will be his aim, in the following essay, to begin by collecting and analysing all the records that have come down to us in relation to the external history of Montanism. Next in order comes an examination into the Tenets of Montanism, and lastly the attempt to distinguish its true historical position, and its ultimate influence upon the Church.

The materials for the work are, in their extent and character, precisely what we find in the case of nearly all obscure departments of history. They are obscure, not less on account of the paucity of original evidence, than from the plethora of subsequent conjecture. The witnesses before the court are few enough, and some of them do not survive cross-examination; but the number of counsel and "amici curiæ" is so vast, that the juryman, wearied by the alternate eloquence of bigotry and paradox, frankly declares himself more puzzled after the learned explanations than before them[2].

First of all, if not in chronology, yet in all other respects, stands Tertullian. Until the seventeenth century he was the only writer in whose pages the prophets of Phrygia appeared in any light but that of fanatics, heretics, and criminals. He is a favourable witness, but the testimonies as well as the controversies of ancient and

---

[1] See Baur's articles in the *Theol. Jahrbücher* of 1851, the substance of which was subsequently incorporated (1853) in his *Christenthum der 3 ersten Jahrhunderte*.

[2] "Hoc commentario lecto, multo incertior sum quam dudum," observes Wernsdorf after reading the notes of the scholiast Balsamon. This, by the way, was only an unconscious paraphrase of Locke's rather irreverent remark upon Biblical commentators in general, itself deriving its origin from Terence (*Phorm.* 459).

6   INTRODUCTION.

INTRODUC- modern times, prove his value to be supreme. It is well
TION.
known that the question as to the period of his lapse to
Montanism is still disputed, although (as will be shewn
subsequently) the controversy has now reached very
narrow limits. It will be necessary, in the course of the
preliminary historical examination, to arrive at distinct
conclusions upon the dates and character of his works,
before quoting them in a later chapter as documents in
the case[1].*

Auctores   Next only in importance, and possibly earlier in date,
ap. Euse-
bium.   come the writers quoted so largely by Eusebius in his
Ecclesiastical History. They are at once the chief witnesses and counsel for the prosecution, and they evince
one and all the thorough detestation of a supposed heretic,
and the readiness to believe anything evil of him, so characteristic of this and many later ages. Neither the
anonymous author of the first book cited[2], nor Apollonius,
nor Serapion, quoted in later chapters[3], attempts to furnish
any complete account of the rise and progress of the sect;
the facts mentioned are vague in the extreme, and nothing
Irenæus. is unquestionable except the animus. Irenæus, although
he lived through the period of the spread and influence of

[1] There is another controversy connected with Tertullian's relation
to Montanism which is discussed in the second book (cf. § 1). This
is the question as to how far his writings present to us Montanistic
tenets pure and simple, and without any colouring from Tertullian's
individual opinions.

* This resolution the writer was compelled to abandon, adopting the
results of Uhlhorn, [*Fund. Chron. Tertull.*]

[2] Supposed by many (Valois, Tillemont, Longerue, Dodwell, Baumgarten-Crusius and Rothe) to have been Asterius Urbanus. Jerome
varies between Rhodon and Apollonius [cf. *de Vir. Illustr.* 37 and 40].
All turns upon the interpretation of the words used by Eusebius—ἐν
τῷ αὐτῷ λόγῳ τῷ κατὰ ᾿Αστέριον Οὐρβανὸν—(*H. E.* lib. v. cap. 16). Rufinus
and Nicephorus declared for Apollinaris, but this seems inadmissible.
Probably, as Schwegler thinks, Eusebius himself was ignorant (*Montanismus*, p. 286).

[3] For what is known of these writers, see *infra*, Book I. § 6. The
quotations from the Anonymous take up the 16th and 17th chapters.
The 18th contains the account of Apollonius, and the following a brief
mention of Serapion's writings.

Montanism, makes only some doubtful references to it in his work against heresies. It has indeed been contested whether the passages in question (*Adv. Hær.* III. 11. 9, IV. 33. 1, II. 32. 4) have in reality a polemical application to the Montanist prophecies, and the ingenious Dr Schwegler is half inclined to claim Irenæus as a Montanist altogether[1]! But one of the passages in question, to which we shall recur later, can have but one natural and reasonable interpretation, viz. as referring to the Montanists.

Introduction.

Hippolytus, thanks to the discovery of the *Philosophumena* in 1842, is a more important witness. Although his career is even now very obscure, we may infer with some confidence that he was born in the second half of the second century, studied under Irenæus, strongly approved of Bishop Victor's severe measures with regard to the Easter-question, but came into antagonism with Zephyrinus and Kallistus on certain points of doctrine and discipline. He wrote his work *Against all Heresies* early in the third century,—say from A.D. 210—220, or even a little later[2].

Hippolytus.

Next in order of chronology is Firmilian, whose epistle to Cyprian has been long an effective weapon in the anti-Papal armoury. He was Bishop of Cæsarea in Cappadocia, and was a great friend of Origen. He unites with some rather vague charges against the teachings of Montanism an important statement as to the position assumed towards the party by the Eastern Churches[3].

Firmilian.

In Cyprian's epistles we find more than one reference

Cyprian.

---

[1] "Seine Ansichten vom Prophetengeiste, sein Chiliasmus, seine Verwerfung der zweiten Ehe, seine praktisch-ascetischen Grundsätze überhaupt, nur diess Alles mit mehr Besonnenheit vorgetragen, lassen seine Verwandtschaft mit dem montanistischen Systeme nicht verkennen." (*Der Montanismus u. die chr. Kirche*, p. 223, note). See *infra*, Book III. § 1, and notes.

[2] Baur believed that the *Philosophumena* were written by the Presbyter Caius.

[3] See Cyprian's Epistles, No. 75.

8   INTRODUCTION.

Introduction. to Montanism as an existent sect, but the pupil of Tertullian who for ever exclaimed "Da magistrum!" would not express openly his objections to a party many of whose opinions he had adopted. [E.g. strong belief in visions, severity on penance, &c.]

Pacian. Pacian, bishop of Barcelona, whose history is very uncertain, inaugurates the list of "hear-say" witnesses[1].

Eusebius. Eusebius probably wrote in the years 338-9, and apart from his quotations from early anti-Montanistic writers (already mentioned) gives us but scanty information. On the point whether the party was still in existence in his own time, he is silent. Far more considerable in volume *Epiphanius.* is the contribution of Epiphanius, written about the year 374. The 48th Heresy in his capacious catalogue is that of Montanus, and in the course of his lengthy dissertation he communicates much valuable information as to the utterances of the prophetesses, interspersed however with an inordinate proportion of homiletical comment. If Eusebius is wanting in the historical sense and method, what shall we say of his successor? Carelessness and inaccuracy in his dates and statements of fact, which frequently contradict one another[2]; ignorance even of his own subject so complete that he includes heathen philosophy among Christian heresies; yet this is the founda-

[1] Pacian is an important witness as proving the opposition of the Western Church to the Montanistic doctrine of penance, which no other writer mentions. [E. g. "So manifold and so diverse are the errors of these men, that in them we have not only to overthrow their peculiar fancies against penance, but to cut off the heads as it were of some Lernæan monster...... How manifold controversies have they raised concerning...... as this also concerning the pardon of penance." *Ep. ad Symphr.* transl. in "Libr. of Fathers."] But the good bishop makes one very comic blunder in including Praxeas among the Montanists.

[2] We shall find, when dealing with the chronology of Montanism, that Epiphanius gives two dates for its commencement, and fixes the death of Maximilla in the year 86, when she was not yet born. Hefele conjectures (*Conciliengeschichte*, I. 71) that this is a clerical error for 186, which is possible. See Lipsius, *Quellenkritik des Epiphanios:* "seine sprüchwörtlich gewordene Leichtgläubigkeit, seine unkritische Willkür in der Benutzung und Verwendung der Stoffe, u. s. w." (Einleitung).

tion upon which the accounts in the majority of popular histories are based.

It will not be necessary to enumerate the Fathers in whose writings are found chance allusions to Montanism[1]. Athanasius was too much occupied with another heresy to be able to spare time for condemning the Montanists, and it is characteristic that the only mention in his genuine works is by way of parallel to the Arians, who are accused of substituting the Emperor's authority (i.e. Constantius) for that of Christ "ὥσπερ ἐκεῖνοι Μαξίμιλλαν καὶ Μοντανόν[2]."

In Cyril of Jerusalem we find a series of denunciations, so serious as to the nature of the charges, and so passionately unreasonable in their manner, that it is necessary to remind ourselves that the "Catechetical Lectures" were delivered when Cyril was but a young man[3]. Gregory of Nazianzus, theologian, orator, and poet, is the first to state rhetorically the ground upon which the Church, in later times, grounded its final anathema on Montanism. Opposed to the Holy Ghost, the true Paraclete, was "τὸ Μοντανοῦ πονηρὸν Πνεῦμα," and hence it easily followed that a baptism, in which the Holy Spirit took no part, could

[1] For instance, in Clemens Alexandrinus (*Strom.* IV. 13, ap. Migne, *Patrol. Græca*, tom. VIII.), who records the nickname ψυχικοί bestowed by the Montanists on their opponents. But the passage—"ταῦτα (sc. idolatrous rites) οἱ Φρύγες τελίσκουσιν Ἄττιδι καὶ Κυβέλῃ καὶ Κορύβασιν" (*Coh. ad Gentes*, cap. II.)—even if written by Clement, can only refer to the Phrygian race. Origen has a solitary reference, to be found in the Apology of Pamphilus:—"Requisierunt sane quidam utrum hæresin an schisma oportet vocari eos qui Cataphrygæ vocantur, observantes falsos prophetas, et dicentes: Ne accedas ad me, quoniam mundus sum: non enim accepi uxorem, nec est sepulcrum patens guttur meum, sed sum Nazaræus Dei, non bibens vinum sicut illi." What Origen's real opinion of Montanism may have been, can hardly be inferred from this passage.

[2] *Epistola de Synodis* (Migne, *Patr. Græca*, XXVI. 688). In the spurious *Synopsis S. Script.* lib. XI. (Migne, XXVIII. 352), we have "οἱ κατὰ Φρύγας παρεισάγοντες προφήτας μετὰ τὸν Κύριον σφάλλονται, καὶ ὡς αἱρετικοὶ κατεκρίθησαν." The equally spurious "Sermo contra omnes Hæreses" describes the opinions as "γρεῶν πτύσματα ἴσως ὡς κεκεπρωμένων" (Migne, XXVIII. 520).

[3] Migne, *Patr. Græca*, XXXIII. 928, and transl. in "Library of the Fathers."

not be regarded as valid. The same idea appears in Gregory's poems[1].

Rather earlier in date, perhaps, than the before-mentioned, comes Didymus Alexandrinus, a staunch champion of orthodoxy against Arianism, which did not prevent him from being finally condemned by the second Nicæan Synod on a charge of Origenistic heresy. In his writings we find a charge of formal error, on the part of the Montanists, with regard to the doctrine of the Trinity[2].

Ambrose[3], Hilary[4], Philaster[5] contribute small shreds of evidence, of course mere tradition, but still, in default of better materials, deserving of careful examination. The last named repeats the atrocious accusations of Cyril, and affords a convenient opportunity for a few words on the character of his historical method, and his credibility as a witness. Notwithstanding the high praise which Augustine (*De Hæres.* cap. 58) has lavished upon him, Philaster cannot be ranked highly. His critical powers may be not unjustly estimated by the fact that he places the Caïnites and Ophites before the Christian era, because he finds traces of Old Testament history in their schemes! He considers it mortal heresy to doubt the Pauline authorship of the Epistle to the Hebrews. Now I wish to disclaim most strongly any desire to speak disrespectfully

---

[1] *Orat.* IV. *Contra Julianum*, and XXII. *De Pace* (Migne, *Series Græca*, XXXV.). See also *Poëmata*, lib. II., "Οἱ Μοντανοῦ τὸ πνεῦμα τιμῶντες κακῶς."

[2] Migne, *S. G.* XXXIX. 720.

[3] *Comment. in Ep. ad Thess.* I. 22 (Migne, XVII. 453). And there is a reference of a somewhat rhetorical order in the 46th sermon, *De Salomone* (ibid. p. 697).

[4] "Hinc et Montanus per insanas feminas suas Paracletum alium defendit."

[5] What Epiphanius had done for the Greek Church, Philaster attempted for the Latin. He wrote about 10 years after his model, whom he certainly used. Montanism is the 49th of the list of heresies (Migne, XII. 1165, 1166), of which there are, thanks to his search, no less than 156, viz. 28 before Christ, and 128 subsequently. The whole subject has been exhaustively treated by Lipsius, in his *Quellenkritik des Epiphanios*, and his *Quellen der ältesten Ketzergeschichte neu untersucht*.

of writers with whose works I have naturally but a small acquaintance. The horde of scribblers in the last century who were enabled to derive from Daillé and Barbeyrac the materials for cheap criticism, discovered in themselves a lower literary depth than that of any Byzantine annalist. And when we find (as I shall have occasion later to point out) a professed contemner of the Fathers guilty of an "economy" in his quotations from Tertullian which cannot be excused by ignorance, we must admit that the blame due to bigotry and deceit must not be bestowed solely upon the early ecclesiastical writers. Still, it is true that a very stringent caution is needed before we accept the statements even of so celebrated a writer as Jerome. The confessed, even boasted, theory of Economies, remains for ever a source of exultation to the enemies of Christianity, and of bitter shame and grief to her friends[1]. And the critical student will not fail to see, as he wades through the pages of Epiphanius or Philaster, how true in substance was the remark of Daillé: "When the Fathers contend with the Valentinians or the Manichæans, they seem to hold the doctrines of Pelagius; but if with the Pelagians, their language is Manichæan: are they striving against the Arians, their arguments are Sabellian, but if against Sabellius, they are at least Semi-Arian[2]." Perhaps a

---

[1] Ribovius (Ribow), a professor of Göttingen at the beginning of the last century, left a treatise on this subject (*De Oeconomia Patrum*), which appears to have been originally delivered as a show-discourse, upon the occasion of a visit from George II.! In this "Black Book,"— for it is far more damaging than the *l'Employ des Pères*, we find the following summing up:—"Integrum omnino Doctoribus et cœtus Christiani antistitibus, esse, ut dolos versent, falsa veris intermisceant, et imprimis religionis hostes fallant, dummodo veritatis commodis et utilitati inserviant." Of his quotations, the most startling is one from Jerome, which is also quoted by Lessing in one of the Anti-Goeze pamphlets:—"Paulus in testimoniis quæ sumit de veteri testamento, quam artifex, quam prudens, quam dissimulator (!) est ejus quod agit."

[2] This was quoted from memory, but with the Latin text before me (Geneva, 1656, p. 147) the expressions are milder. It is "a Sabellio minus esse alicui videntur," and "ad Arium accedere videntur." And

fairer verdict is that delivered by a modern critic, who lays down that their historical standpoint was "to accept every statement that tended to edification[1]." Resuming our survey of the evidence, we find some mention of the latter stages of Montanism in the writings of Optatus Milevensis[2], and a repetition of Cyril's accusations in the epistles of Isidor of Pelusium[3]. The two next writers

the whole accusation is ascribed,—"ut animadvertit Episcopus Bitoutinus, de Augustino in primis."

[1] Schwegler, *Nachapost. Zeitalter*, I. 47: "alles glaublich zu finden, sobald es erbaulicher Natur ist." As to accuracy in detail, there is hardly any reliance to be placed on the writers of the 2nd and 3rd centuries. [See, for Justin Martyr, the list in Semisch's monograph, I. 224 ff.] Even of Tertullian we find the temperate Neander forced to remark: "Der unkritische, und wo er kein besonderes Interesse zu zweifeln hat, leichtgläubige T. ist freilich kein Zeuge von grosser Bedeutung." There is a remark of Schwegler's on the manner of quoting the Fathers which, much as I differ from his conclusions in general, seems to me to hit an unquestionable blot in popular apologetic literature. "Ein unpartheiischer Geschichtschreiber wird also, wenn er die ganze Wahrheit sagen will, nicht blos sagen dürfen, Irenäus bezeugt unsere 4 kanonischen Evangelien, sondern er wird beifügen müssen, sein historischer Beweis für ihre Vierheit ist die Vierheit der Weltgegenden und der Hauptwinde. Er wird nicht blos sagen dürfen: Tertullian bezeugt die Echtheit des Johanneischen Evangeliums, sondern er wird hinzufügen müssen,—derselbe Kirchenvater erzählt auch mit demselben Ernste und gleich festem Glauben die offenbarsten Fabeln über denselben Apostel, z. B. sein Römisches Oelmärtyrthum." (*Nachap. Zeitalter*, I. 50.) Of course it is obvious what all this means and intends, but still truth is truth, and the evidence of a witness who is not crossexamined does not carry overwhelming weight. One flaw in the reasoning of Dr Schwegler is that it proves too much: e. g. it would induce us to reject Bacon on every point, because he believed the earth was stationary. As to the matter of candour, Dr S. might have profited by his precepts when, in the same volume (I. 491) he included Calvin among those who reject utterly the 2nd Epistle of Peter, while in fact the great Reformer only admits doubts as to style, and places it in his Appendix. (See Calvin Soc. Edition, *Comm. on Cath. Epp.* p. 363.)

[2] *De schismate Donatistarum libri VII adversus Parmenianum.* Date doubtful.

[3] Born at Alexandria about middle of fourth century: took part in Cyril's controversies. Left about 2000 epistles on all subjects, of which Nos. 242—245 deal with Montanism, being addressed to Herminus. (See the Paris edition of 1638, I. p. 68.) Isidor talks confidently about

carry far more weight from their personal reputation, than from the substance of the information they give us. Jerome, in his commentary on St Matthew's Gospel, furnishes some details as to the extent of the fasts enjoined by the Montanists, and in one of the letters to Marcella we find a rather declamatory account of the party. In his brief memoirs of illustrious men are included the lives of certain writers against Montanism as well as that of Tertullian; but these, and the last in particular, are extremely superficial[1]. Even the great Bishop of Hippo seems to lose some of his matchless power when he assumes, in his single *Book of Heresies*, the painful office of ecclesiastical scavenger. But it is needless to say that the wild loose declamation, and the rambling hearsay, are conspicuous by their absence. He mentions, it is true, the most horrible of the charges, but without expressing any opinion of his own as to the value of the evidence upon which it was based[2].

The sparse allusions in Ambrosiaster[3], and Marius "adulteries, and the slaughter of children, and the worship of idols, and the possession by fierce demons," as prevailing notes of Montanism. His originality consists in discovering a bond of connection between this party and the Manichæans.

[1] Hieron. Comment. in Matth. ap. Migne, XXVI. 57. See also Ep. LXXV. Ad Marcellam, and the *De Viris Illustribus*, XXIV, XXXVII, XLIII, L, &c. The meagreness of the notice of Tertullian's life, considering Jerome's opportunities for collecting the available materials (cf. the *Catalogus scriptorum ecclesiasticorum*), induced, among other reasons, the amazing hypothesis of Semler, that Tertullian never existed, and that the writings attributed to him, together with those of Irenæus and Justin, were produced at a manufactory of apologetic literature, which he supposed to have flourished at a later time!

[2] *De Hæresibus ad Quodvultdeum liber unus*, in 6th vol. of Froben's ed. of 1542, p. 17. The comparison, in parallel columns, of the accounts of Philaster, Augustine, John of Damascus, and the writer of the "Prædestinatus," convincingly shews that each later writer used his predecessor, and considerably diminishes the cumulative force of the evidence when the accounts agree.

[3] Or the "Pseudo-Ambrosius," the author of a commentary on St Paul's epistles in the second volume of the works of Ambrose of Milan. (Ed. Benedict.) Written about 366—384. He occasionally alludes to the Montanists.

Mercator[1], may be briefly dismissed with a bare mention. Theodoret, however, gives us some valuable evidence, and the honesty with which he confesses some favourable points, gives additional weight to his condemnatory statements on the important question whether or not a branch of later Montanists adopted Sabellian tenets[2]. Last of all the ancient writers, comes Joannes Damascenus, a writer of the eighth century, who naturally can do no more than collate the evidence of his predecessors, although he introduces one or two assertions not met with elsewhere[3]. The genuineness of the book on heresies, called the *Prædestinatus*, has been a subject of too much controversy to enable me to place its writer (as I should be otherwise inclined) among the witnesses of the fifth century. It is clear that there was never an actual sect of Prædestinarians at that time, and equally clear that the book itself is the work of a Semi-Pelagian, who seeks with some ingenuity to damage his opponents by exaggerating their opinions. The book in question furnishes a catalogue of heresies in the style of Epiphanius, the imaginary "Prædestinati" being the last named, and the last but one the Nestorians. Under the 26th head, we have an account of the Montanists, remarkable not only for lucidity but for a studied impartiality of tone[4].*

---

[1] An inhabitant of southern Italy, who flourished in the first half of the fifth century, as we gather from an epistle addressed to Augustine, and a mention in another place of the Eutychian heresy. (*Opera omnia*, ed. Baluze, Par. 1684.)

[2] *Hæret. Fabular.* III. 2, ap. Migne, *Patrol. Græca*, LXXXIII. 401—404. Theodoret was chiefly engaged in the Nestorian controversy. († 457.)

[3] The last of the Greek Fathers, and the gallant defender of images against the iconoclasm of the Emperor Leo. (See his book on heresies, in Migne, XC. 705—708. The 48th Heresy is that of Montanism.) He asserts that the Montanists entrusted the priesthood to women; and as to the sacrifice, he thus improves on the former accounts: "Μυοῦνται δέ τινα κατακεντοῦντες νέον παῖδα ῥαφίσι χαλκαῖς, ὥσπερ οἱ Καταφρυγαστῶν, καὶ τῷ αἵματι αὐτοῦ ἄλευρον φυράσαντες καὶ ἀρτοποιήσαντες, προσφορὰν μεταλαμβάνουσι."

[4] The book is to be found in the tenth volume of Gallandi's *Bibliotheca Patrum*, pp. 366 ff. It was first edited by the learned Jesuit, Jac. Sir-

Passing to modern times, we find no particular im- Introduc-
provement with respect to historic method in the treat- tion.
ment by Baronius and the Magdeburg Centuriators. The Modern
                                                        Writers.
former[1] is naturally desirous to explain away the awkward Baronius,
statements of Tertullian about the recognition of Mon- Magd.
                                                       Centur.
tanism promulgated and then retracted by a Bishop of Tille-
Rome. Tillemont is laborious and avails himself of all mont.
materials, but whether he exercises sufficient judgment in
rejecting unsound statements, will be a matter for later
consideration. At the end of the 17th century two
learned Germans made valuable contributions to ecclesiastical history, and especially to the department of
heresiology. Thomas Ittig (1643—1710) recounted the Ittig.
history of Montanism with much learning and impartiality,
without the slightest tinge of that mania for "rehabilita-
tions" which has made some more recent monographs little
more trustworthy than the pious conjectures and tra-
ditions of a Cyril or a Pacian[2]. In his immediate contemporary, Gottfried Arnold, we find the first writer since Arnold.
Tertullian who places the history and doctrines of the
Montanists in a comparatively favourable light[3]. It is

mond, in the year 1643, a circumstance which caused a suspicion that it
had been manufactured to suit the then raging controversy between the
Jesuits, the Jansenists, and the Dominicans. [Cf. Routh: "Prædestinatus, quem librum *ambiguæ fidei* primus edidit Jac. Sirmondus." *Rel.
Sacr.* II. 378.] Neander believed that it was really written by an eccen-
tric Augustinian, but the internal evidence seems to point in the direction suggested above. See some valuable remarks by W. Möller in Herzog's *Real-Encyclopädie* (sub voce "Semi-Pelagianismus").

* I am now fully satisfied that Pr. can be accepted as a witness of the
fifth century.

[1] See especially Tom. II. p. 261 (ed. Lucæ, 1738). Ritschl points
out (p. 4) that the historians of Magdeburg were the first to recognise
the character of the new ecclesiastical constitution in the 2nd century.

[2] *De Hæresiarchis ævi Apostolici et Apost. proximi dissertatio* (Lips.
1690), Cap. XIII. pp. 219—254, and an Appendix.

[3] *Unpartheyische Kirchen- und Ketzer-Historien*, (Schaffhausen, 1740).
The mystical leanings of this writer led him to regard the Montanists
with especial favour, and he hints in more than one place at the final
verdict on them which has been only recently delivered by Ritschl and
Hilgenfeld. Arnold is in many ways a very interesting personage in

however obvious that Arnold's bias towards mysticism makes him partial in his judgments, and open to the same criticism as his predecessors, though from a different side. It is well, nevertheless, seeing the immense preponderance of voices on the unfavourable side, not to disregard the few which have, from time to time, been raised in defence of the purity and orthodoxy of the Montanists. First of the scientific historians comes Mosheim (1694—1755), who relates the history of the party not only in his narrative of the Events before Constantine, but also in his larger work[1]. It is unnecessary to say that this great writer deals with each portion of his subject with learning and every desire of impartiality, besides the advantage (then first introduced) of a scientific arrangement of his subject. But I am bound to state my honest conviction that Mosheim and his school were, by temperament and training, incapable of doing full justice to a manifestation like Montanism. Their minds were not able to give a "sympathetic" examination, (by which I am far from meaning a favourably partial one). All claims of spiritual insight and revelation become in their eyes mere fanaticism and lunacy. It is curious to compare their impressions of Montanism with those of some bigoted Ultramontane writer, and to mark how very similar are the results. Let us take, for the sake of brevity, the notice in Middleton's *Free Enquiry*, and also that in Gervaise's book, *L'histoire et la vie de S. Epiphane* (Paris, 1738):—

MIDDLETON. (I. 224.)	GERVAISE. (p. 235 ff.)
"Montanus, the heretic, and his female associates, seem to have	"S. Epiphane étudie à faire voir que c'étoient des imposteurs, et il

ecclesiastical history, his career having a considerable influence in the great Pietistic movement in Germany. At last he gave himself entirely to the study of Mystical Theology, and furnished a valuable history of this special subject in his *Historie und Beschreibung der mystischen Theologie* (Frankf. 1703), which, together with Poiret's book, is indispensable to the student of theosophy. His own views were developed in his *Geheimniss der göttlichen Sophia* (Leipz. 1700.)

[1] *De Rebus Christianorum ante C. M.* (Helmst. 1734). The *Church History* has been often edited.

MIDDLETON. (I. 224.)
been the authors of these prophetic trances, towards the end of the 2nd century, and acquired great credit by their visions and ecstasies, in which they acted their part so well, by feigned distortions and convulsive agitations of the body, as to appear to be out of their senses; and in these fits uttered many wild prophecies and predictions, which they imposed upon the people for divine revelations; and by affecting at the same time a peculiar sanctity and severity of discipline, they first raised and propagated in the Church that spirit of enthusiasm, which subsisted in it for near a century, and then gradually sank into utter contempt."

GERVAISE. (p. 235 ff.)
le prouve par deux raisons. La première, c'est qu'il y a déjà, dit-il, plus de deux cent ans que cet hérésiarque et ses Prophétesses sont décédées, cependant le monde subsiste encore, et nous ne voyons aucune marque de sa prochaine destruction. La seconde est que si on compare leurs prétendues Prophéties avec celles de tous les grands saints .... on y trouvera des distances infinies." [The author is quite sure that "Montan et Maximille, poussés par l'esprit de ténèbres qui les agitoit, se fussent pendus."]

The poor Abbé, with his implicit faith in the inspired accuracy of Epiphanius, is by no means so contemptible as the blatant rationalist, who does not even affect an argument, and condemns as heretics and impostors men whose opinions were far beyond entering into his philosophy. There is certainly something not a little comic in Dr Conyers Middleton, to whose profound orthodoxy such unanimous testimony was given by the Church of England, standing up as Inquisitor-General; and the coolness with which he talks of the "feigned distortions" and "affected sanctity" would alone stamp the performance as proceeding from the author of the *Letters from Rome* and the *Free Enquiry*[1]. It is only just to the founder of this school to admit that his own writings were as free from the flippancy and cynicism which marked those of many of his followers, as from their general superficiality in the matter of learning. It is well known that at this period everything that savoured of so-called "Enthusiasm" was under

[1] And of the cowardly attacks on a far greater man. See Monk's *Life of Bentley*.

the united ban of science, theology and society. Half the sermons of the 18th century, to judge by what have come down to us, must have been written against this detestable error; and no doubt much of the contempt lavished upon Montanism and kindred manifestations was intended obliquely for the misguided men who were at this time preaching to the poor a very different Gospel from that of Middleton and Warburton[1].

In this same period, however, we have a series of monographs upon the special subject of Montanism, treated naturally from different standpoints, but in almost each instance by men of reputation[2]. Some of these I have not been able to meet with, but the essay of Theophilus Wernsdorf not only contains a mention of all possible materials, but also an investigation into the opinions (not the external history) conducted with much ingenuity and learning. But this writer is undoubtedly a "counsel for the defence," and in the course of his pleadings he is more than once guilty of a want of candour in his quotations, which is as reprehensible, and indeed more so, than the similar tactics employed occasionally on the other side[3]. The younger

[1] There are some good remarks in Mr Leslie Stephen's *History of Thought in the 18th century.*

[2] Strauch's *De Montano discursus theologico-historicus*, (1680,) is mentioned by Schwegler, also three dissertations by Ruel, "De Montano et Montanistis," in Hartmann's *Concilia Illustrata* (I. 283 ff.), and one by Longerue,—none of which I have been able to consult. They are all doubtless in the University Library at Göttingen.

[3] Theoph. Wernsdorf, *De Montanistis commentatio historica-critica.* (Ged. 1751.) Notwithstanding the fine profession of historical candour, (which I have ventured to copy on my title-page,) Wernsdorf, while attempting to prove the complete agreement of Montanistic tenets with the doctrines of the Primitive Church, more than once quotes as evidence writings of Tertullian, such as the *Ad Martyres*, (p. 128,) which all authorities, and all internal evidence, proclaim to have been written before the "lapse." Now as I firmly believe that his conclusion is sound, and follows from the honest reasonings which I shall attempt imperfectly to set forth in this essay, I feel the more shame that a good cause should have been so disgraced. Dr Réville, surely through an oversight, quotes the *Præscriptio* as embodying Tertullian's Montanistic opinions. (Cf. *Etudes sur T., Nouv. Rev. de Théol.* 1858, p. 53.)

INTRODUCTION.   19

Walch published his *History of Heresies* in 1762, and his INTRODUC-
sober impartiality seems to me very far from deserving TION.
Schwegler's sneer[1]. Schroeckh's vast storehouse of facts Walch.
—more it cannot claim to be—presents once more all that Schroeckh.
industry can furnish[2].

It is needless to enumerate the vast catalogue of modern ecclesiastical histories, very few of which present even a new idea upon the side-paths of their subject. But Neander[3] has the merit, among many others, of having Neander.
first discussed the influence of the Phrygian nationality, early religious and customs, upon the party which originated there. At the same time, two useful monographs appeared; that of Fr. Adolph Heinichen (*De Alogis,* Heinichen.
Theodotianis, atque Artemonitis, Lipsiæ, 1829), in which, following up the previous researches of Merkel (*Ueber die Aloger* &c., Frankf., 1782), he explores a most important appendix to the history of the Montanists; and that of Conrad Kirchner (*De Montanistis...commentatio de eorum* Kirchner.
origine &c. &c., Jenæ, 1832), which, without any claim to originality, furnishes a good synoptical view of the evidence. The controversies which followed the publication in 1834 of Möhler's *Symbolik,* caused much attention to Möhler.
be paid to the movement, which, in the Catholic theologian's opinion, represented the completest and most logical development of the Protestant "ground-idea." His mention of Swedenborg brought into the lists Dr Tafel Tafel.
of Tübingen, who defended the principles of Neo-Montanism against its adversaries[4]. The school of Tübingen

[1] *Entwurf einer vollständigen Historie der Ketzereien.* Leipz. 1762. [Cf. Schwegler, p. 11.]
[2] *Christliche Kirchengeschichte.* Leipz. 1768—1804. (Continued by Tzschirner.)
[3] *Allgemeine Geschichte der christl. Religion u. Kirche.* (Hamburg, 1827.)
[4] J. F. Tafel: *Vergleichende Darstellung und Beurtheilung der Lehrgegensätze der Katholiken und Protestanten.* (Tübingen, 1835.) Möhler was then a professor at the University of Tübingen, but he afterwards accepted a call to München.

began now its investigations into the period succeeding the Apostolic age. In order to avoid the outcry which had followed the publication of the *Leben Jesu*, the trenches were dug in a district where the danger was less to be apprehended: the facts were left alone for a time, while the early witnesses were being discredited. Schwegler's successful essay, in the year 1841, once more brought the importance of Montanism before the bar of criticism. As his work is referred to repeatedly in the following pages, no further mention is here necessary[1]. In 1847, Ritschl published the first edition of his great work on the Primitive Church, in which he developed for the first time the true view that Montanism was a reaction in a conservative sense, rather than a "New Prophecy." He was rather sharply criticised by Baur in the *Theologische Jahrbücher*, who also dissected Neander's views on the same subject, the articles being finally incorporated in his *Kirchengeschichte der 3 ersten Jahrhunderte* (1853). Before this, in 1847, Schwegler had shaped his essay into a larger work, in which his paradoxes were but slightly modified[2]. In 1850, the learned Hilgenfeld published his *Glossolalie in der alten Kirche*, declaring his complete agreement with Ritschl's conclusions, the latter's book appearing in an enlarged form in 1857[3]. In the following year, an interesting essay by Dr Albert Réville appeared in the *Nouvelle Revue de Théologie*, in which the theories of Schwegler and Ritschl were discussed, and a very lucid and impartial sketch of the Montanistic movement furnished[4]. In 1865 Lipsius published the first of his investigations into the nature of the materials used by Epiphanius; a labour (it need scarcely be said) of infinite

---

[1] *Der Montanismus und die christliche Kirche.* (Tüb. 1841.) There had been a competition for a prize offered by the Theological Faculty: Dr Schwegler was successful.

[2] *Das nachapostolische Zeitalter.* (Tüb. 1846.)

[3] *Entstehung der Alt-Katholischen Kirche,* (2te Auflage,) Bonn, 1857.

[4] *Etudes sur Tertullien.* (2.) Le Montanisme, 1858, pp. 49 ff.

INTRODUCTION. 21

importance in connection with Montanism[1]; supplemented quite recently by further researches as to the evidence given by Philaster and other early hereseologers[2]. In addition to these labours, the same writer's monograph upon the chronology of the early bishops of Rome has already been recognised as a standard authority[3]. The last work to be mentioned comes from that well-known magazine of Protestantism, the Theological Faculty of the University of Strasburg. Just before the war of 1870, M. Emile Ströhlin, (a pupil of Colani's,) published an *Essai sur le Montanisme* as his thesis for a degree. Without any pretensions to originality or to exhaustive handling of the topic, M. Ströhlin must be admitted to have furnished a clear and useful résumé of Montanistic history and teaching, his various debts to Schwegler and Ritschl being freely acknowledged[4]. To this list may be added the two articles, each from its own stand-point admirable, by Möller in Herzog's *Real-Encyclopädie*, and by Hefele in the *Freiburger Kirchen-Lexikon*; while the name of the latter theologian cannot be mentioned without a tribute to the assistance furnished to such enquiries by his *Conciliengeschichte*.

INTRODUC-
TION.

Ströh-
lin.

Möller.
Hefele.

From this vast heap of materials it still remains to construct a truly Critical History of Montanism. The first grand step, viz. the application of the keenest analysis to the evidence of Eusebius and Epiphanius, notwithstanding the labours of Lipsius, Volkmar, and Harnack, cannot yet be regarded as complete[5]. If only the tenth part of the labour given to the elucidation of the text of a dramatist, and the chronological order of his works,

[1] *Zur Quellenkritik des Epiphanios.* Wien, 1865.
[2] *Die Quellen der ältesten Ketzergeschichte.* Leipzig, 1875.
[3] *Chronologie der römischen Bischöfe.* Kiel, 1869.
[4] *Essai sur le Montanisme.* Strasbourg, 1870.
[5] See Harnack's *Quellenkritik der Geschichte des Gnosticismus,* Leipzig, 1873, and his criticisms on Lipsius in the *Zeitschrift für historische Theologie,* (1874,) II. 143—226.

could be devoted to such writers as Hippolytus and Tertullian, and with the same impartiality,—what results might we not expect? As for the other requirement, the scientific comparison of Montanism with later spiritual reactions, all that has been done as yet is of the most fragmentary nature.

The writer of this essay, it need not be said, makes no claim to have even attempted these great tasks. Standing on the shoulders of his predecessors, he has tried to form an impartial estimate of their labours, as well as of what remains to be done in the future. But acknowledging that he has worked upon old materials, he claims to have honestly analysed and judged them, and (as Chillingworth puts it) " to have defended truth only, and only by truth."

AUTHORITIES.

[In addition to those already mentioned in the Introduction.]

Patrologies of Migne, Caillau, Gallandi.

On Tertullian.
Hoffmann.—*Dissertatio . . . . . omnia Tertulliani in Montanismo scripta videri.* Witeb. 1739.

Noesselt.—*De vera aetate ac doctrina scriptorum Q. S. F. Tertulliani.* (In his *Opusc. ad Hist. Eccles.* Fasc. 3.)

Kaye.—*Ecclesiastical History of the 2nd and 3rd centuries, illustrated from Tertullian.* London. 1845.

Neander.—*Antignostikus, oder Geist des Tertullians.* Berlin. 1849.

Hesselberg.—*Tertullian's Lehre, entwickelt aus seinen Schriften.* Dorpat. 1848.

Uhlhorn.—*Fundamenta chronologiae Tertullianeae.* Götting. 1852.

[There are also two works, Münter's *Primordia Eccles. Africanae*, and Morcelli's *Africa Christiana*, which I have not been able to consult.]

The Early Church.
Baratier.—*Disquisitio chronologica de successione antiquiss. episcoporum Romanorum.* Ultraject. 1740.

Baur.—*Die christliche Gnosis.* Tübingen. 1835.

Ueber den Ursprung des Episcopats. Tüb. 1838.

Kirchengeschichte der 3 ersten Jahrhunderte. Tüb. 1863.

Beausobre.—*Histoire du Manichéisme.* Amsterdam. 1734—9.

Bingham.—*Antiquities of the Christian Church.* London. 1715.

Bunsen.—*Hippolytus and his age.* London. 1854.
Clinton.—*Fasti Romani.* Oxford. 1845.
Döllinger.—*Hippolytus und Kallistus.* Regensburg. 1853.
   Christenthum und Kirche in der Zeit der Grundlegung. Regensburg. 1868.
Hagenbach.—*Dogmengeschichte.* (5te Auflage.) Leipzig. 1867.
Hase.—*Kirchengeschichte.* (10te Auflage.) Leipz. 1877.
Hilgenfeld.—*Die Glossolalie in der alten Kirche.* Leipz. 1850.
Orsi.—*Dissertatio Apologetica . . . SS. Perpetuae et Felicitatis . . . adversus S. Basnagium.* Florent. 1728.
Pressensé.—*Histoire des 3 premiers Siècles de l'Eglise chrétienne.* Paris. 1858—62.
Rothe.—*Anfänge der christlichen Kirche.* Wittenberg. 1837.
Semisch.—*On the writings of Justin Martyr.* Edinburgh. 1843.
Thiersch.—*Geschichte der christl. Kirche im Alterthum.* Erlangen. 1858.

Chladenius.—*De stationibus vett. Christianorum.* Lipsiae. 1744.
Corrodi.—*Kritische Geschichte des Chiliasmus.* Leipzig. 1781.
Dallaeus.—*De usu Patrum.* Genevae. 1656.
   De Jejuniis. Daventriae. 1654.
Flathe.—*Vorläufer der Reformation.* Leipzig. 1835—6.
Goebel.—*Gesch. des christl. Lebens i. d. Rh. Westph. Kirche.* Leipzig. 1842.
Gunnison.—*History of the Mormons.* Philadelphia. 1852.
Hahn.—*Geschichte der Ketzer im Mittelalter.* Stuttgart. 1845.
   Geschichte der Waldenser, etc. Stuttgart. 1847.
Hase.—*Neue Propheten.* (2te Aufl.) Leipz. 1861.
Hefele.—*Conciliengeschichte.* (1te Aufl.) Tübingen. 1855.
Heinroth.—*Geschichte und Kritik des Mysticismus.* Leipzig. 1830.
Hellferich.—*Die christl. Mystik in ihrer Entwickelung.* Gotha. 1842.
Jortin.—*Remarks on ecclesiastical history.* London. 1810.
Kestner.—*Die Agape, oder der geheime Weltbund der Christen.* Jena. 1819.
Koellner.—*Materien der christl. Kirchengeschichte.* Giessen. 1864.
Lange.—*Tabellen der Kirchengeschichte.* Jena. 1848.
Lee.—*The Inspiration of Holy Scripture.* Dublin. 1865.
Lightfoot.—*St Paul's Ep. to the Philippians.* (Appendix.)
Möhler.—*Symbolik.* (7te Aufl.) Mainz. 1864.
Poiret.—*Bibliotheca Mysticorum selecta.* Amstelod. 1708.
Probst.—*Lehre und Gebet in den 3 ersten Jhrdten.* Tübing. 1871.
   Kirchliche Disciplin in den 3, &c. Tübing. 1873.
Rohrbacher.—*Histoire universelle de l'Eglise catholique.* Paris. 1868.
Routh.—*Reliquiae Sacrae.* Oxford. 1846.
Thomasius.—*Höchstnöthige Cautelen für die Kirchenrechtsgelahrtheit.* Halle. 1728.

Ullmann.—*Reformatoren vor der Reformation.* Gotha. 1866.

Westcott.—*On the Canon of the New Testament.* London. 1875.

⁎⁎⁎ Since writing this notice of the materials, I discovered in the library of the British Museum a curious pamphlet on Montanism, (in fact, the only existing monograph in English,) written by "a Lay Gentleman," no other clue to the author's name being given[1]. It is bound up with a sermon of Dean Hickes on Enthusiasm, and an account of the Camisard Prophets, some of whom had visited England. The "lay gentleman's" partiality (or ignorance) is exemplified by his quoting no single work of Tertullian's except the spurious appendix to the *Praescriptio*. He remarks naïvely: "Had there been any writings of the Montanists remaining at this day, out of which I could have taken my accounts, I should not have concealed anything that they could have said for themselves." One would have thought that Dean Hickes could have informed him as to the existence of such treatises as the *De Monogamia, De Virg. velandis*, and so forth. The book is dated, London, 1709. Its historical value may be estimated from the fact that the writer gravely asserts his belief that the Montanists did not invent the doctrine of Transubstantiation!

[1] Hartley, in his quaint *Paradise Regained*, (London, 1764, p. 176,) speaks of a *History of Montanism*, by Dr Francis Lee, the friend of Pordage, and the leading spirit of the Philadelphian Society. Can this be it? I should hesitate to think that so enlightened a man could have perpetrated so one-sided an account of a religious phenomenon in many respects similar to the movement in which he himself took part.

BOOK I.

THE HISTORY OF MONTANISM.

MORE than a century ago, Mosheim declared that the chronology of Montanism was a matter of such extreme obscurity that he could only claim a fair measure of probability for the view he adopted[1]. The reason lies in the wide diversity, one might fairly say the absolutely contradictory character, of the evidence furnished by the earliest ecclesiastical historians. The chief of these, Eusebius and Epiphanius, furnish statements which hardly any ingenuity can reconcile; and the conclusions of modern writers have been consequently derived from the preference they have given to one or the other of the two historians. Eusebius (in his annals) gives us the year A.D. 172, with the mention (cap. 16) that the first manifestations in Asia Minor took place in the pro-consulate of Gratus, and (in another place) that thirteen years of peace followed the death of Maximilla[2]. Unfortunately, as will be seen, these two last

BOOK I.

§ 1.
Chronology.

---

[1] "Disputant viri docti et sine fine disputabunt de tempore, quo primum factio haec in Phrygia exorta est. Ego quam plerique probant, nec sine rationibus probant sententiam sequutus sum...... (regnante M. Aurelio, medio fere saeculo, &c.)" *De rebus Christianorum ante Const. Magn.* p. 409.

[2] Hefele suggested (*Conciliengeschichte*, I. 71, and see the Prolegomena to the 3rd edition of his *Patres Apostolici*,) that the earliest date was preferable, according to his view, that Hermas, whom he believes to have written certainly before A.D. 151, under Bishop Pius, "bereits den Montanismus zu bekämpfen scheine." Cf. the exhaustive article in the

data afford little help. Epiphanius presents no less than three statements. In the first place, he gives the "93rd year after the Ascension of our Lord," having previously fixed this as the 18th year of Tiberius[1]. This gives us A.D. 135; but in another place[2] he mentions the 19th year of Antoninus Pius, thus postponing the beginning of the heresy until A.D. 157. His third statement[3] is that, from the date of Maximilla's death to the date of his writing, a period of 290 years had elapsed. Now the given year (sc. the 12th of *Valentinian, Valens, & Gratian*) must be not later than A.D. 390, which would carry the beginnings of Montanism into the first century. The *Chronicon Paschale* gives the year 182[4]. In Tertullian's writings we have no help towards the discovery of the date of commencement, but two remarkable statements with regard to the subsequent history of Montanism are found, to which we shall refer later on. It is not necessary to enumerate all the various conjectures which modern writers have made or followed; the first one which attempted a reconciliation of the statements of Epiphanius, due to Petavius, may be briefly stated[5]. He assumed that

---

Freiburg *Kirchen-Lexikon*, VII. 255 ff., and for older authorities, Baronius, II. 266, Tillemont, II. 441, and Routh, II. 97 ff.

[1] Epiph. *Hæres.* LI. § 33. And see Schwegler (*Montanismus*, p. 249 ff.) and Ritschl (*Entstehung*, p. 525).

[2] Ibid. XLVIII. § 1. "Οὗτοι γὰρ γεγόνασι περὶ τὸ ἐννεακαιδέκατον ἔτος Ἀντωνίνου τοῦ Εὐσεβοῦς μετὰ Ἀδριανόν."

[3] Ibid. XLVIII. § 2.

[4] I. 490. (ed. Dindorf.) "Μαμερτίνου καὶ Ῥούφου τὸ γ' ἡ κατὰ Φρύγας ἄθεος προφητεία Μοντανοῦ συνέστη, ἔτι δὲ καὶ Ἀλκιβιάδου καὶ Θεοδότου."

[5] It is sufficient to mention that Pearson, Dodwell, and Neander supported the arguments in favour of the years 156 or 157; Blondel and Longerue, followed in our days by Schwegler and Hefele, declared for A.D. 140 or 141; Tillemont and Walch follow Eusebius in fixing the date at A.D. 172. Baratier, the wonderful child-prodigy, (b. 1721, † 1740) who wrote a Hebrew lexicon at nine years of age, had planned an exhaustive work on the history of the early Church. He only lived to publish a preliminary dissertation on the succession of the Bishops of Rome in the first centuries. He treats at some length in this essay the origin of the Montanistic movement, and concludes that it was far earlier than most

the historian "meant Antoninus the Philosopher," thus arriving at the year 179. But Pearson, in his Minor Works, has exposed the weakness of the assumption.

Looking upon the general character of the evidence, as furnished by Eusebius and Epiphanius, there can hardly be a doubt that the former has far higher claims to credence. But the absolute impossibility of supposing that a sect which only (according to his view) began to exist in Phrygia in 172, should in five years time have reached the situation which elicited the letter of the Gallic Confessors (universally fixed at A.D. 177), makes it necessary to see whether his witnesses really support his conclusion. Let us look at the statements of the Anonymous writer, and the quotations from Apollonius and Serapion, all of whom were most probably contemporaries, or at any rate of the next generation. The Anonymous wrote "more than thirteen years after the death of Maximilla." But this prophetess appears to have survived her companions, from several passages in Epiphanius, (cf. *Euseb.* v. 17,) therefore the beginning of the prophesyings is thrown back to an earlier date, to which we are helped by the additional statement, that "it was forty years" (sc. at the time that Apollonius wrote) "from the first public appearance of Montanus." And we know, moreover, that this writer was a contemporary of Commodus (cap. 18). Put these facts together. It may be fairly concluded :—

(1) That the Anonymous wrote at least 54 years, and perhaps more, after the origin of Montanism.

(2) That he wrote at the beginning of the reign of Commodus, if not under Marcus Aurelius.

Now Miltiades is quoted by Eusebius as mentioning that (contrary to a prediction of Maximilla) " thirteen years have elapsed, and perfect peace prevails." Can this give us a clue? Baratier declares that it does. "Constat ergo

writers have supposed. Many of his results I have adopted in this chapter.

ad Commodi tempus pacem hanc referendam esse. Cœpit nempe Ann. CLXXIX. labente, cum Marcus Imperator Marcomannis victis quiesceret, et duravit usque ad Ann. CXCIII., quo ipsis Cal. Jan. Commodus interficiebatur, vel usque ad Martium ejusdem anni, et Pertinacis mortem, Ann. XIII. et aliquot mensibus." Taking this for granted, the solution is not far off. Miltiades wrote in the year 193, and the death of Maximilla is thus placed in 179, subsequent to the decease of Montanus and Priscilla. Apollonius had written during their lifetime, in other words, not later than A. D. 178. Now we know that 40 years had elapsed from the beginning of the manifestations, which brings us to the year 138 as the date of origin. But it is probable that Maximilla survived Montanus some years, and at least possible that Apollonius did not write immediately after his death. Therefore we are justified in taking 175 as a likely date for Priscilla's decease, and 165 or 166 as that of Apollonius' writing. This brings the origin of all back to the year 126, which may agree with Epiphanius's account of the 93 years after the Ascension, although some calculate this differently. I confess that I cannot follow Baratier in his rather arbitrary emendations of the other statements in Epiphanius[1], nor do I think them necessary for the adoption of his conclusions. All that remains is to fix the interval between the first origin and the establishment of a distinct party, the natural confusion between which is probably the chief cause of obscurity. Baratier gives 10 years for this purpose, and concludes:—"So we may delay the establishment of the Heresy until the year 136, or the

---

[1] "Item idem Epiphanius se anno CXII. post id tempus scribere dicit, *quod mendosum est.* (!) Sed alibi nempe Hæres. XLVIII. § 2. non CXII. annos sed CCXC. habet, quod iterum absurdum. *Sed legendum CCL.* Scribebat enim Ann. CCCLXXVI. Et facilis lapsus a πεντήκοντα in ἐννενήκοντα. (Dindorf, following Petavius, supposed the original numeral to have been εἴκοσιν.) At in Pearsonii Hypothesi forent Ann. CCXX. quod absurdum quoque, quia ex εἴκοσι nemo ἐννενήκοντα exsculpet." (*Disquis. chronol.* p 140 ff.)

19th of Hadrian's reign. And thus we can reconcile Epiphanius's accounts among themselves, and to our own." Without adopting every step of this ingenious reasoning, there can be no doubt that it obviates some (if not all) of the great difficulties which attend the usual Eusebian calculation. It also harmonizes with the statement of "Prædestinatus" that Soter, bishop of Rome, wrote against the Montanists[1]. Now the period of Soter's episcopate is usually reckoned at 167—175, or (as by Vater in his *Tabellen*,) at 161—171. In either case it is quite impossible to suppose that a sect which only had its first beginnings in an obscure Phrygian village in the year 172, could in the following year (the latest possible for Soter), have been deemed formidable enough at Rome to elicit an episcopal manifesto. But by the adoption of a much earlier date, this difficulty vanishes. And, as we shall see later, a very important statement of Tertullian's on the attitude of the Roman See towards Montanism, is also satisfactorily explained[2].

Leaving to a later section our attempt to solve the remaining problems connected with the chronology of the Montanist party, we turn to the second difficulty which meets us at the threshold. This is the extreme diversity of names by which the Montanists are described, and the obvious risk of confounding together descriptions of what might be essentially different objects. The most common designation of the sect applied by ancient writers is that of Phrygians or Cataphrygians, derived from the province

§ 2. Names and nicknames.

---

[1] "Scripsit contra eos librum S. Soter papa urbis, et Apollonius Ephesiorum antistes." (*Liber Prædestinati*, Hæres. XXVI. ap. Galland. *Bibl. Patr.* x. 366.) The same writer adds, it is true, that Tertullian replied to these attacks, "agens contra Soterem supradictum urbis Papam, asserens falsa esse de sanguine infantis, Trinitatem in unitate deitatis, ... &c." Now it is clear that Tertullian wrote no book before the last decade of the 2nd century, and did not become a Montanist until the beginning of the 3rd.

[2] *Adv. Praxean*, cap. I. On this vide infra, in the chapter on the Opponents of Montanism.

Book I. where Montanus began his teachings[1], while all modern writers have preferred to connect the sect with the name of its founder. But the same writers speak of other parties, (whom they variously describe as Quintillianists, Priscillianists, Pepuziani, Tascodrugitæ, Artotyritæ,) in terms which strengthen a suspicion that these were either names of sub-sections of the same sect, if not arbitrary nicknames for the party itself[2]. The subdivision into two parties, the Proculists and the Æschinists, as asserted by the author of the Appendix to Tertullian's *Præscr. adv. Hæreticos,* will be best treated of in our later investi-

[1] For instance, Augustin, *De Hæres.* § 26, "Cataphryges sunt, quorum authores fuerunt Montanus tanquam Paracletus, et duae prophetissae ipsius..... His nomen provincia Phrygia dedit, quia ibi extiterunt." [Basel ed. of 1542, vi. 17.] The name in question is employed by Eusebius, Epiphanius, Hippolytus, Clement of Alexandria, Origen (ap. Pamphil.), Athanasius, (οἱ κατὰ Φρύγας,) Cyril, Gregory Nazianzen, Didymus Alexandrinus, Firmilian, Philaster, Theodoret, and one or two others. Isidor, Hilary, and Ambrose only speak of Montanus. John of Damascus has οἱ Καταφρυγαστῶν. [See his *De Hæres.* § 48. Migne, xciv. 707.]

[2] That the Fathers often exercised their orthodox wit in this way is well known (e. g. the "Alogi," of whom we shall speak later). The Tascodrugitæ were supposed to apply the hand to the nose when praying; the Artotyritæ are said to have offered bread and cheese: (cf. Prædestinatus, "panem et caseum offerunt, dicentes a primis hominibus oblationes Deo de fructibus terrae fuisse celebratas,") and this is said by Epiphanius (*Hæres.* xlix. 2, 1) to have been a rite practised by a very similar sect." The "Pepuziani" were obviously Montanists from the name of the village (Pepuza) in which Montanus first taught, and where some believed he held episcopal authority later. (See Wernsdorf, *de Montanistis,* p. 57.) As Pepuza was a very obscure place, the nickname would carry a certain contempt. The titles "Priscillianists" and "Quintillianists" are not so easy to explain with certainty. It is quite probable that both refer to prophetesses, and that each of these had her special circle of hearers. Of course the "Priscillianists" will not be confounded with the totally distinct Spanish party in the 4th century. And that the title was applied to the Montanists is proved by two penal statutes, in which the same language is employed with regard to both. (Cod. Theod. Tit. *de Hæreticis,* legg. 34, 40, 57, 65, and Cod. Just. lib. i. tit. v. §§ 18—21.) Whether, however, Quintilla was also a Montanistic prophetess, is more open to doubt. Tertullian wrote against her his treatise *de Baptismo,* describing her as one of the Caïnite sect, and Epiphanius gives her the honours of a separate heresy. (Cf. *Hær.* xlviii. 14, xlix. 1. 2, li. 33.)

gations[1], and the catalogue of titles may be concluded by the mention of the noble designation which, according to Tertullian, was sometimes applied as a reproach, but always received as an honour,—that of "Spirituales." ['Nos, quos merito spirituales dici facit agnitio spiritualium charismatum......sed psychicis, non recipientibus spiritum.' *De Monogam.*, cap. I.]

All that can be declared with certainty about Montanus is *that he existed*, that he was originally an inhabitant of Ardaban in Mysia (near the Phrygian frontier), and that about the year A.D. 130 he began to teach a new revelation, and to lay claim to prophetic powers, if not (as his opponents declared) asserting himself to be the Paraclete himself. That he was born of heathen parents, and that he received the office of a presbyter, or even of a bishop, are rumours upon which it is now impossible to decide[2]. He attached to himself a large number of disciples, including several women of high social position, and the opinions he promulgated spread not only through Asia Minor, but obtained acceptance at Rome and at Carthage. He is asserted by some to have left writings, but the sentences quoted have far more the appearance of oral tradition[3]. He has been even claimed as a joint-author

§ 3. Montanus.

---

[1] Pseud.-Tertull. cap. 52: "Sunt enim qui κατὰ Proclum dicuntur, sunt enim qui secundum Aeschinem pronunciantur." The name of this writer, and his period, appear to have never been ascertained. Some suppose it was Hippolytus.

[2] All our details about the person of Montanus are derived either from Eusebius, *H. E.* v. 16—18, or from the 48th Heresy of Epiphanius. Later writers simply copy or write from memory.

[3] Bishop Kaye thinks that "Tertullian's works furnish presumptive proof that the effusions of Montanus... were committed to writing," (*History of second and third centuries*, p. 28,) but the passages he quotes, viz. from cap. 9 and 11 of the *De Fug. in Persec.*, and from the 21st of the *De Pudicitia*, hardly seem to confirm the statement sufficiently to counterbalance the fact that Tertullian does not anywhere mention such writings as proceeding from the pen or dictation of Montanus himself. The first passage: "Spiritum vero si consulas, quid magis sermone illo Spiritus probat? namque omnes pene ad

of the Sibylline Oracles[1]. His opponents declared that he was mad, that he led a disgraceful life[2], and that he finally

Martyrium exhortatur non ad fugam, ut et illius commemoremur, 'Publicaris, inquit: bonum tibi est. Qui enim non publicatur in hominibus, publicatur in Domino.'" Surely this might as easily refer to a traditional as to a written utterance; and it might as probably have been revealed through Maximilla as through Montanus. The quotations made by Epiphanius are also just of that oracular and fragmentary nature to be expected in tradition : and, as Bp Kaye admits, had Tertullian been aware of the existence of such declarations, "he would scarcely have failed in his Treatise against Praxeas to give some explanation of passages, which appear at first sight to identify Montanus with God the Father" (p. 29). The statement of Hippolytus, "τὰ πολλὰ φλύαρα αὐτῶν βιβλία," may well be applied to the apologetic writings of Themiso and Proculus. Tillemont (*Mémoires*, II. 47), and Walch (*Ketzerhistorien*, I. 890), believed in the existence of such writings as Kaye supposes, and thought that Epiphanius must have had access to them. So also Wernsdorf, (*De Montanistis*, p. 133,) who adduces a passage from Theodoret:—Μοντανὸς τὰ τούτων (sc. προφητίδων?) συγγράμματα προφητικὰς προσηγόρευσε βίβλους. He adds, " Atque hoc ipsum diserte confirmat ipse praesul Cyprius, qui verba Montani ex ejus prophetia adducit, λέγει γὰρ ἐν τῇ ἑαυτοῦ λεγομένῃ προφητείᾳ, idemque non uno loco ipsa Maximillae verba transcribit, ut necesse sit, aut hanc Prophetiam continuisse Montani et mulierum oracula conjuncta, aut Maximillam etiam librum reliquisse."—I should certainly not balance my own inferences against so great a weight of authority. But it is difficult to imagine that detached utterances like the famous "Μετ' ἐμὲ προφῆτις οὐκέτι ἔσται, ἀλλὰ συντέλεια," attributed to Maximilla, (Epiph. *Haer*. XLVIII. § 2,) and "'Ακούσατε ὦ παῖδες Χριστοῦ τί λέγει, ἐμοῦ μὴ ἀκούσατε ἀλλὰ Χριστοῦ," (ibid. § 12,) must necessarily have formed part of a book, and could not have been handed down by word of mouth.

[1] This curious notion was supported by Jean le Sueur, (Sudorius,) in his *Histoire de l'Eglise* (p. 466), and also by Blondel. Longerue seems to have thought it not unlikely.

[2] The "evidence to character" in the case of an alleged heretic is always very positive if not always very consistent. For instance, Jerome accuses Montanus of corrupting his hearers by bribery : " M. immundi spiritus praedicator, multas ecclesias per Priscam et Maximillam primum auro corrupit, deinde haeresi polluit," (*Epist*. CXXXIII. *Ad Ctesiph.*). By way of contrast, Apollonius (ap. Euseb. *H. E*. v. 18) charges him with πλεονεξία! Another writer accuses him of adultery and infanticide : ἡ Μοντανοῦ βλασφημία παιδοκτονίαις, μοιχείαις τε καὶ εἰδωλολατρείαις συντίθεται, (Isid. Pelus. I. 242). And Cyril of Jerusalem declares : ὁ Μοντανὸς ὁ ἀθλιώτατος καὶ πάσης ἀκαθαρσίας καὶ ἀσελγείας πεπληρωμένος, (*Catech*. XVI. 8). It must be admitted that the charge of adultery is

committed suicide "after the manner of Judas[1]." Long after his death, when the ecclesiastical opposition had finally developed into active persecution, an Asiatic bishop is said to have exhumed the remains of Montanus, and to have burnt them[2]. All that can be deemed historically certain, I repeat, is that this personage began a religious movement, the full bearing of which he may not have conceived himself, but in which his share is undeniable[3].

hardly compatible with the reproach of being "abscissus et semi-vir," according to Jerome (*Ep. ad Marcell.* XLI.).

[1] The anonymous author quoted by Eusebius (*H. E.* v. 16) observes: "καὶ οὕτω δὲ τελευτῆσαι καὶ τὸν βίον καταστρέψαι Ἰούδα προδότου δίκην."

[2] This is stated by the younger Walch (*Ketzerhistorien*, I. 617), on the authority of "des Bischofs Johannis Kirchenhistorie in Assemann's *Biblioth. Orient.* tom. II. cap. 11."

[3] Schwegler's hypothesis that Montanus is a merely mythical personage, is supported by him on the following grounds: (*a*) the complete obscurity as to the character of the man, apart from the "obligés" attacks of the ecclesiastical writers; (*b*) the universal designation of "Phrygian" instead of "Montanist;" (*c*) the author of the appendix to the *Præscriptio* does not mention him, (nor, he might add, does Hippolytus); (*d*) the vagueness of the statements in Eusebius, stuffed with such words as φασί, λέγεται, λόγος ἐστίν, φήμη ἐστίν, and the like; (*e*) a passage in a spurious homily once attributed to Chrysostom, and included in some editions, in which Montanus is clearly described "als völlig mythische Person;" (*f*) the analogy with the generally admitted non-existence of Ebion. After mentioning these points, Schwegler admits the difficulty that remains: "Dieser Sectenname, weil unabhängig von einem Eigennamen entstanden, müsste irgend welche sachliche Erklärung zulassen. *Allein es findet sich bei keinem der Alten eine Andeutung, durch welche man über den Bereich von Möglichkeiten hinauskäme.* Dass die Donatisten und Novatianer von späteren Geschichtschreibern mit den Montanisten verwechselt, oder als Montenses bezeichnet werden (as in Optat. Milev. *de schism. Donatist.* II. 4; but see Hieron. in Chron. s. a. 356), gibt nichts Sicheres an die Hand" (p. 244). Although this admission goes a good way towards disposing of the theory, it may be remarked that the evidence for the existence of Maximilla and Priscilla, (whom Schwegler suffers to exist,) is precisely of the same character as that affecting Montanus; all three have sayings ascribed to them, and that of Montanus, too characteristic and remarkable to be pure invention. Ritschl thus sums up his argument for the personal existence:—"Wenn der Parteiname 'Montanisten' nicht bei den ältesten Schriftstellern üblich ist, sondern der Name 'Kataphryger,' so geht daraus nur hervor, dass Montanus

Book I.
§ 4.
Prophetesses and disciples.

Of the immediate followers of Montanus in Asia Minor, by far the most notable are the two women, Maximilla and Priscilla, or as she is sometimes called, Prisca. There is hardly a single mention of the leader in which they do not appear, not only as his companions, but as sharers in his alleged spiritual gifts[1]. They are described as having forsaken their husbands and families, and the usual charges of immorality and of final suicide are brought against them[2]. Maximilla seems to have occupied a prominent place of authority among the Montanists, and her prophetic utterances are quoted as well by Tertullian as by the hostile historians in a way which proves that she was one of the recognised organs of spiritual instruction[3]. If we are to accept the statements of Epiphanius, the Quintilla to whom we have already referred[4] was originally a Montanist prophetess, but finally formed a separate sect of Quintillianists, which has been more than once confounded with the main body itself. But a reference to the first chapter of Tertullian's treatise on Baptism, directed against this very Quintilla, will shew that this cannot

nicht etwa eine schöpferische Person war, sondern nur die Kombination vollzog, welche durch die allgemeinen Verhältnisse nothwendig sich aufdrängte." (*Entstehung der Altkath. Kirche*, p. 526.)

[1] Cf. Euseb. *H. E.* iv. 27, and v. 16—18. Also Epiphanius, *Hæres.* xlviii. passim. Also Theodoret, *Hæret. Fabul.* iii. 2. Jerome speaks of the wealth they brought with them. All passages from older writers dealing with the Montanistic prophetesses are collected in Wolf's *Fragmenta mulierum Græcarum*, p. 120 ff.

[2] "Von den Personen der Maximilla und Priscilla hat die Geschichte nichts überliefert als das Prädikat meretrices" (p. 247). Schwegler is here a little unfair, but there is no lack of loose declamation and improbable charges. The account of the suicide in Eusebius, it must be recollected, is considerably qualified by the candid admission, "ἴσως μὲν οὕτως, ἴσως δ' οὐχ' οὕτως," which would be no very inappropriate motto for much of the "history" to be derived from those quarters, (v. 16, § 6).

[3] Augustin is the only writer who seems to place Maximilla in a secondary rank, giving the first place to Priscilla and (?) Quintilla, on account of their vision. Hippolytus makes out Maximilla and Priscilla the real leaders, and suppresses Montanus altogether, viii. 19.

[4] Vide supra, p. 30, note 2.

have been the case[1]. Of the other women whose visions were received as a Divine revelation, the only names that have come down to us are those of the martyrs Perpetua and Felicitas, whose adherence to Montanism, (notwithstanding the well-meant efforts of Orsi and other Roman Catholic writers,) is now generally acknowledged[2]. Among the men prominent in the party, Themiso, Theodotus, Alexander, Alcibiades, Æschines, Proclus (or Proculus,) Lucius, and (according to some modern writers,) Athenagoras. The first-named wrote a "general epistle" to advocate the principles of the New Prophecy[3]. Theodotus, who is not to be confounded with any one of the three other heretics of the same name, is briefly mentioned by Eusebius[4]. Of Alexander and Alcibiades we have no information other than a record of their names in the same work[5]. Æschines and Proclus are noted by the Pseudo-Tertullian as the respective leaders of the two branches into which Montanism broke up in the Third Century, and the latter is also said to have engaged in

[1] He alludes to her as "a viper of the Caïnite heresy, making it her first aim to destroy baptism." That this is a pre-Montanistic treatise appears sufficiently clear from the words, "that most monstrous creature, who had no right to teach even sound doctrine." (See Kaye, p. 43, and Anti-Gnostikus, p. 169 ff.)

[2] Vide infra, II. § 8, and Appendix B. The Cardinal's treatise is based upon the following impregnable syllogism: (1) P. and F. are recognised as martyrs by the Church; (2) all such martyrs must be orthodox; (3) Ergo.

[3] "Ἐτόλμησε μιμούμενος τὸν ἀπόστολον (?) καθολικήν τινα συνταξάμενος ἐπιστολὴν κατηχεῖν μὲν τοὺς ἀμείνον αὐτοῦ πεπιστευκότας, συναγωνίζεσθαι δὲ τοῖς τῆς κενοφωνίας λόγοις, βλασφημῆσαι δὲ εἰς τὸν κύριον καὶ τοὺς ἀποστόλους καὶ τὴν ἁγίαν ἐκκλησίαν." (Apollonius ap. Euseb. H. E. v. 18. 3.)

[4] The younger Walch carefully enumerates (1) "Theodotus der Gärber, aus Byzanz;" (2) "Th. Stifter der Melchisedekiten;" (3) "Th. der Valentinianer;" and finally, (4) "Th. der Montanist." (Hist. der Ketzereien, I. 547.) Eusebius mentions him with Alcibiades as being ἀμφὶ Μοντανὸν (v. 3).

[5] The same authority in one place, (v. 16,) actually describes Montanism as "ἡ τῶν κατὰ Ἀλκιβιάδην λεγομένων αἵρεσις." But Schwegler remarks (Montanismus, p. 243) that the text is doubtful, and that Heinichen's edition reads "Miltiades" in this place.

36   THE HISTORY OF MONTANISM.

BOOK I. a controversy with the presbyter Caius at Rome[1]. Bishop Pacian mentions Blastus as one of the sect, as well as Lucius Carinus[2]. Athenagoras has been included by some on account of his peculiar views on Inspiration; but this and similar questions of internal evidence must be reserved for treatment in the following book.

§ 5. Progress in Asia Minor.

The plan of this essay does not admit of an examination into the causes for the rapid spread of Montanism in Asia Minor. These will be investigated when we deal with the general historical "position" of the party, after having analysed its distinctive tenets. No satisfactory evidence is to be found either in Eusebius or Epiphanius, as to the incidents of this progress. The latter in one place, it is true, asserts that the city of Thyatira was infected with the heresy as early as A.D. 126, a statement which (as we have shewn) it is impossible to reconcile with any consistent theory[3]. A more probable account is found in the anonymous writer so largely quoted by Eusebius. He relates that, owing to the alarming spread of the new opinions, many assemblies of the faithful were convened in order to decide on measures of repression, and that these synods invariably condemned the Montanists[4]. The *Libellus Synodicus* alludes to one council held at Hierapolis by Apollinaris, (the bishop of the town,) and twenty-six other prelates, which fulminated anathemas against Montanus and Maximilla. Also that a "holy and special synod" was held by the Bishop Sotas and twelve

[1] Vide infra, Book III. § 1. And see Tertullian's eulogy on "Proculus noster" (*Adv. Val.* 5).

[2] "Nam puto et Graecus Blastus ipsorum est" (sc. Phrygum). And elsewhere: "ipsi illi Phryges nobiliores, qui se animatos mentiuntur a Leucio, se institutos a Proculo gloriantur" (*Paciani Epist.* I. ad *Symp.* VII. 257 in *Gall.*).

[3] Epiphan. *Hæres.* XLVIII. § 33.

[4] "Τῶν κατὰ τὴν Ἀσίαν πιστῶν πολλάκις καὶ πολλαχῇ τῆς Ἀσίας εἰς τοῦτο συνελθόντων καὶ τοὺς προσφάτους λόγους (sc. of the Montanists) ἐξετασάντων καὶ βεβήλους ἀποφηνάντων καὶ ἀποδοκιμασάντων τὴν αἵρεσιν, οὕτω δὴ τῆς τε ἐκκλησίας ἐξεώθησαν καὶ τῆς κοινωνίας εἴρχθησαν." (*H. E.* lib. V. cap. 16.)

others at Anchialus, on the Black Sea, which council also condemned the Montanists[1]. But these statements have to contend with the difficulty of being reconciled with others supported by far higher authority. If Montanism had been thus summarily condemned, how can we account for the fact that Rome was willing to recognise its orthodoxy not many years later? Or how can we suppose that the confessors of Gaul would have pleaded so earnestly in the face of a solemn decision of the Asiatic Church? These synods are supposed to have been held before A.D. 150, that is, not long after Montanism began to attract the attention of the Church, although twenty years after the first formation at Pepuza. But this seems to be contradicted by a statement in the Libellus, to the effect that the Synod of Hierapolis condemned "Theodotus the tanner" at the same time. Now it is certain that this Theodotus was excommunicated by Victor, Bishop of Rome, near the end of the Second Century, and the only way out of the difficulty is in the supposition, (offered by Hefele,) that the compiler of the Libellus confounded one Theodotus with another[2]. The further events connected with Asia Minor, such as the decision of the Laodicean Council, will be treated of under the head of the decline of Montanism.

§ 6. Montanism at Rome.

In the middle of the Second Century, Rome had already become the intellectual centre of Christendom. Perhaps no historical event had so much importance in shaping the earlier stages of Catholicism as the removal of the head-quarters from Jerusalem to the capital of the Empire. All who wished to influence the Church, or

[1] This *Libellus Synodicus* contains analyses of the Councils of the first nine centuries. It was brought from Greece at the time of the Renaissance by Andreas Darmarius, and was edited by Pappus, (? Pfaff,) a theologian of Strasburg. Harduin reprinted it in his collection, while Mansi separated each portion, placing each under the respective date. Although of no very early date, this *Libellus* is considered to have been based on good information. (See Hefele, *Conciliengeschichte*, I. 70.)

[2] Vide supra, p. 35, and note 4.

to contribute towards the solution of the pending controversies, hastened thither: Valentinus the Gnostic, Justin the Apologist, Hegesippus the Historian, Polycarp the representative of Asiatic orthodoxy, Praxeas the Monarchian, Proclus the Montanist[1]. If the last-named is to be considered the first who proclaimed the New Prophecy at Rome, there can be little doubt that he found the ground prepared for him indirectly by the writings of a remarkable predecessor. The Visions of the "Shepherd" must have been the popular book, for more than a generation, among the secondary Hagiographa[2]. As Ritschl observes: "The real object of these writings is the elevation of the moral code (Sittenstrenge)," and it is difficult to understand the reason why Tertullian (*De Pudic.* 20) speaks of "that apocryphal shepherd of adulterers." Now, we are enabled to infer that it was during the episcopacy of Anicetus that Montanism first appeared at Rome. The evidence is not strong, but it is just sufficient to lend consistency to the view, and very little more can be ever hoped for when one is dealing with the period in question. Our historical points of contact are:—

(*a*) The statement of Prædestinatus that Soter wrote against Montanism[3].

(*b*) The knowledge (derived from Eusebius) that Eleutherus was so unfavourable to the same party as to call forth the letter of the Gallic martyrs; confirmed by—

(*c*) Tertullian's account of the coming of Praxeas to Rome, and his breaking off the amnesty by (doubtless among other objections) reminding "the Bishop" (? Victor) that his predecessors had censured the Montanists.

Let us consider (*b*) and (*c*) more closely. Eusebius relates that the Confessors of Lyons and Vienne (churches which it appears had been founded by Phrygian evangeli-

---

[1] See this worked out in Gfrörer's *Kirchen-Geschichte*, I. 263 ff., and Schwegler's *Nachapost. Zeitalter*, II. 201.

[2] Westcott on *Canon of N. T.* (4th ed.), p. 190 ff. Ritschl, *Entstehung*, 529, 530.

[3] "Scripsit contra Montanistas Soter papa urbis." (*Hæres.* XXVI.)

zation) "sent letters both to their brethren in Asia and Phrygia, and also to Eleutherus, bishop of Rome, advocating peace among the churches[1]." This missive, styled by Eusebius "εὐλαβὴς καὶ ὀρθοδοξοτάτη," was carried by Irenæus, then a presbyter; and knowing the high respect entertained for the authority of confessors, we have no difficulty in believing, especially with the following confirmation, that this embassy was successful in its endeavour. One or two writers, however, have pointed out, and with reason, that this statement is by no means so clear as Schwegler and Ritschl believe, and some have even declined to regard the Gallic epistle as in any way favourable to Montanism[2]. But, apart from the fact that Eusebius's suppression of the letter itself speaks plainly as to the character of its contents—for he would surely have quoted any rebuke to the Montanists "in extenso"—the word ἀδελφοῖς when applied to the same in the other letter (describing the torments of the martyrs), added to "τὴν αὐτὴν πίστιν...ἔχουσιν," and above all, the description of one of their number as "ἔχων τὸν παράκλητον ἐν ἑαυτῷ, τὸ

[1] "Τῶν δὲ ἀμφὶ τὸν Μοντανὸν . . . . περὶ τὴν Φρυγίαν ἄρτι τότε πρῶτον τὴν περὶ τοῦ προφητεύειν ὑπόληψιν παρὰ πολλοῖς ἐκφερομένων, (πλεῖσται γὰρ οὖν καὶ ἄλλαι παραδοξοποιΐαι τοῦ θείου χαρίσματος εἰσέτι τότε κατὰ διαφόρους ἐκκλησίας ἐκτελούμεναι πίστιν παρὰ πολλοῖς τοῦ κἀκείνους προφητεύειν παρεῖχον) καὶ δὴ διαφωνίας ὑπαρχούσης περὶ τῶν δεδηλωμένων, αὖθις οἱ κατὰ τὴν Γαλλίαν ἀδελφοὶ τὴν ἰδίαν κρίσιν καὶ περὶ τούτων εὐλαβῆ καὶ ὀρθοδοξοτάτην ὑποτάττουσιν· ἐκθέμενοι καὶ τῶν παρ' αὐτοῖς τελειωθέντων μαρτύρων διαφόρους ἐπιστολὰς, ἃς ἐν δεσμοῖς ἔτι ὑπάρχοντες τοῖς ἐπ' Ἀσίας καὶ Φρυγίας ἀδελφοῖς διεχάραξαν, οὐ μὴν ἀλλὰ καὶ Ἐλευθέρῳ τῷ τότε Ῥωμαίων ἐπισκόπῳ, τῆς τῶν ἐκκλησιῶν εἰρήνης ἕνεκα πρεσβεύοντες." H. E. lib. v. cap. 3.

[2] Of course Baronius and later R. C. writers indignantly spurn the notion that the martyrs could have sympathised with "heretics." Even the younger Walch is inclined to hold that the epistle may have recommended the Montanists to "restore peace" by ceasing to prophesy. (*Hist. der Ketzereien*, i. 643.) He adds: "Da es ihm (sc. Eusebius) nicht gefallen, zugleich den Inhalt des Urtheils bekannt zu machen; so hat es an mancherlei Muthmassungen neuerer Gelehrten nicht fehlen lassen, da denn jeder die guten Alten so denken lässt, wie er nach seinen eigenen Religionsgesinnungen denken würde." (i. 643.) Schwegler seems, in this instance, to have drawn only a fair conclusion from the evidence. (*Montanismus*, p. 253.)

πνεῦμα πλεῖον τοῦ Ζαχαρίου[1];" all these details fairly support the theory in question. That Irenæus should have regarded Montanism at first with far more favourable eyes than later, will not surprise those who study the very slight allusions to the New Prophets in his book against Gnosticism, and we can only suppose that he supported the petition with his already not inconsiderable influence. The date of this mission is now universally fixed at A.D. 177[2].

Our next piece of evidence is derived from Tertullian, and is of such vast importance in the history of Montanism that it needs to be transcribed: "For after the Bishop of Rome had acknowledged the prophetic gifts of Montanus, Prisca, and Maximilla, and in consequence of the acknowledgment, had bestowed his peace on the churches of Asia and Phrygia, he" (sc. Praxeas, already mentioned as having brought his heresy from Asia to Rome), "by importunately urging false accusations against the prophets themselves and their churches, and insisting on the authority of the bishop's predecessors in the see, compelled him to recall the pacific letter which he had issued, as well as to desist from his purpose of acknowledging the [said] gifts. By this, Praxeas did a twofold service for the devil at Rome; he drove away prophecy, and he brought in heresy; he put to flight the Paraclete, and he crucified the Father. Praxeas' tares had been moreover sown, and had produced their fruit here also, while many were asleep in their simplicity of doctrine...We indeed, on our part, subsequently withdrew from the carnally-minded on our acknow-

---

[1] H. E. lib. v. cap. 1. Ritschl does not go quite so far as Schwegler in his estimate of the pro-Montanistic character of the epistle. He may be right in thinking that the passage here quoted does not *necessarily* imply what is here inferred, but it is remarkable, to say the least, that an instance of ascetic practice, quite Montanistic in its character, is quoted with regard to Alcibiades, (not to be confounded with the Phrygian of that name). See v. 3.

[2] 17th year of Marcus Aurelius. Cf. Sulpicius Sev. *H. Sacr.* II. 46. "Tum primum inter Gallias martyria visa, serius trans Alpes Dei religione suscepta."

ledgment and maintenance of the Paraclete[1]." Who was this Bishop of Rome? Although many singular guesses may be found in the different histories and monographs, the later and more critical writers[2] are divided between two names only, Eleutherus and Victor. It must be premised that the imperfect chronology of the Roman bishops in the 2nd century defies any pretence at complete accuracy, and in the following statement of the argument on both sides, I adopt the dates commonly accepted in general works of reference[3]. It is clear that, in order to explain Tertullian's "praecessores," Anicetus and Soter are inadmissible. For Eleutherus the chief ground is the probability that the intercession of the Gallic confessors and of Irenæus had the effect of making peace, and obtaining recognition for the Montanistic χαρίσματα. Only as there is not a scrap of confirmatory evidence, the supporters are bound to urge other reasons drawn from what is known of Victor's

[1] "Idem tunc episcopum Romanum, agnoscentem jam prophetias (*adv.* Montani, Priscae, Maximillae, et ex ea agnitione pacem ecclesiis Asiae et *Prax.* cap. Phrygiae inferentem, falsa de ipsis prophetis et ecclesiis eorum adseve- 1.) rando et praecessorum ejus auctoritates defendendo coëgit, et literas pacis revocare jam emissas, et a proposito recipiendorum charismatum concessare. Ita duo negotia diaboli Praxeas Romae procuravit, prophetiam expulit, et haeresem intulit; Paracletum fugavit et Patrem crucifixit. Fruticaverunt avenae Praxeanae, hic quoque superseminatae, dormientibus multis in simplicitate doctrinae; . . . . . . Et nos quidem postea agnitio Paracleti atque defensio disjunxit a Psychicis."

[2] Baronius, Rigaltius (see Prolegg. to his ed. of Tertullian), declare for Anicetus, of course with the purpose of minimizing the papal mistake; Schwegler and Ritschl are in favour of Eleutherus; Neander is doubtful; Pagi (*Annot. ad Baron.*), Tillemont (*Mém.* II. 869), and Routh (*Rel. Sacr.* I. 261), prefer Victor. Dodwell (ap. Pearson, *Opp. posth.* App. 168,) suggested Zephyrinus.

[3] That is to say:—Pius, (142—157); Anicetus, (157—168); Soter, (168 —173); Eleutherus, (173—189); Victor, (189—201); Zephyrinus, (201— 218). Vater in his *Tabellen*, still a standard authority in Germany, differs considerably from the above: e. g. he places Soter's accession in 161, that of Eleutherus in 171, and Victor's in 182. Certainly this latter calculation is more convenient for those who suppose that Tertullian's bishop was Eleutherus, as it bestows five more years on him. The latest investigator, Lipsius, differs slightly in his results from the first enumeration. (See Appendix E.)

character. "His hostile attitude towards Jewish Christianity," says Schwegler, "and his overbearing conduct to the Asiatic Church, are well known. This might agree well with the final condemnation of Montanism, but not with a previous desire for reconciliation[1]." But this would depend, as the same writer admits, on the question whether the Montanists of Rome had retained the Asiatic rule for keeping Easter, or had adopted that of the Western Church. Prædestinatus says distinctly "unum Pascha nobiscum[2]," and Schwegler has no resource but to reject his evidence as untrustworthy. It is true that the evidence on this point is very conflicting, and that Socrates[3], Sozomen[4], and the Pseudo-Chrysostom[5] assert that the Montanists held to the Asiatic rule. But there is another aspect of the question, to which very little attention seems to have been paid. By examining the records of the Monarchian heresy, always identified with Praxeas, we find no small grounds for supposing that Victor must have been this bishop. For instance, the author of the Appendix to Tertullian's *Præscriptio* says: "But after all

---

[1] *Montanismus*, p. 250. Neander seems to have wavered between the two:—"Wir wissen nicht, welche Umstände den starren, von einem hierarchischen Geist beseelten Victor für den Montanismus günstig stimmen könnten. Es passt wohl zur Charakteristik desselben, dass er seinen beiden Vorgängern nicht widersprechen wollte, und dass daher Praxeas ihn dadurch gegen die montanistischen Gemeinden sich zu erklären bewog, dass er ihm das Ansehen seiner Vorgänger entgegenhielt." (*Anti-Gnostikus*, 2nd ed. p. 441, note; and see also *All. K. G.* I. 3. 896.)

[2] *Hæres.* XXVI. Schwegler finds it convenient to discredit this witness here, after using him elsewhere. (Cf. p. 254.) "Indem uns nämlich der Prädestinatus mit der Nachricht *zu Hülfe kommt.*"

[3] *Hist. Eccl.* IV. 28. [He is dealing with a later period, when the Montanists had fused with the Novatianists.]

[4] Sozom. *Hist. Eccl.* VII. 18. Sabbatius introduced the Jewish custom to the Novatianists: "καὶ πολλοὺς τοὺς ζηλοῦντας ἔσχε, καὶ μάλιστα Φρύγας καὶ Γαλάτας," &c.

[5] In the spurious 7th Oration, "In Pascha," (Chrysost. *Opp.* Tom. VIII. App. 276, ed. Montfauc.,) we find that, among those who belonged to the heresy of σὺν Ἰουδαίων ποιοῦντες τὸ πάσχα, is included the party of τῶν Μοντανιστῶν. [But cf. the 7th and 8th Canons of the Council of Laodicea.]

these things, one Praxeas introduced a heresy, which Victorinus was careful to corroborate[1]." Who was Victorinus? Many high authorities, such as Fabricius in his comments on Philaster[2], and, in our own times, Oehler, believe that this name is simply a mistake for that of Victor. But in neither case can we suppose that the intervention of Praxeas caused a complete breach and excommunication. We know, for instance, that the Montanist Proclus conducted a controversy with the presbyter Caius, the latter being placed by Eusebius in the period of Zephyrinus[3]. And this bishop was probably the "pontifex maximus" and "episcopus episcoporum," whose claims to absolve all crimes incurred the severity of Tertullian's satire[4]. In fact, the Montanists during the remainder of Victor's reign may be reasonably supposed to have remained in an ambiguous position, disowned and yet not formally and officially condemned: as with the Jansenists in France between the "Paix de l'Eglise" in 1668, and the renewal of persecution in 1702. The time was not yet ripe for declaring those men heretics who opposed the growing encroachments of ecclesiastical machinery, and the consequent "quenching of the Spirit." But this result, which will be further discussed in another chapter, was inevitable. At the beginning of the third century, the Montanists at Rome were completely isolated from the

[1] "Post hos omnes etiam Praxeas quidam hæresin intulit, quam Victorinus corroborare curavit." (Cap. 53.)
[2] Oehler supposed (*Annot. in Tertull.*) that the name of Victor's successor, Zephyrinus, had been also written, either originally, or by way of correction; and that a subsequent transcriber, as so often was the case, added the termination of the latter name to the former.
[3] Eusebius, *H. E.* lib. II. 25; III. 31; VI. 20. (Vide infra, II. § 7.) Although the writings in this controversy are lost, we can gather from the subject as described by Eusebius, that the last extremities of power had not yet been employed by the majority.
[4] "Audio etiam edictum esse propositum, et quidem peremptorium. Pontifex scilicet maximus edicit: 'Ego et mœchiæ et fornicationis delicta pœnitentia functis dimitto.' O edictum, cui adscribi non poterit: bonum factum!" (*De Pudic.* cap. 1.)

Book I. rest of the Church. A few generations later they became the mark for unanimous hatred and contempt.

§ 7. Montanism in Africa.
After Montanism had been rejected at Rome, it took fresh root in Africa. This is not the place to speak of the many causes which combined to fit the nature and proclivities of the national temperament for the new opinions; we can judge of the effects upon the surest and completest evidence. To the great champion of the New Prophecy at Carthage the next section is devoted. His contemporaries, the martyrs Perpetua and Felicitas, the account of whose sufferings constitutes one of the most interesting portions of Christian history, are now generally considered to have been undoubtedly attached to the same party; and I confess that I cannot understand the possibility of any other conclusion[1]. They have visions, and they expect them; they convey a mild but unmistakable reproof to their bishop; they even seem to recognise that peculiarity of ritual which several witnesses ascribed to Montanism, viz. the offering of cheese[2]. The date of their martyrdom has now, thanks to the labours of Uhlhorn, been fixed with tolerable certainty in the year A.D. 203, though he himself, with commendable caution, prefers to allow a possibility of a rather later date[3]. On the episodes of the martyrdom itself, deeply pathetic as they are, the limits and object of this essay forbid me to enter; but there are several incidents in the preliminary narrative which cast light on the situation of the Carthaginian Church, and on the extent of the Montanistic progress. In the 11th chapter, the martyr Saturus relates a vision, in which he was carried, together with Perpetua, into heaven. There

[1] See the controversy in Orsi, Basnage (*Hist. Eccl.* XVIII. 9), Wernsdorf, *de Montanistis*, p. 52 ff., and 126, Ritschl, *Entstehung*, p. 545 ff.; Schwegler, *Montanismus*, p. 65, Uhlhorn's *Fundamenta*.

[2] On this point I certainly should lay no stress. See Appendix B.

[3] "Persecutio Severiana .... jam ann. 205 vel 206 defervisse. Martyrium autem SS. Perpetuae et Felicitatis primum jam impetum persecutionis prodere videtur." (Uhlhorn, *Fundamenta Chron. Tertull.* p. 13.) See the whole chapter.

they found their bishop, Optatus, and the presbyter
Aspasius, apparently in sadness. These at once fell at the
feet of Perpetua and her companion, and besought them
to restore peace. The future martyrs, though disclaiming
this authority, yet began to console them; and angels,
coming in, exhorted Optatus to "correct his flock[1]." Now
it is known that Optatus was Bishop of Carthage. Aspasius
is called "doctor" as well as "presbyter," from being
probably the teacher of catechumens. That the dissension
was upon the subject of Montanism appears the only
reasonable conclusion[2]. The "corrige plebem tuam" must
certainly have referred to the question of discipline, always
foremost in the relations of the Montanists to the church-
rulers. And finally the simile employed by the angels,
"quasi de circo redeuntes et de factionibus certantes," can
only be explained as an oblique condemnation of the amusements which laxer Christians enjoyed or excused, but
which the Montanists invariably denounced as mortally
sinful.

Our knowledge of this great man's life is almost solely derived from a meagre sketch left by Jerome, and from allusions in his own works. We infer with certainty that his literary activity took place in the reigns of Severus and Caracalla, (A.D. 193—216,) but we can only conjecture that he was born about the middle of the Second Century[3], and survived until 220 or 230[4]. Jerome tells us that he

§ 8. Tertul-
lian.

---

[1] [See the whole passage in Appendix D.] Ritschl paraphrases the "quia sic ad te conveniunt quasi de circo redeuntes, &c." thus: "(denn die Glieder derselben kämen zu ihm,) als wenn sie von der Rennbahn zurückkehrten, *und an den auf die Spiele bezüglichen Parteien theilnäh- men.*" Uhlhorn also takes this meaning for "factiones," against Hol- stenius and Münter, who thought that ecclesiastical factions were meant. (*Fundamenta*, p. 18.)

[2] Uhlhorn quotes Münter, (*Primord. eccl. Afr.* p. 25,) and Morcelli, (*Africa Christiana*, II. 53.) The latter even fixed the duration of Optatus's episcopate at from A.D. 200 to 204.

[3] Allix placed his birth about the year 145 or 150.

[4] Jerome reports that "he is said to have lived to a very advanced age." (*Catal. Scr. Eccl.*)

was a native of Carthage, and the son of a proconsular centurion[1], and it is impossible not to recognise in the writings which have come down to us the evident traces of legal as well as rhetorical education. Eusebius informs us that Tertullian was thoroughly acquainted with the Roman Law[2], and we may suppose that he practised as an advocate on reaching manhood. But the bent of his mind towards religious speculation seems to have found an early vent in a treatise on the state of marriage[3], and such a nature was not likely to watch without deep interest, nor without ultimate choice of side, the then widening gulf between the Montanists and the hierarchy at Rome. It seems probable that he was born a heathen, and in his early life may not have been free from the moral corruption of the time and place[4]. But when the time of conversion came, it was deep and decisive. The fierce, stern African character made valiant soldiers, if not always discreet teachers, in the service of God. Its intellectual bent was far removed indeed from the dreamy, Oriental musings upon the origin of the world: but it welcomed the ardent hopes of Christ's speedy coming; it revelled in the austerities which at once diminished the terrors of persecution and opened visions of the future reward; it was prepared to acknowledge the religion of the New Prophets as the pure, unadulterated Gospel, and their utterances as the voice of the Spirit. Tertullian was always combating; first with the heathen, next against

[1] Kaye explains this office as equivalent to our modern "aide-de-camp." He refers to a note of Valesius in Euseb. *H. E.* II. 2.

[2] "Τοὺς Ῥωμαίων νόμους ἠκριβωκὼς ἀνήρ" (II. 2), which, as Neander suggests, should be taken together with the following: "τάτε ἄλλα ἔνδοξος, καὶ τῶν μάλιστα ἐπὶ Ῥώμης λαμπρῶν." (See *Anti-Gnostikus*, p. 7 ff.)

[3] "Als Jüngling richtete er an einen heidnischen Philosophen (cf. Hieron. ep. 22 *ad Eustoch.*) eine nach Art der rhetorischen Deklamation verfasste Schrift über die Schwierigkeit des Ehestandes." (See also *Adv. Jovinian.* I. 13.)

[4] So Neander infers from a passage in the *De resurr. carn.* cap. 59; as well as from the allusions to former visits to the gladiatorial combats. (*Antign.* p. 9, and note.)

the "carnal-christians," lastly against heretics. The scanty fragments of report as to his life may be briefly reviewed here: that he became, after his conversion, a presbyter in the Christian Church, is asserted by Jerome expressly, and is contradicted nowhere[1]. His decided acceptance of Montanism, and consequent separation from the Church about the year 203[2], decided the remaining course of his life. A visit to Rome (perhaps more than once), as to the period or duration of which even conjecture is wasted, alone marks what may have been externally a very uneventful life. His writings, however, with but a few exceptions, are ours[3]; and from them it now remains to extract such preliminary knowledge as may enable us to quote them rightly[4]. [See Book II. § 1.]

Most of the names of the adversaries of the Montanists have been already mentioned in the course of the preceding narrative. In fact, concerning the "Anonymous" writer, Apollonius, Serapion, Apollinaris, Zoticus, and Sotas, nothing is known in addition to the brief facts stated. Praxeas also is only known by an outline of his heresy, and by the incidents recorded by Tertullian. Two remain, however, concerning whom something is to be said. Miltiades, who is called scornfully "the sophist

§ 9. Assailants of Montanism.

[1] Naturally, the undoubted fact of Tertullian's marriage has caused all R. C. writers to contest the statement of Jerome. It has been the custom of these critics to put forth such passages as, " Nonne et Laici Sacerdotes sumus?" (*De Exhort. Cast.* c. 7). And one in the *De Monogamia* c. 12: " ...tunc unum omnes sumus, tunc omnes Sacerdotes, quia Sacerdotes nos Deo et Patri fecit." I cannot see that such an employment of the term carries any more weight on one side, than the narrative in the *De Anima* (where T. mentions his stopping to hear a revelation in the Church " dimissa plebe "), on the other side.

[2] The date is fixed by Uhlhorn in A.D. 202 (or 203), by Noesselt in 199, by Hesselberg in the following year. 199 seems the year most commonly followed, and it is probably as nearly right as we can hope for.

[3] See list in Kaye, p. 59 ff. Also in Oehler's *Prolegomena*. The seven books *On Ecstasy* are indeed a terrible loss to the historian of Montanism!

[4] I reserve the question of doctrine to the following Book.

of the Churches" by Tertullian[1], is known to have written a book against the Montanistic Prophecies[2]. The presbyter Caius is known to us, through Eusebius, as (*a*) writing against the Montanist Proculus; (*b*) denying (probably in the same work,) the Pauline authorship of the Epistle to the Hebrews; (*c*) describing the works of Cerinthus in a manner which led some to suppose that he included the Apocalypse among them[3]. This last feature induced Storr and Eichhorn to class Caius with the strange and little-understood party,—the Alogi, which we shall describe later. Photius relates of him "$\chi\epsilon\iota\rho o\tau o\nu\eta\theta\hat{\eta}\nu a\iota$ $a\mathring{v}\tau\grave{o}\nu$ $\kappa a\grave{\iota}$ $\grave{\epsilon}\theta\nu\hat{\omega}\nu$ $\grave{\epsilon}\pi\acute{\iota}\sigma\kappa o\pi o\nu$[4]," which Schwegler would explain as denoting an intimate connection between Caius and the anti-Jewish party. In what way the authorship of the Epistle to the Hebrews became a subject of controversy between Catholic and Montanist, I confess, I am utterly unable to conjecture.

---

[1] According to Eusebius, (*H. E.* lib. v. c. 17,) the title or subject was: "$\pi\epsilon\rho\grave{\iota}$ $\tauο\hat{v}$ $\mu\grave{\eta}$ $\delta\epsilon\hat{\iota}\nu$ $\pi\rho o\phi\acute{\eta}\tau\eta\nu$ $\grave{\epsilon}\nu$ $\grave{\epsilon}\kappa\sigma\tau\acute{a}\sigma\epsilon\iota$ $\lambda a\lambda\epsilon\hat{\iota}\nu$." Tertullian includes him, in the 5th chapter of his book against the Valentinians, among the writers who had already written against these heretics; but his expression "ecclesiarum sophista," does not evince any admiration in other respects.

[2] It would be possible to construct some ingenious theories in connection with the passage in the Muratorian Fragment:—"Arsinoi autem seu Valentini, vel *Mitiadis* (sic), nihil in totum recipimus, qui etiam novum Psalmorum librum Marcioni conscripserunt una cum Basilide Assianum Catafrygum constitutorem." But all critics that I have been able to consult dismiss it as hopelessly obscure. (See Schwegler, p. 219, note.)

[3] Euseb. *H. E.* lib. vi. c. 20; and lib. iii. c. 28. Prof. Westcott (*Canon of N. T.* 275, note), expresses his "decided belief that Caius is not speaking of the Apocalypse of St John, but of books written by Cerinthus in imitation of it." Volkmar (*Hippo'ytus u. die röm. Zeitgenossen*, p. 60, ff.) is inclined to place the very existence of the $\grave{\epsilon}\kappa\kappa\lambda\eta\sigma\iota a\sigma\tau\iota\kappa\grave{o}\varsigma$ $\grave{a}\nu\acute{\eta}\rho$ in doubt. A writer in the *Lit. Centralblatt* (1854, p. 35) attempted to prove that Caius "als der Gegenbischof gemeint sein könne, wogegen denn auch Hippolytus gestritten habe." The whole matter seems to be hopelessly obscure.

[4] Phot. Cod. 48. Pag. 12. (Bekker.) Quoted by Schwegler, *Montanismus*, p. 287, note.

EXCURSUS UPON THE ALOGIAN HERESY.

Mindful of Hug's caustic, and perhaps not ill-deserved com- The Alogi.
ment¹, I shall compress these remarks into the briefest compass.
The sources for our knowledge of this heresy are as follows :—

(a) Original writers :
I. Dionysius Alexandrinus (ap. Euseb. *H. E.*, v. 25), also
III. 28.
II. Epiphanius (*Hæres.* LI.).
[Mentions also in Josephus, Augustin, John of Damascus,
&c.]

(b) Modern compilers :—
I. Petrus Wesselingius. *Probabilium liber singularis, in quo
insunt vindiciæ...verborum Johannis*, &c. Ultraject. 1731.
II. Koerneri *De Auctoritate Apocalypseos Johannis ab
Alogis impugnata*, &c. Lips. 1751.
III. Schroeckh. *Christliche Kirchengeschichte* (tom. III. p.
176 seq.).
IV. Walch. *Hist. der Ketzereien* (I. 569 seq.).
V. Merkel. *Historisch-kritische Aufklärung der Streitigkeit
der Aloger und anderer alten Lehrer über die Apokalypsis im
zweiten Jahrhunderte*. Frankfurt, 1782.
VI. Heinichen. *De Alogis, Theodotianis, atque Artemonitis*. Lipsiæ, 1829.
[See also Schwegler, p. 267 ff., Harnack, (*Zeitschr. für
hist. Theol.* 1874,) and Lipsius, *Quellen der aeltesten Ketzergeschichte*, p. 93 ff.]

THE NAME. We have already seen how easily names of
heresies were invented or varied. The Tascodrugitæ for instance, (v. supra, I. § 2,) are also called Ascodrogitæ, Ascodrutæ,
Ascodrupitæ, Ascitæ. And Theodoret (*Hær. fab.* II. 4) says of
Artemon, "'Ἀρτέμων...ὅν τινες Ἀρτεμᾶν ὀνομάζουσιν." Kœrner
considered the term "Alogi" a pure nickname, an opinion
concurred in by Walch, who says :—" Der Witz der Kirchen-
lehrer, Ketzern Spottnahmen beyzulegen, ist hier offenbar."
(I. 569.) Even in modern times this inclination has been

¹ "Die Secte der Aloger, über welche man desto mehr geschrieben
hat, je weniger man von ihnen weiss." (Hug, *Einleitung in das N. T.*
II. 588.)

BOOK I. manifested, and Heinichen (p. 6) mentions a pamphlet entitled *Die Akephaler unserer Zeit.* (Lips. 1825.)

LOCALITY AND DURATION. According to Epiphanius, Asia Minor, especially Lydia. He mentions the city of Thyatira. (Heinichen, p. 8.) This heresy cannot be dated before the end of the Second Century, nor is there any trace after the middle of the Third. Epiphanius declares that 112 years had elapsed since the sect had disappeared. Now it is known that he wrote his history of heresies in the twelfth year of Valentinian's reign, *i. e.* about A.D. 375 or 376. This places the end of the Alogi about A.D. 263. But we cannot be certain[1].

OPINIONS. According to Epiphanius, the rejection of the Logos doctrine, and in general of St John's writings, particularly the *Apocalypse*. No doubt Epiphanius's Alogi, Irenæus's rejectors of prophecy, and the sect described by Dionysius of Alexandria (ap. Euseb. *H. E.* VII. 25) are identical. The last-named, as we have seen before, ascribes the origin of the error to Cerinthus; although, strangely enough, the later heretics chose to accuse him of having forged writings which he certainly did not accept. The Apocalypse was rejected as possessing no internal claims to reception: (τί με ὠφελεῖ ἡ ἀποκάλυψις Ἰωάννου, λέγουσά μοι περὶ ἑπτὰ ἀγγέλων καὶ ἑπτὰ σαλπίγγων; Ep. *Hær.* LI. 32). Irenæus (*adv. Hær.* III. 9, 11) evidently condemns the same party on two grounds: (1) "qui vel plures, quam dictæ sunt, vel rursus pauciores inferunt personas (πρώσωπα) Evangelii:" and (2) "qui donum Spiritus frustrentur, quod in novissimis diebus secundum placitum patris effusum est in humanum genus." This shews us another part of the Alogistic grounds for rejecting St John's writings: they found in them so strong a bulwark for the Montanistic claims that they had no alternative. There seems every probability that Praxeas was a member of this party. As Schwegler has pointed out, "he came from Asia Minor, opposed the Logos doctrine, does not allude to the Holy Spirit, and opposes the Montanists bitterly." Of Epiphanius' statement that Theodotus the tanner was ἀπόσπασμα ἐκ τῆς Ἀλόγου αἱρέσεως, we can only say that it labours under much antecedent improbability, as we know that the so-called Theodotians appealed to the

---

[1] "As we have no evidence of the tenets attributed to the Alogi being entertained in the time of Eleutherius," says Storr, "we should place the sect later, in the times of Victor or Zephyrinus." I think that the passages of Irenæus quoted above (and written, as he admits, under Eleutherius) do distinctly refer to the Alogi, whether they had the name then or not. It was this rationalizing party which, working into the hands of the ambitious hierarchy, finally drove out the Montanists.

Gospel of John (ch. viii. 40) in their attempt to prove the sole humanity of Christ's nature[1].   *Book I.*

In a former section (§ 5) we saw that certain synods were held in Asia Minor, about the years 150—160, which resulted in the local condemnation of the Montanists; such anathemas, however, not preventing the saintly Confessors of Lyons from openly advocating the aspersed cause. The next trace of a synod dealing with the question is found in the famous Epistle of Firmilian to Cyprian. In it he says: "Since some doubted as to the efficacy of the baptism of those who receive the new prophets, but nevertheless acknowledge the equality of Father and Son with us,...we have diligently examined the question, and have determined that no baptism beyond the limits of the Church is to be received[2]. In ascertaining the exact period to which this Synod belongs, we are aided by two points in his narrative. Firstly the phrases, "we assembled at Iconium," "we examined the question," etc. etc., shew us that Firmilian himself took part as a bishop in the conferences. And, as Hefele has pointed out, the use of "jam pridem" supports the inference that the Synod took place in the first years of Firmilian's prelacy, and consequently in the years A.D. 230—235[3]. We find that, during   *§ 10. Decisions of Councils.*   *1. Iconium.*   *2. Carthage.*

[1] See Eichhorn's *Einleitung*, II. 385, Heinichen, pp. 31—35, Schwegler, 270. On the other hand, Lipsius holds that "die Aloger des Epiphanios, wenn auch nicht gerade die Theodotianer, so doch eine mit diesen aufs Engste verwandte Partei waren." (*Quellen der aeltesten Ketzergeschichte*, p. 105.)

[2] Cyprian, *Epist.* LXXV.

[3] "Einen weitern Anhaltspunct für die Zeitbestimmung der Synode von Iconium in den zwei Stellen......... Zugleich berechtigt uns das *jam pridem* zu der Annahme, dass unsere Synode wohl in die ersten Jahre der bischöflichen Amtsführung Firmilians zu versetzen sei. Aus Eusebius aber (VI. 26) wissen wir dass Firmilian schon unter Kaiser Alexander Severus (222—235) als Bischof von Cäsarea blühte, weshalb wir keinen Anstand nehmen, mit Valesius und Pagi die Abhaltung der Synode in die Jahre 230—235 zu verlegen." (Hefele, *Conciliengeschichte*, I. 82.)— That this implied sentence on Montanism was not recognised by the Church, appears from the action taken at Nicæa.

4—2

the controversies on the same question which were raging in the years 255, 256, between Stephen of Rome and Cyprian, two or three Synods were held, and the Roman Bishop declared the Montanistic baptism to be valid. It is well known that the Council of Nicæa passed over the Montanists in silence, thus confirming, tacitly at least, this decision of Stephen; while the Paulianists (i. e. followers of Paul of Samosata) were ordered to be re-baptized upon admission. But the last link was broken in the Synod which met at Laodicea in the latter part of the Fourth Century[1], held at the time of a truce in the Arian campaign, which accounts for the predominant reference to questions of discipline. The 8th Canon enacts:—"That those who return from the heresy of the so-called Phrygians, even if they belonged to its clergy, and were the most distinguished, yet must be carefully catechised, and baptized by the bishops and presbyters of the Church." Now in the former Canon (§ 7), it was expressly stated that the Novatianists and Quartodecimans needed no re-baptism. This final condemnation was once more endorsed by the Œcumenical Synod of Constantinople (A.D. 381), the 7th Canon of which includes this provision:—"The Montanists or Phrygians, and the Sabellians, we receive as we do Pagans, namely, the first day we make them Christians, the second catechumens, the third day we exorcise them by breathing thrice into their face and ears, and make them continue a good while in the Church and hear the Scriptures, and afterwards we baptize them[2]." Such was the epitaph on the tomb of the New Prophets!

BOOK I.

3. *Nicæa.*

4. *Laodicea.*

5. *Constantinople.*

---

[1] Hefele declares himself unable to fix this Synod with any chronological precision. It must have been after A.D. 343, and before 381. (*Conciliengeschichte*, I. 724 ff.)

[2] "...Μοντανιστὰς τοὺς ἐνταῦθα λεγομένους Φρύγας, καὶ Σαβελλιανοὺς τοὺς υἱοπατορίαν διδάσκοντας, καὶ ἕτερά τινα χαλεπὰ ποιοῦντας· καὶ τὰς ἄλλας πάσας αἱρέσεις· πάντας τοὺς ἀπ' αὐτῶν θέλοντας προστίθεσθαι τῇ ὀρθοδοξίᾳ ὡς Ἕλληνας δεχόμεθα, καὶ τὴν πρώτην ἡμέραν ποιοῦμεν αὐτοὺς Χριστιανούς, τὴν δὲ δευτέραν κατηχουμένους, εἶτα τὴν τρίτην ἐξορκίζομεν αὐτοὺς μετὰ τοῦ ἐμφυσᾷν τρίτον εἰς τὸ πρόσωπον καὶ εἰς τὰ ὦτα αὐτῶν.

Augustin is the only writer who furnishes us with any tidings concerning the later fortunes of the African Montanists. It is true that elements of Montanistic ethical severity transfused themselves into other sects, and that the blunders of ecclesiastical annalists confuse together frequently manifestations of a very dissimilar character, such as Donatism. Augustin's account[1] conveys to us the impression that a separate sect of Tertullianists had been formed; but this notion is so utterly contrary to what we know of the Catholic spirit pervading that teacher's writings, that we must conclude that a later generation adopted the title. Still there is one witness, Prædestinatus, who would place this schism in Tertullian's own life-time[2], and the same writer in another place mentions that Tertullian, in later life, attempted a reconciliation between his own opinions and those of the Church[3]. The natural process of decomposition would take its course as soon as the last links of Catholicity were broken. It is possible that, in the middle of the Third Century, two main divisions already existed:—viz. (a) the orthodox Montanists, otherwise Proculists, or (in Africa) Tertullianists, who added nothing to the received faith but a belief in the prophetic gifts, and in the

καὶ οὕτως κατηχοῦμεν αὐτούς, καὶ ποιοῦμεν αὐτοὺς χρονίζειν εἰς τὴν ἐκκλησίαν, καὶ ἀκροᾶσθαι τῶν γραφῶν. καὶ τότε αὐτοὺς βαπτίζομεν." [As to the value of this evidence of the fusion of Montanism and Sabellianism, vide infra, Book III.

[1] "Tertullianistæ a Tertulliano, usque ad nostrum tempus paulatim deficientes, in extremis reliquiis durare potuerunt in urbe Carthaginiensi. Me autem ibi posito ante aliquot annos omni ex parte consumti sunt. Paucissimi enim, qui remanserunt, in catholicam transierunt, suamque basilicam, quæ nunc etiam notissima est, catholicæ tradiderunt." August. *Hæres.* 86.

[2] "Tertullianus a Cataphrygis postea divisus fudit a se omnem Phrygiae vanitatem, et Tertullianistarum conventicula propagavit, nihil tamen in fide mutavit." Præd. *Hær.* 86.

[3] Ibid. 26. But this might perhaps refer to the line which Tertullian adopts throughout, viz. maintaining that the Pneumatici had prescription on their side, and were the true Catholics.

value of ascetic observances; (b) the Æschinists, who had gradually adopted Sabellian views, just as, in our own times, many Presbyterian congregations in England gradually lapsed into Unitarianism. Montanism was practically dead when its prophets ceased to find successors[1], though relics of the party are found alluded to in ecclesiastical history as far as the Sixth Century[2], and in the edicts of Honorius, Theodosius, and Justinian. Having now reviewed the historical facts of Montanism, we turn to an examination of its doctrines.

[1] Epiphanius points to the fact that, in his time, the Montanists could point to no prophet (*Hær.* XLVIII. § 2). In fact, the last appearance that I can trace in history, is that of the prophetess mentioned by Firmilian, who does not indeed apply the name Montanist to her, but whose account admits of no other conclusion. He writes to Cyprian:— "In Cappadocia subito emersit atque in ecstasi constituta se prætulit et quasi S. Spiritu plena sic agebat, mirabilia quædam et portentosa perficiens; dicebat enim in Judæam festinare, fingens tanquam inde venisset. Huic exorcista quidam inspiratus Dei gratia fortiter restitit, et esse illum nequissimum spiritum, qui prius sanctus putabatur, ostendit. Illa mulier etiam hoc frequenter ausa est, ut invocatione non contemptibili sanctificare se panem et eucharistiam facere simularet, et sacrificium Domino non sine sacramento solitæ prædicationis offerret, baptizaret quoque multos usitata et legitima verba interrogationis usurpans." The period of this woman's appearance may be thus fixed. Firmilian tells us that it was "viginti et duos fere annos" before he wrote (which was during the Baptism Controversy, 253—257), so that we may conclude that it was about A.D. 235. [See Ritschl, *Entstehung*, p. 551 ff.] Wernsdorf contends that this woman was no Montanist, (p. 54 ff.), but a mere enthusiast. Apart from their belief in continued revelations, the later Montanists would easily have coalesced with the Novatianist and kindred sects.

[2] Gregory of Nazianzum declares (*Orat.* 14): " ἡ Φρυγῶν εἰσέται καὶ νῦν μανία." (Cf. Schwegler, p. 306, note.) But on the other hand, we find Optatus declaring that Montanism was a dead heresy:—"Marcion, Praxeas, Sabellius, et ceteri usque ad Cataphrygas temporibus suis...... ab assertoribus ecclesiæ catholicæ superati sunt. Ut quid bellum cum mortuis geram, quod ad negotium temporis nostri non pertinet?" (Opt. Mil. *de Schism. Donat.* I. 9.) For the edicts referred to, see list of references in Gieseler's *Church History*.

BOOK II.

THE TENETS OF MONTANISM.

THE historical student who has pledged himself to carry no preconceived ideas with him into his investigations, contends with one especial difficulty which, in the case of Montanism, can hardly be exaggerated. Recognising very soon that the accounts of the heresiologists afford but little help, owing to their fragmentary and often contradictory character, and that therefore it is from Tertullian's writings almost alone that his conclusions must be drawn, he finds himself in danger of entering a vicious circle. For he has first to decide which books of Tertullian's are Montanistic, and then to examine the charges of the adversaries by this self-made criterion. The dangers which may attend the course are only too obvious; accordingly the very strictest care is necessary in establishing this preliminary criterion. Now, by confining ourselves to the employment of the following Canon, the work seems susceptible of due performance: "Those opinions shall alone be deemed Montanistic which are asserted to be such by one or more of the ecclesiastical writers, and expressly admitted by Tertullian." It need hardly be said that our investigations will need to extend considerably beyond this tether afterwards, but not until a sufficient foundation has been laid in the ground of undoubted facts.

One of the soberest of German critics pointed out,

many years ago, the danger of confounding individual opinions of Tertullian with the general creed of Montanism[1]. But his caution, if carried out literally in practice, would prevent us absolutely from using our materials. On the contrary, a candid comparison of the passages where Tertullian makes especial reference to the inspiration from the Paraclete, with the statements in other writers, leads us to the conclusion, as Schwegler observed, "that Tertullian made no radical alteration whatsoever in the principles he accepted." That his strong individuality colours the outlines, and that his fiery African temperament grasps certain forms of reasoning differently from the dreamy and ecstatic Phrygians; this is inevitable. But the writer who has always in his mind the double ideal—the ancient as opposed to the innovations of heresy, and the spiritual as hostile to the carnal and external— would be under special restraints, both as regards the matter and the form of his utterances[2]. And once admitting him as witness, and, if any prefer it, counsel in the cause, no one can think that Montanism runs danger of condemnation because there are so many voices on the other side[3]. Such a champion is indeed a host in himself:

"Si Pergama dextra
Defendi possent, etiam hac defensa fuissent!"

[1] "Sehr gewöhnlich hat man Meinungen des Tertullian dem Montanismus zugeschrieben, und damit sowohl die Beurtheilung von diesem, als von Tertullians Schriften erschwert. Es durfte diess selbst da nicht geschehen, wenn Tertullian in montanistischen Formeln redet." Baumgarten-Crusius, *Dogmengesch.* I. 179. [And see Schwegler, p. 7 ff.]

[2] Most students of Tertullian's writings will, I think, have been struck by the fact that he is never less fiery and *exalté* than when speaking of Montanistic tenets and revelations. Take, for instance, the strongest of the anti-Psychic writings, as the *De Monogamia*, *De Pudicitia*, or *De Jejuniis*, and note how much less violent is the tone than when he is defending common Catholic truths against Praxeas or the Valentinians. It might be said that in the latter case he spoke from deeper-rooted convictions: I should draw a totally opposite conclusion.

[3] Nothing is a more curious study than to watch the solicitude with which a R. C. editor, such as Rigaltius, strives to manufacture a com-

THE TENETS OF MONTANISM.

Now without prejudice to the coming investigation, we may separate at once the writings of Tertullian into two divisions: (a) those in which topics within the Montanistic orbit are dealt with; and (b) those referring (as the *Ad Nationes, Apologeticus, De Oratione*, &c.) to subjects on which no difference arose between Catholic and Montanist. By comparing the bills of indictment in Eusebius, Epiphanius, Philaster, &c. we can limit the former topics as follows:

I. The doctrine of the Trinity (for while Epiphanius and Philaster declare that the Montanists were orthodox, many other writers accuse them of Sabellianism).

II. The work of the Spirit (especially as to prophecy and inspiration).

III. The theory of the Church (and the character of the sacerdotal office).

IV. The Sacraments (both as regards the charge of using unauthorised elements, e.g. Artotyritism, and of the horrible accusations already mentioned).

V. Discipline, and the application of religion to life (fasting, penance, marriage).

VI. Eschatology.

Upon these subjects we find that the following works of Tertullian treat, with more or less of fulness:

On I. Chiefly the treatise *Adversus Praxeam*, but references in the *Præscriptio Hæreticorum*.

II. Almost every treatise, especially *De Fuga in Persecutione, De Pudicitia, De Monogamia, Adv. Praxeam, De Virg. velandis, De Res. Carnis, De Jejuniis, Adv. Marcionem, De Anima, De Idololatria, De Spectaculis, De Cor. Militis.*

III. Chiefly *De Monogamia, De Pudicitia, De Virg. velandis, De Exh. Castitatis.*

IV. Only the treatise *De Baptismo* (which all authorities, as we shall find, consider præ-Montanistic).

pletely orthodox witness out of Tertullian. [See the note on *Adv. Prax.* 1.]

V. *De Monogamia, De Jejuniis, De Virg. velandis, De Exh. Castitatis, De Pudicitia, Ad Uxorem, De Fuga in Persecutione, De Cultu Feminarum.*

VI. *De Oratione, Apologeticus, De Spectaculis, De Res. Carnis, Monogamia*, and in the "regula fidei" contained in the *Praescriptio* (c. 13).

We proceed, then, in the first place, to ascertain the general form and character of the opinions in question, upon the plan proposed. Subsequently we shall take each of the sections in turn, attempting to work out more fully not only the substance of each particular tenet, but its connection with the whole system; concluding with the endeavour to fix the historical position of Montanism in relation not only to the Catholic Church, but to the contemporary phenomena of Gnosticism, and the possible derivation in part from forms of Phrygian worship[1].

§ 2. The New Revelation.

Montanus and his followers claimed to have received a revelation of God, of a nature supplementary to that communicated by Christ and His apostles. Its foundation is to be found in a literal and exclusive acceptation of the promise of the Paraclete, "who will guide you into all truth," and "shew you things to come" (John xvi. 13). The belief in the superiority of this new revelation is put very clearly by Tertullian. "If Christ abrogated what Moses commanded, because from the beginning it was not so...why should not the Paraclete alter what Paul permitted[2]?" The same order of development is defined in

---

[1] An able German critic [Hauber, in the *Studien u. Kritiken*, 1845, pp. 607—662] attempted to prove that Tertullian ought not to be admitted as a high authority, or rather, not as a representative of Montanistic teaching, seeing that he appears unable "sich mit den neuen Prophetenstimmen zu beruhigen, sondern es ist ihm beständiges Bedürfniss, in die frühere Zeit zurückzugehen, und .... bald aus dem Paradiese, bald aus den Patriarchen, Priestern u.s.w. Bestätigung, und bei Jesus und den Aposteln theils Bestätigung theils Entschuldigung zu suchen" (p. 608). This argument is effectively met by Ritschl. [*Entstehung*, pp. 511, 512.]

[2] "Si enim Christus abstulit quod Moyses praecepit, quia ab initio

another of Tertullian's treatises, as (1) the prophetic voice of the Old Testament; (2) the "disciplina Domini;" and (3) the Holy Spirit by (the mouth of) the holy prophetess Prisca[1]. This is also the view reprobated by the opponents of Montanism, who strove to aggravate what they declared heresy by asserting that the prophets claimed to be not merely the mouth-piece, but the very incarnation of the Paraclete. This point will be specially discussed afterwards; at present it will be sufficient to quote three witnesses in support of the former position.

Hippolytus.	Philaster.	Augustin.
"They are beguiled by two females whom they consider prophetesses. . . . They pretend that these see certain things by means of the Paraclete in them. They implicitly believe what these utter, and give out that they learnt more from their revelations than from the law, the prophets, and the gospels." *Adv. omn. Hær.* VIII. 19.	"They hold that the full gift (plenitudinem) of the Holy Spirit was not granted by Christ to His Apostles, but to their false prophets, and thus separate themselves from the Catholic Church." *Liber de Hæres.* XLIX. (Migne, XII. 1165.)	"They declare that the promised advent of the Holy Spirit took place in themselves, rather than in the case of the Apostles." *Hæres.* XXVI. (*Opp.* VI. 17.)

Tertullian never loses an opportunity of asserting in unqualified terms the superior insight enjoyed by those who hearkened to the Paraclete through the mouth of the prophets or prophetesses. He understands the mysterious

non fuit sic, nec ideo ab alia venisse virtute reputabitur Christus, cur non et Paracletus abstulerit quod Paulus indulsit." (*De Monogamia*, cap. 14.) Although, strictly speaking, Tertullian is only treating of one special point, viz. the permission of second marriages by St Paul, all writers (Mosheim, Wernsdorf, Neander, Kaye, Schwegler, Ritschl) agree that this may be taken as a general axiom, put in the form of a question.

[1] "Prophetica vox veteris Testamenti, . . . disciplina Domini, . . . Spiritus Sanctus per sanctam prophetidem Priscam." *De Exhort. Castit.* c. 10.

οἰκονομία of the Trinity, as better instructed by the Paraclete[1]. He declares himself the pupil of no man, but only of the same divine instructor[2]. He accepts the visible coming of the New Jerusalem on the same authority[3]. The Paraclete counsels martyrdom[4]; finally, the Paraclete teaches those things which the apostles even were not able to understand[5]. And yet there is no revolution organized against the institutions which, in their first form, undoubtedly furnished the fittest media for the agency of the Holy Spirit. The prophetic office, commended so highly by St Paul, and witnessed to by Justin and Irenæus, this was no innovation. Nor does Tertullian shrink from a criterion of true or false prophetic claim, which he states thus. He had imagined an opponent to moot the very pertinent objection : "It follows that, by this line of argument, anything you please which is novel and burthensome may be ascribed to the Paraclete, even if it have come from the adversary spirit." "No (replies the Montanist), for the adversary spirit would be apparent from the diversity of his preaching, beginning by adulterating the rule of faith, and so (going on to) adulterating the order of discipline[6]." Accordingly it is to the practical effects in life of the new teachings that he appeals, just as he and

---

[1] "Nos et semper, et nunc magis, *ut instructiores per Paracletum*, deductorem scilicet omnis veritatis, unicum quidem Deum credimus, sub hac tamen dispensatione, quam œconomiam dicimus, ut sermo ex ipso processerit, qui deinde miserit a Patre Spiritum Sanctum Paracletum." [*Adv. Prax.* cap. 2.]

[2] "Nos, qui et tempora et causas scripturarum per Dei gratiam inspicimus, *maxime Paracleti non hominum discipuli.*" [*Ibid.* cap. 13.]

[3] "Hierosolymam de cœlo delatam, qui apud fidem nostram est, *novæ propheticæ sermo testatur.*" [*Adv. Marc.* III. 24.]

[4] "Si pro Deo occumbas, ut Paracletus monet, in martyriis, &c." [*De Anima*, cap. 55.]

[5] Cf. the 2nd chapter (passim) of the *De Monogamia*.

[6] "Ergo hac argumentatione quidvis novum Paracleto adscribi poterit; etsi ab adversario spiritu fuerit. Non utique; adversarius enim spiritus ex diversitate prædicationis appareret, primo regulam adulterans fidei, et ita ordinem adulterans disciplinæ." [*De Monog.* cap. 2.]

his fellow apologists had appealed to the heathen world in the same way. Thus the spirits might be proved, whether they were of God or not. Nor even does Tertullian admit, as valid against himself, the stern legal rule of Præscription, which he had wielded with such inexorable rigour against heretics. Or rather, he claims its benefit once more! "Paracletus solus antecessor, quia solus post Christum[1]!" Accordingly the last stage is merely a revival of what was truly first, and unites the strength of youth with the dignity of age. Tertullian states the problem of revelation by stages by aid of a splendid image, which will best complete this sketch: "Nothing is without stages of growth; all things await their season...Look how creation itself advances little by little to fructification! First comes the grain, and from the grain arises the shoot, and from the shoot struggles out the shrub; thereafter boughs and leaves gather strength, and the whole that we call a tree expands; then follows the swelling of the bud, and from the bud bursts the flower, and from the flower the fruit opens; that fruit itself, rude for a while, and unshapely, little by little, keeping the straight course of its development, is trained to the mellowness of its flavour. So too righteousness (for the God of righteousness and of creation is the same) was first in a rudimentary state, having a natural fear of God; from that stage it advanced, through the Law and the Prophets, to infancy; from that stage it passed, through the Gospel, to the fervour of youth; now, through the Paraclete, it is settling into maturity. He will be, after Christ, the only one to be called and revered as Master; for He speaks not from Himself, but what is commanded by Christ....They who have received him set truth before custom[2]." Such was

---

[1] *De Virg. velandis*, cap. 1.

[2] *Ibid.* Twice in this chapter Tertullian repeats the noble thought, the great truth, that *Christ is Truth rather than Tradition*. ["Sed Dominus noster Christus veritatem se, non consuetudinem cognominavit."] Möhler made no error when he saw in the combat between Mon-

the faith, such the claims, of the New Prophets[1]. The next point in the investigation is the "Form" of these alleged revelations. In pursuance of our plan, let us first cite the following witnesses:—

Anonymus (ap. Euseb.).	Epiphanius.	Miltiades (ap. Euseb.).
"So then he [sc. Montanus] was carried away in spirit, and wrought up into a certain kind of frenzy and irregular ecstasy, raving, and speaking, and uttering strange things, and proclaiming what was contrary to the institutions that had prevailed in the Church. .... He excited two others, females, and filled them with the spirit of delusion, so that they also spake like the former, in a kind of ecstasy, out of all season, and in a manner strange and novel."	"Behold, [—this is the Paraclete speaking through Montanus,] man is as a lyre, and I hover round him as the plectrum; the man sleeps and I watch; behold, it is the Lord who transports the hearts of men, and gives hearts to men[2]." *Hæres.* xlviii. § 4. [Maximilla says: "ἀπέστειλέ με κύριος ἠναγκασμένον, θέλοντα καὶ μὴ θέλοντα."] *Ibid.* § 13.	[After mentioning the work of Miltiades on the subject "περὶ τοῦ μὴ δεῖν προφήτην ἐν ἐκστάσει λαλεῖν," Eusebius quotes him as saying:—] "But the false prophet *is carried away by a vehement ecstasy*, accompanied by want of all shame and fear. Beginning, indeed, with a designed ignorance, and terminating, as before said, *in involuntary madness*. They will never be able to shew that any of the Old or New Testament were thus agitated and carried away."
H. E. lib. v. cap. 16.		*H. E.* lib. v. cap. 17[3].

Our next step is to consult Tertullian, in order to see tanism and the Church the first (and perhaps the most logical) expression of the eternal opposition between the Protestant Idea in its highest sense, and what he called the "Catholic" principle.

[1] See Baronius, ii. 267; Mosheim, *De Rebus*, &c. p. 416; Walch, i. 620; Wernsdorf, p. 11 ff.; Ritschl, p. 462 ff.; Schwegler, 15 ff.

[2] I am not sure whether my translation of the last clause is correct. The original passage is as follows: "'Ἰδοὺ ἄνθρωπος ὡσεὶ λύρα, κἀγὼ ἵπταμαι ὡσεὶ πλῆκτρον· ὁ ἄνθρωπος κοιμᾶται, κἀγὼ γρηγορῶ, ἰδοὺ κύριός ἐστιν ὁ ἐκστάνων καρδίας ἀνθρώπων, καὶ διδοὺς καρδίας ἀνθρώποις." [In another place we have: "ἐφίσταμαι καὶ πλήσσω, καὶ γρηγορῶ, καὶ ἐξιστᾷ κύριος καρδίας."] Is the sense, "the Lord who created men's hearts, also can excite or transport them"?

[3] Many writers consider the speaker thus quoted to be not Miltiades, [in any case "*Alcibiades*" is wrong,] but the Anonymus of the former chapter. I confess that I cannot agree with them.

whether he admits or traverses these statements. The first passage quoted shall be the narrative which he gives us in his treatise *De Anima*, concerning a prophetic vision. This is specially important as furnishing us, at first hand, with a complete notion of the manner in which these alleged revelations were received, both by the "medium," and by the congregation or those to whom it was revealed. "We have now," Tertullian relates[1], "amongst us a sister whose lot it has been to be favoured with certain gifts of revelation, which she experiences in the Spirit by ecstatic vision ["per ecstasin in spiritu,"] amidst the sacred rites of the Lord's day in the Church: she converses with angels, and sometimes even with the Lord; she both sees and hears mysterious communications [sacramenta]; some men's hearts she understands, and to them who are in need she distributes remedies. Whether it be in the reading of the Scriptures, or in the chanting of Psalms, or in the preaching of sermons, or in the offering up of prayers, in all these religious services matter and opportunity are afforded to her of seeing visions. It may possibly have happened to us, whilst this sister of ours was rapt in the Spirit, that we had discoursed about the soul. After the people are dismissed at the conclusion of the services, she is in the habit of relating to us whatever things she may have seen in vision; for all her communications are most carefully examined, in order that they may be proved[2]."

[1] *De Anima*, cap. 9. The special value of this evidence is that Tertullian gives it, as it were parenthetically, and does not indulge in any rhetoric. His object is to explain his curious theory about the nature of the soul.
[2] "Est hodie soror apud nos revelationum charismata sortita, quas in ecclesia inter dominica solemnia per ecstasin in spiritu patitur; conversatur cum angelis, aliquando etiam cum Domino, et videt et audit sacramenta, et quorundam corda dignoscit, et medicinas desiderantibus submittit. Jam vero prout scripturae leguntur, aut Psalmi canuntur, aut adlocutiones proferuntur, aut petitiones delegantur, ita inde materiae visionibus subministrantur. Forte nescio quid de anima disseruimus,

Tertullian expressly admits here the complete passivity of the prophetess: the only element other than the operation of the Spirit being the subject of the prayer or discourse. We can compare other of his statements on the same subject: "The soul receives motion from some other thing when it is swayed (from the outside, of course, by something else) by prophetic influence or by madness[1]." Even Adam is supposed to have experienced the same influence and ecstasy, as well as all the prophets[2]; in fact, nothing is more clear than Tertullian's confidence not only in the genuineness of the condition, but also of its agreement with God's will and dispensation. It must be added that Tertullian places the Divine origin of all visions and dreams upon an equally lofty foundation:— "But from God, who has promised to pour out the grace of His Holy Spirit upon all flesh, and has ordained that His servants and His handmaids should see visions as well as utter prophecies [Joel iii. 1], must all these visions be regarded as emanating, which may be compared to the actual grace of God, as being honest, holy, prophetic, inspired, instructive, inviting to virtue, the bountiful nature of which causes them to overflow even to the profane[3], &c." There was no monopoly claimed for Priscilla or Maximilla. Tertullian mentions in no place having received any such Divine intimations himself[4], but he frequently records

cum ea soror in spiritu erat. Post transacta solennia, dimissa plebe, quo usu solet nobis renuntiare quæ viderit, nam et diligentissime digeruntur, ut etiam probentur." After relating the vision itself, to which we shall recur later, Tertullian concludes with the emphatic asseveration: "visio et Deus testis et Apostolus charismatum in ecclesia futurorum idoneus sponsor."

[1] "Ostendimus... moveri animam ab alio, cum vaticinatur, cum furit, utique extrinsecus." (*De Anim.* c. 6.)

[2] "Accidentiam spiritus passus est; occidit enim ecstasis super illum, sancti spiritus vis, operatrix propheticæ." (Cap. 11.) And, "In illum Deus amentiam immisit, spiritualem vim, qua constat prophetia." (Cap. 21.)

[3] *De Anima*, cap. 47.

[4] It is impossible not to think of Edward Irving as a parallel

THE TENETS OF MONTANISM.

the experiences of others. He relates how "a brother was chastised in a vision, because on the announcement of public rejoicings his servants had decorated his gates[1]." This is mentioned as "a witness on the authority of God." The Acts of Martyrdom of Perpetua and Felicitas relate many other instances of the same nature[2], and they must have been considered of common occurrence.

Seeing then that the facts are undisputed, the only question remaining is the theological one, or rather two questions of this nature arise:— *Primitive theory of inspiration.*

I. Did, or did not, the Primitive Church, up to the time of Montanus, admit the gift of prophecy and vision to all its members?

II. Was the character of this prophetic inspiration recognised as passive, or were the individual faculties active?

The former of these questions hardly needs discussion. It is indisputable that Clement, Ignatius, Hermas, Justin Martyr, and Irenæus, unanimously affirm their belief in, or even their experience of, the continued distribution of these *charismata*[3]. In fact the earlier opponents of Montanism were too prudent to take issue on the point at all, or else denounced, not the claim of prophetic gift, but its discontinuance. The writer quoted by Eusebius demands:—"If, after Quadratus and Ammia in Philadelphia, the women that followed Montanus succeeded in the gift of prophecy, let them shew us what women among them succeeded Montanus and his women.

instance, never laying claim himself to the gifts, but gladly welcoming them in others. Another case is that of Petersen (cf. Appendix C.), who received the higher light through the Fräulein von Asseburg.

[1] "Scio fratrem per visionem castigatum graviter, quod januam ejus, subito annunciatis gaudiis publicis, servi coronassent." (*De Idolol.* cap. 15.) See also *De Spectac.* 26.

[2] There are many collected in Noesselt's treatise on the Writings of Tertullian. (*De vera ætate*, &c. p. 184 ff.)]

[3] See the old authorities collected and discussed in John Smith's famous *Select Discourses*, No. 6, and also Hagenbach's *Dogmengeschichte*, and other collections.

H. E. 5

THE TENETS OF MONTANISM.

For the apostle shows that the gift of prophecy should be in all the church until the coming of the Lord, but they can by no means shew any one at this time, the 14th year from the death of Maximilla[1]." In a later section we may notice the remarkable change of opinion in the Church on this point; we now turn to the other. What was the theory of Inspiration recognised by writers of the Second Century? Did they reject as impious the claims of "ecstatic vision," of complete passivity under spiritual influence?

Athenagoras presented his Apology to the emperors Aurelius and Commodus about A.D. 176, when the manifestations of Montanism were fully known. He describes the inspiration of the Prophets in an often-quoted passage:—"...Moses, or Isaiah, or Jeremiah, and the other prophets who, lifted in ecstasy above the natural operations of their minds by the impulses of the Divine Spirit, uttered the things with which they were inspired, the Spirit making use of them as a flute-player breathes into a flute[2]."

Justin Martyr expresses the same view with equal clearness. He did not consider that inspiration was a mere increase in the productivity of human intelligence, nor did he allow to human faculties any share other than simple reproduction of the truth received[3]. He asserted that the prophets never delivered their own thoughts, but only what they had received by Divine revelation[4]. Like Athenagoras, he compared their state during the

---

[1] Miltiades (?) ap. Eusebius, *H. E.* lib. v. cap. 17.

[2] "οἱ προφῆται κατ᾽ ἔκστασιν τῶν ἐν αὐτοῖς λογισμῶν, κινήσαντος αὐτοὺς τοῦ θείου πνεύματος, ἃ ἐνηργοῦντο, ἐξεφώνησαν· συγχρησαμένου τοῦ πνεύματος, ὡσεὶ καὶ αὐλητὴς αὐλὸν ἐμπνεύσαι." (*Legat.* cap. 9.) The same image occurs in the 7th chapter, "... θεοῦ πνεύματι ὡς ὄργανα κεκινηκότι τὰ τῶν προφητῶν στόματα."

[3] I am indebted for my references in Justin to Semisch's able monograph. (Vol. 1. pp. 263 ff.)

[4] "Μηδὲν ἀπὸ τῆς ἰδίας αὐτῶν φαντασίας διδάξαντες ἡμᾶς..... ἀλλ᾽ ἀφιλονείκως καὶ ἀστασιάστως τὴν παρὰ θεοῦ δεξαμένου γνῶσιν καὶ ταύτην διδάσκοντες ἡμᾶς." *Coh. ad Græc.* cap. 8. [And see *Dial. c. Tr.* cap. 7.]

period of inspiration by the image of the lyre struck by the plectrum; he denied in fact that they retained any natural consciousness during inspiration: in other words, it was a state of ecstasy[1]. It is clear, then, that Justin and Athenagoras held no other doctrine of inspiration than that which the Montanists asserted, and for asserting have been condemned as heretics by the Church since the Fourth Century[2]. The defenders of the "Quod semper, quod ubique," are reduced to lamentable straits in the matter; but, what is more surprising, not a few Protestant theologians have failed or refused to see this change of front. The writer of a modern text-book thus deals with the difficulty:—"It is true that Athenagoras considers the Prophets of the Old Testament to have uttered their predictions while in a state of ecstasy, thus adopting the sentiments of Philo; but that he held, on any point, the extravagant opinions of Montanus, cannot, I apprehend, be alleged with any justice[3]." Now assertions of this sort

[1] "Τοὺς ἁγίους ἄνδρας ..... οἷς οὐ λόγον ἐδέησε τέχνης .... ἀλλ' κιθαροὺς ἑαυτοὺς τῇ τοῦ θείου πνεύματος παρασχεῖν ἐνεργείᾳ, ἵν' αὐτὸ τὸ θεῖον ἐξ οὐρανοῦ κατιὸν πλῆκτρον, ὥσπερ ὀργάνῳ κιθάρας τινὸς ἢ λύρας τοῖς δικαίοις ἀνδράσι χρώμενον, τὴν τῶν θείων ἡμῖν καὶ οὐρανίων ἀποκαλύψῃ γνῶσιν." [Coh. ad Gr. c. 8.] The same view is expressed with even greater plainness in the Dialogue; where the revelation to Zechariah is declared to have "not been when unexcited, but when in ecstasy." [τὸν διάβολον καὶ τὸν τοῦ κυρίου ἄγγελον οὐκ αὐτοψίᾳ, ἐν καταστάσει ὤν, ἑωράκει, ἀλλ' ἐν ἐκστάσει, ἀποκαλύψεως αὐτῷ γεγενημένης. Dial. c. Tr. cap. 115.]

[2] In addition to Justin and Athenagoras, (not to mention Tertullian,) we find that Theophilus [cf. Ad Autol. II. 9, 10], Clement Alex. [Strom. VI. 18], and Macarius [Homil. XLVII. 14], adopt the same view of inspiration. The last-named writer employs the identical image:—"Πλῆκτρον τῆς θείας χάριτος, ... ὡς γὰρ διὰ τοῦ αὐλοῦ τὸ πνεῦμα διερχόμενον λαλεῖ, οὕτω διὰ τῶν ἁγίων καὶ πνευματοφόρων ἀνθρώπων τὸ πνεῦμα τὸ ἅγιόν ἐστιν ὑμνοῦν."

[3] Lee, On the Inspiration of Holy Scripture, (4th edition,) p. 78 ff. Anything so astounding as the "argument" adopted by Dr Lee I have never met. He ignores the perfect agreement of Justin Martyr with the Montanistic view, and he actually appeals to Hippolytus as a witness to the Church's antagonism to the "ecstatic" view. Now Hippolytus does not touch the question at all: his only words on the subject of the inspiration claimed for the prophetesses are: "They pretend that these see

may be safely left to battle with inexorable facts which we have already adduced, and really deserve no refutation. We have seen that the work of Miltiades, itself a mere private treatise, and carrying with it no character of authority, was the very first declaration against the previous universal and orthodox sentiment. Later, in the Third Century (although even here the catenas are dubious) and in the Fourth, it is quite true that a vast change had taken place. The once orthodox doctrine of Justin and Athenagoras and Montanus was now branded as a heresy; and that which had been undoubtedly the private αἵρεσις of Miltiades was now the doctrine of the Catholic Church. From this time it is easy to collect a most unanimous list. Epiphanius is perhaps the first to lay down, as a canon and criterion of true prophecy, that it must be conscious and intelligent. ["Ὅσα οἱ προφῆται εἰρήκασι, μετὰ συνέσεως παρακολουθοῦντος," or "μετὰ καταστάσεως λογισμοῦ καὶ παρακολουθήσεως ... ἐφθέγγοντο." Epiph. *Hæres.* XLVIII. § 2, 3.] This was adopted universally, and no doubt is, theologically, more correct than the opinion which it opposed. But we are concerned here only with the truth of history; and it would involve the grossest departure from that truth were we to slur over, or attempt to explain away, the remarkable facts which have been the subject of this chapter.

§ 3.
Montanism and the Trinity.

Epiphanius commences his account of the Montanists with the following admission:—"They receive the whole of the Scriptures, both Old and New Testament, and certain things by means of the Paraclete in them." [*Adv. omn. Hæres.* VIII. 19.] Dr Lee's theory is that the ecstatic view is derived from the heathen idea of the μάντις, and that the Christian church opposed it uncompromisingly *from the very first!* "With reasoning similar to that adopted when rejecting the heathen divination, the Church rose in opposition to this fanaticism, (sc. that of the Montanists,) and here also it was argued that the exercise of a state of unconsciousness proved that Montanism was, in no sort, allied to the true prophetic spirit." (*Ibid.*) Dr Westcott admits freely that "the language of Athenagoras has been regarded, *with good reason,* as expressing the doctrine of Montanism." [Quoted by Lee, *Ibid.*]

believe the resurrection of the dead: also concerning the Father, the Son, and the Holy Ghost, they agree with the holy Catholic Church[1]." Firmilian, at an earlier date, had certified that, "although they receive new prophets, yet they appear to accept the same Father and Son with us[2]." Hippolytus had declared that "they acknowledge God to be the Father and Creator of all things, as the Church does, and what the Gospel testifies respecting Christ[3]." He adds, it is true, somewhat later:—"Some of them belong to the sect of the Noetians, saying that the Father himself is the Son, and that the former has been subjected to suffering and death." This contradictory statement naturally deprives the evidence of Hippolytus of the weight to which its date, and the probable impartiality of the writer, would entitle it. Philaster testifies that the Montanists "acknowledge the Father, Son, and Spirit, and the resurrection, as also the Catholic Church[4]." In Theodoret as well as the author of the Appendix to Tertullian's Prescription, we have a distinct intimation that some of the Montanists had adopted Sabellian views; finally Prædestinatus appears to leave the question open, admitting that charges of dogmatic heresy were alleged, but mentioning the indignant denial by Tertullian[5]. The difficulty of reconciling these different statements is greatly enhanced by the confusion so frequently made between the opinions on prophetic inspiration, and those concerning

[1] Epiph. *Hæres.* XLVIII. § 1.
[2] *Ep. ad Cyprian.* (inter opp. Cypr. *Ep.* LXXV.)
[3] *Adv. omn. Hæres.* VIII. 19.
[4] "Isti prophetas et legem accipiunt, Patrem et Filium, et Spiritum confitentur, carnis resurrectionem exspectant, quæ et Catholica Ecclesia prædicat." *Liber de Hæresibus,* § XLIX.
[5] *Fabul. Hær.* III. 2. The passage of the Pseudo-Tertullian (cap. 52) in which it is asserted that the Montanists were divided at last into two subsections; the followers of Proculus holding the orthodox belief on the Trinity; the "Aeschinists" believing that "Christum ipsum esse Filium et Patrem." Prædestinatus appears to doubt (cf. *Hær.* XXVI.) the Montanist orthodoxy; saying of Tertullian's defence "in hoc se reprehensibilem fecit."

the nature of the Holy Spirit. Some of the later fathers, it is true, accused the Montanists of identifying their founder with the very person of the Paraclete, if not of God the Father; but this tremendous accusation can hardly be compatible with Epiphanius's unqualified statement[1].

Our resource, as before, is to turn to Tertullian; and fortunately we find among his works an important treatise, the *Adversus Praxeam*, which not only deals with the very topic under discussion, but was undoubtedly composed after his acceptance of the New Prophecies. In the beginning of the second chapter, Tertullian enunciates the creed which (as he says) "we indeed always have believed, and more especially since we have been better instructed by the Paraclete, who leads men into all truth." "We believe," he continues, "that there is one only God, but under the following dispensation, or οἰκονομία, as it is called; that this one only God has also a Son, His Word, who proceeded from Himself, by whom all things were made, and without whom nothing was made. Him (we believe) to have been sent by the Father into the Virgin,

---

[1] For instance Cyril, in his Catechetical Lectures (Migne, xxxiii. 928), says that "Μοντανὸς ἐτόλμησεν ἑαυτὸν λέγειν εἶναι τὸ ἅγιον πνεῦμα." Basil declares "εἰς τὸ πνεῦμα τὸ ἅγιον ἐβλασφήμησαν, Μοντανῷ καὶ Πρισκίλλῃ τὴν τοῦ Παρακλήτου προσηγορίαν ἀναισχύντως ἐπιφημίσαντες." (*Ep. ad Amphiloch.*) Jerome, on the other hand, who never misses an opportunity of attacking the Montanistic theory of the form of inspiration, (cf. "neque ut Montanus cum insanis feminis somniat, prophetae in ecstasi sunt locuti, etc." *Praef. in Isai.*), even he has the fairness to admit that "Paracletum *in* Montanum venisse contendunt," (*contr. Vigil.*), which is in fact the only view of the Montanistic claim compatible with the evidence. A whole volume might be filled with the contradictions of the Fathers about the Montanists, and certainly no other verdict but that of "Not Proven" could be returned upon their evidence. For instance, Basil, in the epistle cited above, declares that they baptized εἰς πατέρα καὶ υἱὸν καὶ Μοντανὸν καὶ Πρισκίλλαν!! Schwegler, who quotes this, (*Montanismus*, p. 174, note,) contrasts with it the following from another treatise by the same writer:—"Μοντανὸς τοσοῦτον ἐμάνη κατὰ τοῦ πνεύματος καὶ ὀνόμασιν αὐτὸ ταπεινῶς καθύβρισε καὶ τὴν φύσιν αὐτοῦ τοσοῦτον ἐξευτέλισεν, ὥστε ἀδοξίαν εἰπεῖν τῷ πεποιηκότι προστρίβεσθαι." (*Adv. Eunom.* II.)

and to have been born of her, being both man and God, and to have been called by the name of Jesus Christ; (we believe) Him to have suffered, died, and been buried, according to the Scriptures, and, after He had been raised again by the Father and taken back into Heaven, to be sitting at the right hand of the Father, (and) that He will come to judge the quick and the dead; who sent also from Heaven from the Father, according to His own promise, the Holy Ghost, the Paraclete, the sanctifier of the faith of those who believe in the Father, and in the Son, and in the Holy Ghost[1]." Later in the same chapter, there is an amplification of considerable importance with regard to the relation ascribed by Tertullian to the Divine Persons. After describing the heresy of Praxeas, "which supposes itself to possess the pure truth, in thinking that one cannot believe in one only God in any other way than by saying that the Father, Son, and the Holy Ghost are the very selfsame person," he declares, "that all are of one, by unity of substance; while the mystery of the οἰκονομία is still guarded, which distributes the Unity into a Trinity, placing in their order the three (Persons)—the Father, the Son, and the Holy Ghost: three however not in condition (*statu*), but in degree; not in substance, but in form; not in power, but in aspect (*specie*); yet of one substance and of one condition, and of one power, inasmuch as He is One God, from whom these degrees and forms and aspects are reckoned, under the name of the Father, and of the Son, and of the Holy Ghost[2]." It is impossible here to enter

---

[1] *Adv. Prax.* c. 2. Comparing this creed with the unquestionably pre-Montanistic one in the Præscriptio, the only difference traceable is that the language in the later form is more precise and more clear. Neander even goes so far as to assert: "Tertullian *war der erste*, der in dem Streite mit den Monarchianern auch die Lehre vom heiligen Geist hervorhob. Praxeas scheint sich darauf gar nicht eingelassen zu haben." (*Antignost.* 2nd ed. p. 451.) See also Kaye's *Tertullian*, p. 494 ff., and Hesselberg (*Tertullian's Lehre, &c.*) p. 217.

[2] *Ibid.*

upon the question of how far this "hypostatic" doctrine agrees with the developments of later times, whatever date be assumed for the Athanasian Creed. What I shall attempt to prove will be simply :—

I. That, in the beginning of the third century, no official or (in any sense) universal choice had been made between Monarchianism and the doctrine supported by Tertullian.

II. That, although the influence of Montanism in the development of the Trinitarian doctrine was slight, it was in favour of that side which is now acknowledged to have been orthodox and scriptural.

Tertullian admits freely that the arguments he was bringing forward were by no means universally received. "The simple (whom I will not call unwise and unlearned) ...are startled at the οἰκονομία on the ground that their very creed withdraws them from the world's plurality of gods to the one only true God, &c.[1]" This was a very natural difficulty. The attempt at a strict separation of Persons in the Divine Trias led to a system of subordination (as we have seen in our review of Justin)[2], according to which the Son was placed under the Father, and the Holy Spirit beneath the Father and the Son, and this, to the popular mind, carried with it an appearance of Tritheism. To guard against the objection, some inclined to soften the language employed; while others, like Origen in a later period, exaggerated the ideas of separation and subordina-

---

[1] "Simplices quique, ne dixerim imprudentes et idiotæ, quæ major semper credentium pars est, quoniam et ipsa regula fidei a pluribus diis seculi ad unicum et verum Deum transfert, non intelligentes, unicum quidem sed cum sua œconomia esse credendum, expavescunt ad œconomiam. Numerum et dispositionem trinitatis divisionem præsumunt unitatis . . . . . Itaque duos et tres jam jactitant a nobis prædicari, se vero unius dei cultores præsumunt: monarchiam, inquiunt, tenemus." (*Ibid.* c. 3.)

[2] Justin expressly laid down:..."Τἱὸν αὐτοῦ τοῦ ὄντως Θεοῦ μαθόντες (sc. τὸν Ἰησοῦν Χριστὸν) καὶ ἐν δευτέρᾳ χώρᾳ ἔχοντες, πνεῦμά τε προφητικὸν ἐν τρίτῃ τάξει." (*Apol.* 1. 13.) Once more Montanism stands or falls with Justin!

THE TENETS OF MONTANISM. 73

tion, so as to lay the foundation for the Arian controversies of a later day[1]. Now Tertullian's doctrine was a necessary corollary to the Montanistic theory of the three stages, already described, and its effect was to neutralize any tendency to subordinate the Third Person either in respect of condition (status) or work. The Paraclete was now instructing the τέλειοι, as it had not been permitted even to the Apostles after Pentecost to instruct[2], and this single aspect, constantly pressed upon their hearers by the new prophets, would alone contribute greatly to strengthen the cause of Trinitarianism against Monarchian attacks. It is, as we have before attempted to shew, an impossible task to prove that the "Church" had declared itself on one side or another. In the third century it is now well known that, under Kallistus, Monarchianism became predominant for a time, even if that bishop did not favour the grossest excesses of Patripassianism[3]. There was still free play for investigation and conjecture as to the mode of οἰκονομία; all that was fixed was the simple assertion of the Three in One, which not even Praxeas attempted to deny. We must now touch, as it were parenthetically, upon a historical point for which, intimately connected as it is with matters of doctrine, no fitting place could be found in the former book. It has been asserted by a recent and very able

[1] For instance, the Son is δεύτερος θεός, (*Contr. Cels.* v. 608,) and "ἄξιος τῆς δευτερευούσης μετὰ τὸν θεὸν τῶν ὅλων τιμῆς." And cf. *De Oratione*, "Ἕτερος κατ' οὐσίαν καὶ ὑποκείμενός ἐστιν ὁ υἱὸς τοῦ πατρός. According to Hagenbach, Origen's view amounted to this: "Der Bereich des Vaters erstreckt sich auf das ganze Weltall, der des Sohnes auf die vernünftigen Geschöpfe, der des heiligen Geistes auf die Heiligen." (*Dogmengeschichte*, p. 103.) He refers to *De Princ.* I. 3. 5.

[2] That the Montanists asserted that the Apostles *themselves* had not received full revelation from the Paraclete, though asserted by some of the Fathers, seems to have been totally unfounded. Tertullian expressly says: "Proprie enim apostoli Spiritum sanctum habent in operibus prophetiæ et efficacia virtutum atque documentis linguarum, *non ex parte*, *quod ceteri.*" (*De exhort. Cast.* c. 4.)

[3] Hippolytus is very clear on the point: and all Döllinger's ingenuity to save the orthodoxy as well as the moral character of this "Pope" avails little. (Cf. *Hippolytus und Kallistus*, Regensburg, 1853.)

writer that the Asiatic Montanists were themselves Monarchians, since they are described as attributing their inspiration now to God the Father, at another time to Christ, and elsewhere to the Spirit[1]. It is impossible to deny that, by accepting literally the assertions of Epiphanius, and those of the Pseudo-Tertullian and others concerning a later body of Aeschinists who adopted Noetian or Sabellian opinions, a very symmetrical account can be constructed. But it has one flaw: the person and writings of Tertullian must be practically ignored. Can we suppose that he would have passed over such a fact with a mere gentle reproof ("*imprudentes et idiotæ* &c."), and could he have entered upon the campaign against Praxeas with such confidence? Even the conduct of Praxeas would be inexplicable then. Coming (as we know) from Asia, knowing that—according to this hypothesis, the Montanists there sympathised with him in his views—what motive could he have had to act in hostility to their interests at Rome? History proves that few religious parties can long avoid division: but if Montanism could subsist under conditions such as these, we must seek in vain for a parallel case in all the annals of Christianity[2].

[1] Ritschl, *Entstehung der altk. Kirche*, p. 488. "Diese Ansicht ist nicht, wie Schwegler annimmt, als ein Rückfall von der Hypostasenlehre zu betrachten, sondern als die theologische Theorie des ursprünglichen kleinasiatischen Montanismus. Denn eben die Identität des Vaters, Sohns, und Geistes liegt allen prophetischen Aussprüchen des Montanus und seiner beiden Begleiterinnen zu Grunde." It is quite true that Epiphanius makes Maximilla say: 'Ακούσατε ὦ παῖδες Χριστοῦ τί λέγει, ἐμοῦ μὴ ἀκούσατε ἀλλὰ Χριστοῦ. (*Hæres.* XLVIII. § 12.) And in the former section (§ 11) Montanus is supposed to declare himself inspired by God the Father, "ἐγὼ κύριος ὁ θεὸς ὁ παντοκράτωρ καταγενόμενος ἐν ἀνθρώπῳ· οὔτε ἄγγελος οὔτε πρέσβυς, ἀλλὰ ἐγὼ κύριος ὁ θεὸς πατὴρ ἦλθον," but that these vague utterances, reported on the strength of doubtful tradition, two centuries later, and by a hostile critic, should be regarded as conclusive, is more than I feel at liberty to admit. Tertullian must be regarded as the safer informant, and it is perfectly gratuitous to suppose that the "imprudentes et idiotæ" were necessarily a section of Montanists.

[2] Schwegler's account (cf. *Montanismus*, 152 ff.) seems, in this instance, far more probable.

How, then, do we account for the statements that the Montanists, in later times, held erroneous opinions on the subject of the Trinity? In the first place let us regard this evidence a little more closely. The earliest writers are Hippolytus and Eusebius's Anonymus. The former of these, as we have seen, declares generally that the Montanists were orthodox (in his sense, most certainly anti-Monarchian), but he qualifies this statement by the remark that some belonged to the sect of the Noetians[1]. The Anonymus is silent on the subject; nor does Eusebius quote any corroborative statement from either Miltiades or Serapion or Apollonius. Epiphanius, we have seen, knows nothing of such heresies, and would be the last man to have concealed or palliated them: in fact we must pass to Theodoret in order to find the next witness. It is most significant, and to me conclusive, that neither Philaster nor Augustin accuses the Montanists of formal heresy on this subject. Theodoret, it is true, confirms the statement of Hippolytus[2], and his account was usually copied by later writers[3]. All that seems proved, therefore, is the existence of a popular suspicion against the Montanists as a body, justified possibly by the fact that a small minority did fall away from the original faith. This suspicion gained strength only when Montanism was virtually extinct: for instance, in the fourth century, Socrates declares that some

---

[1] "Τινὲς δὲ αὐτῶν τῇ τῶν Νοητιανῶν αἱρέσει συντιθέμενοι τὸν πατέρα αὐτὸν εἶναι τὸν υἱὸν λέγουσι." (*Refut.* VIII. 19.)

[2] "Τινὲς τῶν Μοντανιστῶν τὰς τρεῖς ὑποστάσεις τῆς θεότητος Σαβελλίῳ παραπλησίως ἠρνήσαντο, τὸν αὐτὸν εἶναι λέγοντες καὶ πατέρα καὶ υἱὸν καὶ ἅγιον πνεῦμα, παραπλησίως τῷ Ἀσιανῷ Νοητῷ." (Theodor. *Hær. Fabul.* III. 2.)

[3] Jerome appears at times to imply something of the sort, (cf. *Ep. ad Marcellam*,) but it is not easy to distinguish whether he speaks of the Inspiration-theory, or of the independent doctrine of the Trinity. Marius Mercator, about the middle of the fifth century, is said by Wernsdorf (*De Montanistis*, p. 33,) to support the charge; and also that very incoherent Father, Isidor of Pelusium. (*Epist.* I. 67, and cf. I. 242 ff.)—Harnack believes that the Pseudo-Tertullian's Monarchian Montanists were in reality the Alogi of Epiphanius and Philaster. See this theory ably discussed, and (to my mind) satisfactorily answered by Lipsius. (*Quellen*, p. 93 ff.)

BOOK II. refused the Ὁμοούσιον as "partaking somewhat of Montanism and Sabellianism[1]," which is alone a proof of the second of my two propositions, viz. that the influence of Montanism worked in the direction which (on this point alone) the Church subsequently adopted.

Returning finally to Tertullian for the only statement of Montanistic belief free from obscurity[2], we may derive the following articles from his writings:—

I. The Son (*Sermo*) and the Spirit (*Sophia*) were substantially existent before the worlds, in the Godhead; [*Adv. Prax.* passim, *Adv. Hermog., Adv. Valentin.* &c.]

II. But there was no personal and titular separation until the universe was planned, and subsequently when that plan was effected. [Hæc est nativitas perfecta Sermonis, dum ex Deo procedit: conditus ab eo primum ad cogitatum in nomine Sophiæ...dehinc generatus ad effectum[3]."]

Adv. Prax. c. 7.

III. The occasional ambiguity in his language concerning the Holy Spirit may be ascribed to the variety of senses in which the word "spiritus" is used, often for the Divine Nature in Christ (see quotations in Bull, *D.F.N.* sect. 1, chap. 2). That he considered It a separate, independent Person, and the source of spiritual knowledge to the faithful, has been sufficiently shewn.

---

[1] *Hist. Eccl.* I. 23. "Οἱ μὲν γὰρ τοῦ ὁμοουσίου τὴν λέξιν ἐκκλίνοντες, τὴν Σαβελλίου καὶ Μοντανοῦ δόξαν εἰσηνεῖσθαι αὐτὴν τοὺς προσδεχομένους ἐνόμιζον." Valesius (in loc. cit.) wonders hugely at the juxtaposition. It may be noted that the 7th Canon of the Constantinopolitan Council specially grouped the Montanists and Sabellians:—"καὶ Μοντανιστὰς τοὺς ἐνταῦθα λεγομένους Φρύγας, καὶ Σαβελλιανοὺς τοὺς υἱοπατορίαν διδάσκοντας." But this could hardly be adduced as an argument.

[2] That there are ambiguous expressions in Tertullian cannot be denied. Take, for instance, that passage in the *De Oratione* (cap. 3):—"Jam enim filius *novum* patris nomen est." Neander, in his first edition of the Antignostikus, proposed to read "notum" for "novum." Even this was better than his translation: "denn mit dem Sohne ist auch der neue Name des Vaters gegeben." (*Antignost.* 2nd ed. p. 158.)

[3] Kaye quotes the remarkable passage, "Fuit autem tempus quum et delictum *et Filius non fuit*, quod judicem et qui Deum Patrem faceret." (P. 522, and see *Antignostikus*, p. 444 ff.)

THE TENETS OF MONTANISM.

IV. That there was a principle of Subordination: but that this was no introduction of Montanism, since it is to be found in Justin as well as others, and remained a popular doctrine until the last and final development of opinions in the fifth century.

Among the opinions denounced as heretical by Epiphanius must be included the earnest and precisely-formed expectations of a speedy coming of the Lord. He condemns them in the first place for reverencing the town of Pepuza, as the very place where the Παρουσία should happen[1], and for declaring (as he makes the prophetess Maximilla) that after them there should be the end of things[2]. But in addition to these particular notions, it is impossible not to recognise his distaste for the Millennarianism which the Montanists as a body undoubtedly embraced. Tertullian appears to have held these views as strongly before becoming a Montanist as after. His treatise *De Oratione*, which all critics regard as pre-Montanistic, includes a passionate invocation of the Great Change—"the prayer of Christians, the confusion of the nations, the exultation of angels" (cap. 5). In the later, and unquestionably Montanistic work "against Marcion," he narrates (with full belief in its truth) the story of a miraculous apparition which was alleged to have appeared in Judea. This was a city suspended in the air, according to his account the New Jerusalem, destined for the reception of the Saints during their reign of a thousand years on earth, in the course of which period their resurrection would be effected according to their different degrees of merit,

Book II.

§ 4. Eschatology.

---

[1] "Τιμῶσι γὰρ καὶ τόπον τινὰ ἔρημον ἐν τῇ Φρυγίᾳ, Πέπουζάν ποτε καλουμένην πόλιν, νῦν δὲ ἠδαφισμένην. Καὶ φασιν ἐκεῖσε κατιέναι τὴν ἄνω Ἱερουσαλήμ." (*Hæres*. XLIX. 1.) This notion is also expressed in the narration of Quintilla (or Priscilla?) that Christ appeared to her, and had revealed "τουτονὶ τὸν τόπον εἶναι ἅγιον καὶ ὧδε τὴν Ἱερουσαλὴμ ἐκ τοῦ οὐρανοῦ κατιέναι." (Apollonius *ap. Euseb*. v. 18.) Cyril of Jerusalem describes Pepuza as "κωμίδιον ἐν τῇ Φρυγίᾳ καταλαβὼν καὶ ψευδῶς Ἱερουσαλὴμ ὀνομάσας." (*Catech*. XVI. 8.)

[2] "Μετ' ἐμὲ προφῆτις οὐκέτι ἔσται, ἀλλὰ συντέλεια." (Epiph. *Hær*. XLVIII. 2.)

and which was to be followed by the conflagration of the world and the general judgment[1]. Although in one place Tertullian declares that he had attempted in his [lost] work, *De Spe Fidelibus*, to spiritualize the utterances of the Prophets with respect to the Millennium, the passage just cited is hardly treated in such a manner, and fully justifies us in including Tertullian as holding the ordinary Montanistic tenet, although he never alludes to Pepuza by name. After the investigations of so many able critics, we need not quote once more the catena of passages which prove that this opinion, although condemned as heretical by the Church from the fourth century onwards, was held by writers whose orthodoxy is unimpugned. When Bishop Kaye gravely declared that "the more judicious and sober-minded Christians would naturally take alarm at the open avowal of tenets, the necessary effect of which must be to render their religion obnoxious to the ruling powers &c.[2]," he was of course well aware that he was placing Justin Martyr, Papias, and Irenæus in the category of those who were not "judicious" nor "sober-minded[3]." If, indeed, I

---

[1] Kaye, p. 345 ff. The passage referred to is in the third Book (*Adv. Marcionem*) and is as follows:—" Constat enim, Ethnicis quoque testibus, in Judea per dies quadraginta matutinis momentis civitatem de cœlo pependisse, omni mœniorum habitu, evanescentem de profectu diei et alias de proximo nullam. Hanc dicimus excipiendis resurrectione Sanctis et refovendis omnium bonorum utique spiritalium copia, in compensationem eorum quæ in seculo vel despeximus vel amisimus, a Deo prospectam. Siquidem et justum et Deo dignum illic quoque exsultare famulos ejus, ubi sunt et afflicti in nomine ipsius. Hæc ratio regni terreni: post cujus mille annos, intra quam ætatem concluditur Sanctorum resurrectio pro meritis maturius vel tardius resurgentium, tunc et mundi destructione et judicii conflagratione commissa, demutati in atomo in angelicam substantiam, scilicet per illud incorruptelæ superindumentum transferemur in cœleste regnum." (*Adv. Marc.* lib. III. cap. 24.) I confess that I cannot follow Bishop Kaye in understanding Tertullian's meaning as "wholly spiritual."

[2] P. 20. It is true that he is speaking more particularly of the predictions of the ruins of the Roman Empire.

[3] The special passages are: Justin, *Dial. c. Tryph.* cap. 80, (the famous passage); Irenæus, *c. Hær.* v. 32, 33; and Papias (ap. Euseb.

am right in accepting the first-named of these writers as a fair representative of the Church's views in the second century, the Montanists are indeed the victims of the irony of history. "Cette proposition serait Catholique dans une autre bouche," said one of Pascal's Jesuits, "ce n'est que dans M. Arnauld que la Sorbonne l'a condamnée." (3me L. Prov.) As one ponders on this crying injustice, one is tempted almost to conclude with the same writer: "Laissons là leurs différends. Ce sont des disputes de théologiens, et non pas de théologie!"

If, as we have seen, Hippolytus expressed himself doubtfully on the question of formal heresy, he is precise in his statement and condemnation of the changes (or reformations) which the Montanists attempted to introduce into the external life; and his censures were almost unanimously followed by later writers. We shall find in this case no difficulty about facts: never did culprit plead guilty with more triumphant confidence than does Tertullian when he accepts the charges of his opponents on the subject of fasting, of marriage, and of penance. Here the Paraclete had ordained new rules, and had authoritatively abrogated the old: in fact his principal title is *Novae Disciplinae Institutor*[1].

Now the injunctions of the Gospel and of the Apostles, and especially those of St Paul in his epistles, were intended for the mass of general believers, and included many concessions to the weakness of the flesh. To take one instance, the Apostle admitted the unconscious partaking of sacrificed meat as harmless, only recommending that, should the character of the food be declared, the Christian in that case should abstain [1 Cor. x. 27—29]. The Montanists, adopting a reasoning totally opposed to that of St Paul, affixed an objective impurity to the

§ 5.
Ascetic-
ism.

H. E. III. 39). (Cf. Schwegler, p. 71 ff.; Ritschl, p. 485 ff.; Semisch, I. 304.)

[1] So in *De Monogam.* c. 11. In the *De Pudic.* c. 11 it is "Spiritus sanctus ipsius disciplinæ determinator."

Book II. various heathen symbols, and built upon this idea a
series of stringent regulations[1].

Fasting. Although, as we have mentioned, there is no difficulty
in ascertaining the actual rules and restrictions imposed
upon themselves by the Montanists, still for the purpose
of afterwards analysing the influence of this asceticism
upon the Church itself, we will proceed as before to quote
the witnesses in chronological order, before proceeding to
examine Tertullian's own account.

APOLLONIUS (ap. Euseb.).	HIPPOLYTUS.	JEROME.
"But who is this new teacher? His works and his doctrines sufficiently show it. This is he that taught the dissolutions of marriages, he that imposed laws of fasting."	"But they introduce new fasts and festivals, and the practice of eating dry things and radishes, pretending that these females (sc. M^lla. & Pr^lla.) have enjoined them."	"The Montanists keep three Lents in the year." (*Ep. ad Marcell.* 41.) "Even after Pentecost they keep Lent, on the ground that the bridegroom is taken away."
(*H. E.* lib. v. cap. 18.)	(*Refut.* lib. viii. cap. 19.)	(*Comm. in Matth.* ix. 15.)

These testimonies will be sufficient for our purpose:
and we can now turn to Tertullian[2]. He states the question and answers it clearly: "It is on this account that
the New Prophecies are rejected: not that Montanus and
Maximilla and Priscilla preach another God, nor that they

---

[1] This is well worked out by Ritschl (*Entstehung*, p. 493 ff.): "Ein solches Streben kann nun erstens keine Adiaphora dulden, das heisst, solche Lebensäusserungen, deren sittlicher Werth nicht in ihnen selbst, sondern nur in ihrer Beziehung zum Subjekte liegt, welches sie ausübt. Vielmehr werden alle einzelne Punkte nur entweder als *gebotene* oder als *verbotene*, bezeichnet worden." Tertullian condemns those who acted on the rule, "Quod non prohibetur, ultro permissum est," and lays down inexorably: "Imo prohibetur quod non ultro est permissum." (*De Cor. Mil.* c. 2.) Neander (*Antignost.* p. 280 ff.) also expatiates upon the strange inconsistency which caused the Montanists to outbid the Church in Judaistic formalism.

[2] Other references may be found in Epiphanius (*Hær.* xlviii. 8), he accuses them of disdaining food sent by God; and in Theodoret. (*Fabul. hær.* iii. 2.) It is somewhat singular that Philaster and Augustin do not mention the topic.

overturn any particular rule of faith or hope, but that they plainly teach more frequent fasting than marrying[1]." And in a later chapter he exclaims:—"How small is the extent of our restrictions! Two weeks of *xerophagiae* in the year (and not the whole of these, for the Sabbaths and the Lord's days are excepted)—these we offer to God, abstaining from things which we do not reject, but defer[2]."

Without furnishing a complete abstract of this remarkable treatise, we may summarize its contents as follows. The Christian Church regarded the institution of fasting as Scriptural and binding, but left a large measure of liberty to the individual. Montanist and Catholic started from the same general scheme[3], but the former (acting on the dictates of the Paraclete,) desired to restrain this liberty, or perhaps rather to mark out rules by which it might be profitably utilized. But the real purpose of the treatise is not so much to defend the rules themselves, which were in reality but little more stringent than the simple "custom" of the Church: it was the underlying principle that he ardently advocates. This principle is chiefly utilitarian in its character: temperance, even want, is the bodily state most conducive to holiness. In the fifth chapter, Tertullian reviews the history of Israel, and shows that (as in Adam's case) sensual appetite was the chief source of sin. The rejection of manna is their contempt for the heavenly *xerophagia*. Moses and Elijah are instances of the aid which fasting gives to spiritual elevation, as well as Anna in the New Testament [cap.

[1] *De Jejuniis*, cap. 1.
[2] *Ibid.* cap. 15.
[3] "Pascha celebramus annuo circulo (including the preliminary Quadragesima) stationibus quartam et sextam sabbati dicamus et jejuniis parasceven." (Cap. 14.) He adds that the Catholics sometimes extended the fast to the Sabbath. [It is curious that Bp Cosin, in his *Religion of the Realm of England*, declares that "the Fridays and Saturdays of each week are fast-days of the Anglican Church." Meyrick's edition, p. 53.]

Book II. v.—VIII.]. Then Tertullian discusses the advantage of the partial fast on dry meats, and also the institution of "Stations[1]." Little by little the defence of the one system changes into a fierce attack upon the other, " which reigns in wealth and satiety, not making inroads upon such sins as fasts diminish, nor feeling need of such visions as *xerophagiae* extort, nor apprehending such wars of your own as Stations dispel" [cap. XII.]. After a rapid transition once more to the question of prescription against novelty, and claiming true antiquity for his own views, Tertullian concludes with a stirring peroration upon the need of fasts in the present persecution [sc. that of Marcus Aurelius]. "Even to encounter beasts, it will be a Christian's duty to practise emaciation!" [cap. XVII.]

[1] Of all the writers on Montanism, Wernsdorf seems to have devoted most learning to the very difficult subject of the special fasts. His conclusion is that the Montanists had "duas proprias sibi ac peculiares quadragesimas, unam mensis Junii post Pentecosten, alteram Decembris ante Nat. Christi, quarum quælibet quinque dies absolvebat a feria secunda ad sextam, ita celebrabant, ut siccis tantum cibis et potu aquæ uterentur, non abstinentes ab omnibus sed a delicatioribus cibis, non ab omni potione sed vini, non ' recusantes' sed 'diminuantes et resecantes' cibum." (*De Montanistis*, p. 69.) Tertullian's own definition of the *Xerophagia* is:—" siccantes cibum ab omni carne et omni jurulentia et uvidioribus quibusque pomis ne quid vinositatis vel ederent vel biberent." (Cap. 1.) Much difference of opinion still prevails as to the exact nature of the *Statio*. An old writer, Chladenius (*De Stationibus rett. Christianorum*. Lipsiæ, 1744), held that the Stations were not necessarily fasts, or joined to them, and remarked that the Montanists "sabbati die solo voram præstitisse stationem." He defines the Station as "...diem aut insignem diei partem, quam quis privatim...precibus piisque meditationibus, libero destinaverit." (p. 43.) Petavius, Rigaltius, and Daillé, all high authorities, thought that the *Stationes* were fixed days of special devotion, with an invariable fast until the 9th hour. As to this, a passage in Hermas seems clear:—" Quid tam mane venisti? Respondi, quoniam stationem habeo. Quid est, inquit, statio? Et dixi, jejunium." (Lib. III. Sim. 5.) And even if Hermas be rejected as a doubtful authority (as Chladenius insists), we have both Clemens Alexandr. and Origen, who distinctly explain that "Stationes = $νηστείαι$." Tertullian's own words are really sufficient by themselves: "Hæc erit statio sera, quæ ad vesperam jejunans, pinguiorem orationem Deo immolat." (*De Jej.* cap. x.)

THE TENETS OF MONTANISM.

It is not necessary to devote any space here to recount and refute the particular slanders which the imagination of later writers evolved concerning the Montanistic theory of Marriage. These, with others of a similar character, will be dealt with in a note at the end of this book[1]. Nor need we recount the arguments in detail with which the champion of the New Prophecy strove to prove that the reforms were more ancient than the customs attacked. The nature of this reasoning we have seen in the former section. We need only regard the particular facts, and the relation which these Montanistic opinions bore to those held generally in the Christian Church.

The Montanistic position is defined in the opening words of the treatise *De Monogamia*:—"Heretics do away with marriages; the 'Psychici' accumulate them. The former marry not even once: the latter not only once. What dost thou, Law of the Creator?" And, a few lines further on:—"We admit one marriage, just as we do one God." This is perfectly in harmony with the (pre-Montanistic) treatise *Ad Uxorem*, where he extols in the highest terms the holy union "quod ecclesia conciliat, oblatio confirmat, obsignat benedictio, angeli renuntiant[2]." Here, although a second marriage is not denounced as a crime, as a "decent adultery," it is urgently deprecated as a departure from God's original dispensation. Still, in the second Book, even those cases where a second marriage has been contracted are dealt with, and such persons (assumed to have acted under infirmity) are enjoined to marry only "in the Lord[3]." This portion also deals at

---

[1] Vide infra, § 9.
[2] *Ad Uxor.* II. 8. Wernsdorf, by assuming against all internal evidence, that the 2nd book was written after Tertullian had embraced Montanism, attempts to prove that Montanism admitted second marriages in exceptional cases. Against such a hypothesis, the treatise *De Monogamia* is decisive.
[3] "Spiritus sanctus, qui viduas et innuptas integritati perseverare mavult, qui nos ad exemplum sui hortatur, nullam aliam formam repetendarum nuptiarum, nisi in Domino praescribit. Huic soli conditioni

length with the dangerous consequences of marriage between Christian and Heathen, not necessarily for the second time. The tone is far more decided and severe in the treatise *De exhortatione Castitatis*, culminating in the ninth chapter, where Tertullian concludes that " if we look deeply into his [sc. St Paul's: he had been examining 1 Cor. ix. 5] meanings, and interpret them, second marriage will have to be termed no other than a species of fornication." But still here the argument is to a great extent utilitarian, based on the spiritual and even temporal advantages of leading a single life after the first widowhood, if not throughout life. This standpoint is utterly abandoned in the final work already named, and the second marriage becomes an evil in itself, only suffered for a time on account of the hardness of men's hearts, and now forbidden by the Paraclete to His followers. Tertullian revels as usual in a historical review of Biblical history. If Cain's was the first crime after his parent's disobedience, Lamech's double marriage was hardly less culpable[1]. From Abraham's case, denied as a precedent, he passes to the provisions of the Mosaic law; and here his arbitrary selection of rules to which he ascribes a permanently binding force, and those which he regards as abrogated, can hardly be defended[2]. The

---

incontinentiæ detrimenta concedit. Tantum, inquit, in Domino. Adjecit pondus legi suæ: tantum!" (*Ad Uxor.* II. 2.)

[1] " Post primum scelus, homicidium, tam dignum secundo loco scelus non fuit, quam duæ nuptiæ. Neque enim refert, duas quis uxores singulas habuerit, an pariter singulæ duas fecerint. Idem numerus conjunctorum et separatorum." (*De Monogam.* c. 4.)

[2] " Während Tertullian die Vielweiberei der Patriarchen bei Seite setzt, als einer überwundenen Offenbarungsstufe angehörig, benutzt er das Mosaische Priestergesetz für seinen Zweck, weil nichts dagegen sei, von den alten Vorbildern das anzuerkennen, was mit seinen eigenen Tendenzen übereinstimme." (Ritschl, *Entstehung*, p. 503.) I cannot say that I go so far as Ritschl in attributing to Montanism, as expounded by Tertullian, " not a new ethical code, but ONLY the execution of the old one, as found in Old and New Testament." (*Ibid.*)—This is " protesting too much."

teaching of our Lord and of St Paul is then examined, and the utterances favourable to celibacy held forth and insisted on [cap. IX.—XIV.]. Finally, those pleas of "infirmity," so gently reasoned with in the early treatise, are now dissected with indignant scorn. "Such infirmity is equal to a third, and a fourth, and even (perhaps) a seventh marriage; as increasing its strength as often as its weakness; but which will no longer have an apostle's authority, but of some Hermogenes,—wont to marry more women than he paints[1]." One question only remains: was Tertullian as sincere and vigorous in his war against the Gnostic heresy which condemned marriage in itself, as against the digamists? Probably he was; but still it was rather the premises of Marcion that he detested than this especial practical conclusion. Celibacy is to the married state not as good to evil, but as the more favoured condition to the less[2]. But then this permitted monogamy is hedged in by such minute restrictions, and the praise bestowed on it is so much outweighed by the enthusiastic exaltation of virginity, that the lesson intended for the hearer cannot be doubted[3].

Finally, we ask whether on this question any gulf existed between the opinions of Montanism, and those of the primitive Church in the 2nd century. Tertullian everywhere disclaims the slightest departure from the principles of Christianity. How is he confirmed by other writers? Athenagoras declares that "the remaining in virginity and in the state of a eunuch brings nearer to God," and that many of his contemporaries "grow old unmarried, in the hope of living in closer communion with God." And in the same chapter occurs the completely Montanistic utterance:—"a person should either remain

---

[1] *De Monogam.* cap. XVI.
[2] "Sanctitatem sine nuptiarum damnatione novimus, et sectamur, et præferimus; non ut malo bonum, sed ut bono melius." (*Adv. Marcion*, I. 29.)
[3] See this worked out in the most masterly manner by Neander. (*Antignostikus*, 2d ed. p. 245 ff.)

BOOK II.

as he was born, or be content with one marriage; for a second marriage is only a specious adultery[1]." Theophilus gives evidence to the universal feeling in favour of monogamy[2]; Irenæus declares repeated marriages to be so many fornications[3]; even Clement of Alexandria deems them distinct marks of Christian imperfection[4]. Our conclusion, then, can only be that Montanism may have pressed to excess the doctrine which it found in the Church, but cannot justly be accused of introducing it.

§ 7. Penance.

In this most important branch of the subject, we are deprived of one portion of the evidence hitherto compared with the rest. For with the exception of a doubtful allusion by a writer quoted in Eusebius's history[5], there is no reference to be found in any writer except Tertullian to the special opinions entertained by the Montanists upon repentance and the power of the keys. Fortunately his writings include two treatises, one most obviously composed before his adoption of Montanism, the other as unquestionably subsequent to that step. A comparison of these works will be amply sufficient for our purpose.

The first of these is a fitting sequel to the tract *De Baptismo*. The subject is Repentance, that is to say, the means offered by the Church to those who had sinned

---

[1] Τὸ ἐν παρθενίᾳ καὶ εὐνουχίᾳ μεῖναι μᾶλλον παρίστησι τῷ θεῷ.... Ὁ δεύτερος γάμος εὐπρεπής ἐστι μοιχεία. (*Legat.* c. xxxiii.)

[2] Παρ' οἷς (τοῖς χριστιανοῖς) σωφροσύνη πάρεστιν, ἐγκράτεια ἀσκεῖται, μονογαμία τηρεῖται, ἁγνεία φυλάσσεται. (*Ad Autolyc.* iii. 15.)

[3] "Samaritana praevaricatrix, quae in uno viro non mansit, sed fornicata est in multis nuptiis." (c. *Haer.* iii. 17. 2.)

[4] *Stromata*, iii. 12. 82. [And see Herm. *Past.* Mand. iv. 4.] And Justin Martyr has a remarkable passage: "by means of virgins, marriage, made lawless (ἄνομος) by lust, is destroyed." But notwithstanding Semisch, this Fragment cannot be deemed quite indubitably Justin's. (*Fragm. Resurr.* cap. iii.)

[5] The evidently ironical question, "Does the prophetess forgive the martyr his robberies? Or the martyr forgive the prophetess her avarice?" (Apollonius ap. Euseb. v. 18), can hardly be described as throwing much light on the matter, as Ritschl thinks. Cf. *Entstehung*, p. 518.

after baptism. The treatise begins with a general review of Repentance in the abstract, an investigation into its origin, as well as into the laws which regulate it. In the seventh chapter the real matter is reached, and it is approached (as it were) with reluctance. "It is irksome," says Tertullian, "to make mention of a second,—in that case, the last—hope; lest, by treating of a remedy yet in reserve, we seem to be pointing to a yet further space for sinning[1]." This mention of a "last hope" appears certainly to be modified by what follows: "Let no one be less, because God is more good, by repeating his sin as often as he is forgiven. Otherwise he will find, be sure, an end of escaping, when he shall not find one of sinning. We have escaped once: thus far [and no farther] let us commit ourselves to perils, even if we seem likely to escape a second time[2]." This broader and freer view is endorsed by the earnest recommendations which follow:— "Dread by all means to sin again, but do not shrink from repenting again! Guard yourself from incurring peril, but not from being rescued from it. Let none be ashamed. Repeated sickness must have repeated medicine. ... You have offended, but you can still be reconciled. You have One whom you may satisfy, and Him willing [to accept the satisfaction]." These admirable words, breathing as they do the purest spirit of Christianity, are fitly followed up in the next chapter, where the lessons of the prodigal son, the lost drachma, and the pardon offered to the erring Asiatic Churches, are pointed out and enforced. Next comes the outward means, the ceremony called in the Church the Ἐξομολόγησις. "It commands [the penitent] to lie in sackcloth and ashes, to cover his body in mourning (*sordibus*), to lay his spirit low in sadness, to exchange for severities the sins he has committed; moreover, to know no food or drink but such as is plain,......

---

[1] *De Pænitentia*, cap. VII.
[2] *Ibid.* Cf. *Antignostikus*, p. 199 ff.

to groan, to weep and cry unto the Lord their God; to fall at the feet of the presbyters, and kneel to God's dear ones. ...... All this Exomologesis [does] that it may enhance repentance[1]." The treatise concludes with an earnest appeal to sinners to embrace this salutary humiliation.

Now, the first thing that strikes the reader is the diametrically opposed principle (to that of Montanism) which is furnished. Here the absolute necessity of an outward ceremony is insisted on, and the worthlessness of mere inward resolutions exposed. "But some say that God is satisfied if He be looked up to with the heart and the mind, even if this be not done in act....... These dispositions are ever wont to spring from the seed of hypocrites, whose repentance is never sincere[2]." But we saw in the two previous sections the strange inconsistency between the creed of spiritual liberty and the strict neo-Judaic code upon fasts and marriage. The discussion of the cause for this phenomenon we reserve for a later section: it is sufficient to note here that no very wide gulf had to be passed to make these opinions Montanistic. Save only in one point: the limit for post-baptismal repentance was now drawn very close, and at times it seems to be excluded.

The subject of the treatise *De Pudicitia* was an episcopal edict, issued by Zephyrinus, which announced absolution to those adulterers and fornicators who had complied with the requirements of ecclesiastical discipline. "Oh edict," exclaims Tertullian, "which cannot be characterized as a worthy act[3]!" At first, this work hardly seems to desert the stand-point of the former one, for he is undoubtedly right in contrasting the spirit of this edict

[1] *De Pœnitentia*, cap. ix.
[2] *Ibid.* cap. v.
[3] "Audio etiam edictum esse propositum, et quidem peremtorium. Pontifex scilicet maximus edicit: 'Ego et mœchiæ et fornicationis delicta pœnitentia functis dimitto.' O edictum, cui adscribi non poterit: bonum factum!" (*Ibid.* cap. 1.)

THE TENETS OF MONTANISM. 89

with "the primary discipline of the Christian name," BOOK II. most rigorous in the case of these sins. But soon the influence of the new opinions shews itself:—" Why then do they grant indulgence, under the name of repentance, to crimes for which they furnish remedies by their law of multinuptialism[1]?" The next chapter is an attempt to refute his own position (previously assumed in the *De Pœnitentia*), as to the freedom and unlimited nature of the Divine grace. This culminates in a division of offences into the pardonable and the deadly[2], not as affecting God's power, but the discretion entrusted to the visible Church[3]. It is a mistake to suppose that Tertullian and the Montanists ever limited the power of the Church in this matter: "'You say, the Church has the power of forgiving sins.' This I acknowledge and sanction [so much the rather] as I have the Paraclete Himself in the persons of the new prophets, saying: 'The Church has the power to forgive sins; but I will not do it, lest they err again[4].'"

[1] *Ibid.* cap. 1.
[2] "Sunt quædam delicta quotidianæ incursionis, quibus omnes sumus objecti. Cui enim non accidit, aut irasci inique, et ultra solis occasum, aut et manum immittere, aut facile maledicere, aut temere jurare......ut si nulla sit venia istorum, nemini salus competat. Horum ergo erit venia per exoratum patris Christum." And in Cap. II.: "Alia delicta sunt remissibilia, alia irremissibilia, secundum quod nemini dubium est, alia castigationem mereri, alia damnationem. Secundum hanc differentiam delictorum pœnitentiæ quoque conditio discriminatur. Alia erit, quæ veniam consequi possit, in delicto scilicet remissibili. Alia, quæ consequi nullo modo possit, in delicto scilicet irremissibili."
[3] Werusdorf was the first, I think, to see this clearly. "Quæstio non erat de foro Dei, sed de foro ecclesiæ." (*De Montanistis*, p. 91.) Tertullian puts this very clearly (at the same time attempting to remove any inconsistency with his earlier position) in the 3rd chapter:— "Quantum ad nos, qui solum Dominum meminimus delicta concedere, et utique mortalia, non frustra agetur. Ad Dominum enim remissa, et illi exinde prostrata, hoc ipso magis operabitur veniam, quod eam a solo Deo exorat, quod delicto suo humanam pacem sufficere non credit, quod ecclesiæ mavult erubescere quam communicare......Et si hic pacem non metit, apud Dominum seminat."
[4] *Ibid.* cap. XXI. The Bishop of Winchester must have temporarily

THE TENETS OF MONTANISM.

BOOK II.   Met by the not unreasonable query, how he can expect repentance if he refuses an assurance of pardon, he answers that the repentance, if genuine, will not be in vain, [*non frustra agetur,*] but the pardon cannot expediently be declared by the Church, lest license to sin be imagined.

The second point of importance was the nature of the sins to be included in the category of mortal offences. It appears that some who were ready to treat with the utmost rigour murder and idolatry, were not disposed to regard sins of impurity with equal severity[1]. We can readily understand that the ascetic principles of Montanism would sternly oppose any such exception, if they did not place fornication and adultery in the worst category of all, i.e. with premeditated murder. At any rate they were *peccata mortalia,* while those guilty of nameless sins were to be excluded even from the ranks of public penitents[2]. Tertullian's objections to the exercise of the absolving power on the part of the bishops took their root in his conception of the Church, to which we devote a special section. He considered them as indeed successors of the Apostles in teaching, but not necessarily (or even probably) in the possession of spiritual power and insight, the unfailing marks of Apostleship. These

---

forgotten this passage, I think, when he wrote "The Montanists did not allow the Church the power of forgiving great sins after Baptism, even once." (On Art. XVI.) The practical distinction might be almost non-existent; but the logical difference is obvious between a power which it is not expedient to employ, and absolute impotence.

[1] "Idololatram quidem et homicidam semel damnas, mœchum vero de medio excipis, idololatriæ successorem, homicidæ antecessorem, utriusque collegam? Personæ acceptatio est, miserabiliores pœnitentias reliquisti." (*Ibid.* cap. v.)

[2] It is not easy to decide whether these last-named were only excluded from the interior of the Church, the class of so-called χειμαζόμενοι, (as Neander thinks, *Antign.* 262,) or banished altogether. Tertullian's words are: "Reliquas autem libidinum furias impias ..... non modo limine, verum omni ecclesiæ tecto submovemus, quia non sunt delicta sed monstra." (*Ibid.* cap. IV.)

THE TENETS OF MONTANISM. 91

he demands from those who claim the accompanying privilege. "Exhibit to me, apostolic Sir, prophetic evidences, that I may recognise your divine virtue, and vindicate to yourself the power of remitting such sins!" [cap. XXI.] Accordingly, the "Church" which has the power of so doing, is the Spiritual Church, enlightened by new revelations, and purged by the new discipline[1].

We have reached a stage in the investigations where it is possible to form the first general idea of the Montanistic principle, and the character of its opposition to the Church. It is true that, as we have seen, the Paraclete introduced no changes in formal doctrine,—still His presence and His revelations were new facts. It is likewise true that the asceticism of Montanism differed only in degree from the moral code universally accepted in the Christian Church—nevertheless the alteration involved a claim, and that claim was the certain cause of ultimate disunion and separation.

What, then, was the idea of the Church entertained by those who believed that the Paraclete spoke by the mouth of Montanus and Maximilla? In the first place, there was the division of those who believed these revelations,—the "Pneumatici" or *Spirituales*, and those who rejected them,—the "Psychici." Between these bodies peace might well prevail, for they comprise one church. "We share with them," says Tertullian in the Montanistic treatise on the Veiling of Virgins,—"the law of peace, and the name of brotherhood. They and we have one faith, one Christ, one God, the same hope, the same baptismal sacraments; let me say it once for all, WE ARE ONE CHURCH[2]. This view was by no means reciprocated

---

[1] Tertullian makes the same demand to Marcion: "Edat aliquem psalmum, aliquem visionem, aliquam orationem, duntaxat spiritualem, in ecstasi, si qua linguæ interpretatio accessit." (*Adv. Marc.* v. 8.)

[2] "Communicamus cum Psychicis jus pacis et nomen fraternitatis. Una nobis et illis fides, unus Deus, idem Christus, eadem spes, eadem lavacri sacramenta. Semel dixerim, UNA ECCLESIA SUMUS." (*De Virg. Veland.* cap. 2.)

on the other side; the Montanists were reviled, and finally driven by force from the Church[1]. Themison is declared to "blaspheme against the holy church" because he wrote in favour of the Prophets[2]. And certainly it would have needed no small measure of Christian meekness to have submitted in silence to the title of "Carnal Christians" thus applied. The origin of the name was obvious: Ψυχικὸς ἄνθρωπος (said the Apostle in his First Epistle to the Corinthians) οὐ δέχεται τὰ τοῦ πνεύματος τοῦ Θεοῦ. The Psychic Christian had the Scriptures, but only their letter; he had the Church, but only the outward framework or polity; and a system of machinery which, unless directed in obedience to the Paraclete, might do more harm than good. For the Spiritual Christian, although he submitted gladly to the outward forms of the Church, there was much more within. He was himself a priest: he might be a prophet, an apostle. In his eyes, as Tertullian says:—"The Church is, properly and principally, the Spirit Himself, in whom is the Trinity of the One Divinity. [The Spirit] combines that church which the Lord has made to consist in 'three.' And thus, from that time forward, every number [of persons] who may have combined together into this faith is accounted a 'church,' from the Author and Consecrator[3]." And from these premises he drew the conclusion: "The Church, then, will truly forgive sins: but it [will be] the Church of the Spirit,...not the church which consists of bishops."

---

[1] Ὀλίγοι ἦσαν οὗτοι τῶν Φρυγῶν ἐξηπατημένοι, τὴν δὲ καθόλου καὶ πᾶσαν τὴν ὑπὸ τὸν οὐρανὸν ἐκκλησίαν (sc. the Catholic Church), βλασφημεῖν διδάσκοντες τοῦ ἀπηυθαδισμένου πνεύματος κ.τ.λ. (Anonymus ap. Euseb. *H. E.* v. 16.)

[2] .... βλασφημῆσαι δὲ εἰς τὸν κύριον καὶ τοὺς ἀποστόλους καὶ τὴν ἁγίαν ἐκκλησίαν. (Apollonius ap. Euseb. v. 18.)

[3] "Ecclesia proprie et principaliter est ipse spiritus. Illam ecclesiam congregat, quam Dominus in tribus posuit." (*De Pudic.* cap. xxi.) In the treatise *De Jejuniis* (cap. 11) the Catholic Church is described as "gloriosissima multitudo psychicorum."

THE TENETS OF MONTANISM.

Thus, while in theory the Pneumatic Church was situated concentrically within the Psychic: in reality this relation was soon lost. In Tertullian's writings we can trace the gradual change of tone, sometimes even in the same treatise. Perhaps it might be possible, by help of the same minute criticism which recent research has bestowed on the writings of Shakspere, to ascertain the order of Tertullian's works, following the change of tone with regard to the Visible Church. By such a canon we should place very late the *Exhortation to Chastity*, notwithstanding other reasons against the course, for there the naked extreme of Montanism appears. "Are not even we laymen priests?...... Where three are, a church is, albeit of laymen. For each individual lives by his own faith, nor is there acceptation of persons with God.... Therefore, if you have the right of a priest in your own person, in cases of necessity, it behoves you to have likewise the discipline of a priest[1]." The more the Church tended in the direction of externalism, the more openly were these counter-claims put forth, and often without moderation of language or even adherence to scriptural ordinance. Points of difference, too, were added to the materials already existing, in themselves of slight moment, but capable of being magnified in the heat of controversy. Two of these may be here touched upon, as illustrations of the struggle.

It is unquestionable that all parties in the Church regarded martyrdom as the crowning glory of a Christian's career. The follies, even the crimes, of past life were considered as triumphantly condoned. Even the Confessor, who had manfully undergone torture or imprisonment, gained a personal distinction and authority not always beneficial either to the Church at large or to the individual. It was natural that the Montanists should yield an excessive regard to a testimony which corresponded exactly with their ascetic ideas. The scriptural

[1] *De exhort. Castit.* cap. VII.

rule "when they persecute you in this city, flee ye into another" (Matth. x. 23), was now derided as an unworthy cloak for weakness, and martyrdom, from being a privilege, was erected into a duty. One motive was obvious. If the Spirit of God were truly with the Pneumatici, He would sustain them under the pangs of death. And had the Montanists not been eager to dare the ordeal, we can imagine that bitter taunts would not have been wanting[1]. As however they did seek, and (in the majority of cases) endure martyrdom, the accusation took another turn, which we must notice. They were charged with (a) provoking, and counselling to provoke persecution; (b) denying the right to flee to another city; (c) passing off as martyrs those who had suffered as criminals; and finally, (d) preferring and teaching to prefer apostacy under torment to flight. The two first charges are not easy to refute, and it can only be alleged that similar theories were held by certain Christians doubtless from the very earliest times[2]. The third rests on the evidence of Apollonius (ap. Euseb.) and the Anonymus, the former of whom declares that a certain Montanist named Alexander, "who called himself a martyr,...was punished for robberies and other crimes[3]." It is by no means asserted here that Alexander had not suffered as a Confessor as well, which in fact is admitted in the case of Themison. [We know that the words "martyr" and "martyrdom" were often employed as if convertible with what was more strictly "confessorship."] And perhaps the least agreeable side of the controversy is the taunting comparison and

---

[1] The Anonymous writer admits that "ὅταν ἐν πᾶσι τοῖς εἰρημένοις ἐλεγχθέντες ἀπορήσωσιν, ἐπὶ τοὺς μάρτυρας καταφεύγειν πειρῶνται, λέγοντες πολλοὺς ἔχειν μάρτυρας καὶ τοῦτο εἶναι τεκμήριον πιστὸν τῆς δυνάμεως τοῦ παρ' αὐτοῖς λεγομένου προφητικοῦ πνεύματος." (Ap. Euseb. H. E. v. 16.)

[2] It is clear that many who were not Montanists shared these opinions. "The Fathers ...... represented martyrdom as an object to be ambitiously sought." (Kaye, p. 144.)

[3] H. E. v. 18.

mutual depreciation of the character and motives of those who had endured punishment as Christians[1].

The fourth and most serious charge is only found in the writings of modern assailants of Montanism. Tillemont states it thus: "Tertullian, in his *De Fuga in Persecutione* (cap. 10), puts into the mouth of a pious Christian, evidently a 'Pneumaticus,' these words:—'It is the Lord, He is mighty...If it be His pleasure that I die, let Him destroy me Himself, while I save myself for Him. I had rather bring odium upon Him by dying at His will, than wrath by escaping through my own[2]." This Tillemont explains as meaning:—"I will face martyrdom even should I apostatize under torture, rather than escape." Surely, however, this is a grossly unfair comment. The sense of the passage is, obviously, that the Christian should not desert his post, but look to God for aid. Wernsdorf, as usual, attempts to explain matters by quoting the pre-Montanistic treatise *Ad Uxorem* (lib. I. cap. 3), which of course has no pertinence[3]. Finally, it is untrue to suppose that the Montanists exaggerated the merit of the mere act of martyrdom. It is, of course, possible to find detached passages in Tertullian's writings[4] seeming to bear out the view, but none, at any rate, which might not be matched in his orthodox successors. But, on the other hand, he speaks on more than one occasion of the worthlessness of

[1] The Anonymus admits that there were very many Montanistic Martyrs, and is reduced to the rather dangerous resource of pleading that many heretical sects, such as the Marcionites, had numerous martyrs also. (*Ibid.* v. 16.)

[2] "Dominus est, potens est, omnia illius sunt: ubi fuero, in manu ejus sum, faciat quod vult, non discedo; et si perire me volet, ipse me perdat, dum me ego servo illi: *malo invidiam ei facere per voluntatem ipsius pereundo, quam bilem, per meam evadendo.*"

[3] "Etiam in persecutionibus, melius est ex permissu fugere de oppido, quam comprehensum et distortum negare." No doubt Tertullian always held to this sensible maxim: but unless Wernsdorf agreed with Hoffmann that all Tertullian's writings were Montanistic, he should not have quoted this one.

[4] Such as "tota Paradisi clavis tuus sanguis est." (*De Anima*, 55.)

such an act when it is not the result of deep faith and conviction. He ridicules the pretensions of those who, on the strength of a few weeks' imprisonment, flaunted their vanity in the Church. And his satirical pen reaches a terrible bitterness when he describes the unhappy end of those who (as it is to be feared was sometimes the case) sustained or replaced their failing courage in a disgraceful way[1].

Another dispute arose upon the question of the dress of virgins when in the church: the custom hitherto permitting these to keep the head uncovered, or but slightly veiled, while the Montanists strenuously enjoined the complete covering, as in the case of the married and widows. That the root of the controversy was far beneath the surface, is clear to any one who studies Tertullian's masterly analysis of the relation between Tradition and Truth, which he prefixes to his exhortation, although he also appeals to the authority of St Paul, to reasons of good taste, and to a very singular vision[2]. Other treatises, such as the *Soldiers' Crown*, and *On Theatres*, only involved, as regards their Montanistic colouring, a slight exaggeration of principles bound up in the spirit of Early Christianity. It is significant that not even an Epiphanius found any capital in this department.

§ 9. Sacraments and Ritual.

Once more we have to work on materials of a one-sided character, the accusations of writers who lived in later times, and with but slender assistance from Tertullian.

---

[1] Praxeas is "above all inflated with the pride of Confessorship, simply and solely because he had to bear for a short time the annoyance of a prison; on which occasion, 'had he given his body to be burned, it would have profited him nothing,' not having the love of God, whose very gifts he resisted and destroyed." (*Adv. Prax.* c. 1.) The account of the death of Pristinus, "your martyr, but no Christian one," could not be matched with anything in Juvenal or Swift. It does not bear quotation. (*De Jejuniis*, cap. 12.)

[2] It is recorded in the 17th chapter. Wernsdorf calls it "visio satis lepida." And indeed it must have been a trial to the gravity of some hearers to learn that "nobis Dominus etiam revelationibus velaminis spatia metatus est."

THE TENETS OF MONTANISM. 97

The question to be discussed in this section is, Did the Montanists introduce any changes into the outward service of the Church, or into the Sacraments? The best arrangement will be to treat, one after another, the accusations of wilful and radical innovation made by Epiphanius, Augustin, and many others.

The first-named expressly asserts that women filled the offices of presbyters and even of bishops among the Montanists[1]. Augustin appears to endorse the opinion. Here fortunately Tertullian is precise, and it is easy to understand the cause of the error. That women were allowed by the Montanists to prophesy in the Church, there can be no doubt. Even if the practice, as is probable, had been disused in the Church, its antiquity shielded it from any charge of heresy or innovation[2]. But we have evidence that a Montanist prophetess only revealed her visions "dimissa plebe," i.e. after the regular service, and when only the select faithful remained behind[3]. And we also have a very precise statement in the treatise *De virg. velandis*, to the effect that "it is not permitted to a woman either to speak or teach, or baptize, or offer [the Eucharist], nor any other masculine function[4]." In this Tertullian shews no change from the views expressed in the earlier tracts (that on Baptism and the Prescription of Heretics), written certainly before he had embraced Montanism[5]. The next point has been already

BOOK II.

1. *Women in the church.*

2. *Easter.*

[1] 'Επίσκοποι παρ' αὐτοῖς γυναῖκες καὶ πρεσβύτεροι γυναῖκες καὶ τὰ ἄλλα ..... αἱ καθισταμέναι παρ' αὐτοῖς γυναῖκες ἐν κλήρῳ. (Epiph. *Hær.* XLIX. 2.) And see Augustin, *Liber de Hæres.* § 27, and Wernsdorf, *de Montanistis,* p. 54 ff.

[2] Neander has some good remarks on 1 Cor. xi. 5 in his *Auslegung der Corintherbriefe.* (Berlin, 1859, p. 175.)

[3] See the whole passage (*De Anima,* cap. IX.) quoted supra, p. 63, note (2).

[4] "Non permittitur mulieri in ecclesia loqui, sed nec docere, nec tingere, nec offerre, neque ullius virilis muneris, nedum sacerdotis officii sortem sibi vindicare." (Cap. 9.)

[5] In the latter treatise he condemns certain heretics among whom "ipsæ mulieres quam procaces! quæ audeant docere, contendere, exor-

98   THE TENETS OF MONTANISM.

BOOK II. discussed in a former section[1]. It was there shewn, (*a*)
that the keeping of Easter according to Roman or Asiatic
use could never have become a note of Montanism;
(*b*) that the evidence as to the rite adopted is at best conflicting; and (*c*) that the better opinion seems to be that
the Montanists did adopt the Roman use[2].

Sacra- *Baptism.* Did the Montanists baptize "for the dead"?
ments. The accusation is made by Philaster alone[3], of whom the
irreverent Wernsdorf remarks, "*vir simplex, fortassè pius,
sed scriptor ineptus*" (p. 51). The learned German suggests
that Philaster blundered between the Marcionites and the
Montanists, which would not involve, I imagine, any excessive want of charity to believe[4]. Tertullian alludes
twice to the passage in the First Epistle to the Corinthians
(xv. 29), and though he certainly utters no specific condemnation of the practice, he in no way approves it[5]. "It
is certain," says Tertullian, "that they adopted this
[practice] with such a presumption as made them suppose
that this vicarious baptism would be beneficial to the flesh
of another in anticipation of the resurrection." This is
not the language of a man who treats of a rite still exercised by a party to which he belongs, notwithstanding
vehement attacks. Accordingly our conclusion must be
to reject the statement of Philaster.

---

cismos agere, curationes repromittere, forsitan et tingere." (Cap. 41.)
And see *De Baptismo*, cap. 17.

[1] Vide supra, pp. 42 and notes 2—5.

[2] The fact of the Synod of Laodicea specially separating the Phrygians and the Quartodecimans, (for the former were to be rebaptized,
the latter not,) I now think almost conclusive on this point. Cf. the
Canons 7 and 8, and Hefele, I. 729.

[3] "Hi mortuos baptizant." (Philastr. *de Hæres.* 49.)

[4] "Marcionitas voluit nominare *bonus vir*, quorum baptismus vica-
rius satis notus est, neque aliam habuit confusionis causam, quam quod
utriusque sectæ nomen ab eodem elemento inchoatur." (The analogy,
I presume, of Monmouth and Macedon.)

[5] Cf. *Adv. Marc.* v. 10, and *De res. carnis*, c. 48 (quoted above).
Besides Wernsdorf, the subject is fully treated in Arnold's *Unpartheyische Ketzerhistorien*, p. 77 ff.

Were any unauthorized elements distributed in the Eucharist? According to Epiphanius, Philaster, and Augustin, cheese was partaken of; and the statement seems to find confirmation in an episode of the vision which appeared to the martyr Perpetua. She relates that she found herself in a spacious garden, in which sat a man with white hair, in the garb of a shepherd, milking his sheep....He gave her a morsel of cheese (*casei buccella*), upon which "I received it with folded hands, and ate it; and all the saints around exclaimed, Amen." This, together with Augustin's positive statement[1], and the absence of any evidence or assertion on the other side, would leave at least a strong presumption in favour of the idea. But in some cases a writer's silence is more positive than even his utterance; and we can hardly believe that Tertullian's combative honesty would have suffered him to pass over in silence so remarkable an innovation. It seems probable, then, that the cheese was not adopted as a Eucharistic element, but as an oblation: perhaps to be partaken of in the *Agapè*, but not in the solemn ceremony of the Church[2].

Book II. The Eucharist.

Lastly we must deal with a topic which, were it possible, we would gladly pass over in silence. We must consider now the evidence upon which Epiphanius, Cyril, Philaster, Augustin, Isidor, and Theodoret accuse the party to which Tertullian and Perpetua belonged of participation in crimes so horrible that, if the charges be believed, Montanism deserves to the end of time to be the object of detestation[3]. It would be easy to reject the evidence at

Mysteries.

[1] He distinctly identifies them with the Artotyritæ: "Artotyritæ sunt, (sc. Phryges,) .... offerunt enim panem et caseum, dicentes a primis hominibus oblationes de fructibus terræ et ovium fuisse celebratas." (*Hær.* 26.) And compare Epiphanius, XLIX. 2, and Philaster (*Hæres.* LXXIV.).

[2] This solution I found in Wernsdorf. (P. 53.) It must be recollected that Epiphanius is doubtful whether the Artotyritæ were Montanists or a separate sect. And Timotheus Presbyter (quoted by Fabricius in his notes on Philaster) makes them out to have been Marcionites.

[3] See Epiphanius (*Hær.* XLVIII.); Cyril (*Catech.* XVI. 4); Philaster

once by the simple process of quoting the different accounts side by side, and pointing out the variations and contradictions involved; but such a course, allowable in jurisprudence, is not admissible in history. Besides, on one point all witnesses agree; and that is in the fact of Infanticide. A "fact," at least, if these holy writers have spoken truly, which we must be so presumptuous as now to investigate[1].

First let it be noted that neither Hippolytus nor the writers quoted by Eusebius know anything of these enormities. Clement, Origen, and Cyprian, all of whom mention Montanism in one way or another, are equally silent; so also is Athanasius. Cyril, in the middle of the fourth century, is the first to make the accusation. Let us transcribe his words:—"Montanus, most miserable of men,...cutting the throats of wretched little children, and chopping them up into horrid food, for the purposes of their so-called mysteries[2]." Philaster, who wrote later, is vague in his details, but positive as to his facts. "And there [sc. at Pepuza] were celebrated the cynical mysteries, and the horrible impiety with the child. For they say that [the Montanists] at Eastertide mingled the blood of a child with their sacrifice[3]." The story gains, as might well be expected, immensely in graphic detail, by the end of

(*Hær.* XLIX.); Augustin (*Hær.* XXVI.); Isidor of Pelusium (lib. I. ep. 242); Theodoret (*Fabul. hær.* III. 2); &c. &c.

[1] This investigation would no doubt seem very presumptuous in the eyes of a certain modern school, whose writers speak of S. Philaster, S. Isidor, and so on, (cf. Canon Bright's *History*, and others,) and who possibly wrote S. Kallistus, before the discovery of the *Philosophumena* revealed this distinguished person in his true light.

[2] "Ὁ Μοντανὸς ἀθλιώτατα παιδία γυναικῶν μικρὰ σφάττων καὶ κατακόπτων εἰς ἀθέμιτον βρῶσιν, προφάσει τῶν καλουμένων παρ' αὐτοῖς μυστηρίων." (*Catech.* XVI. 4.)

[3] "Ubi et mysterium Cynicorum, et infantis exsecranda celebratur impietas. *Dicunt* enim eos de infantis sanguine in Pascha miscere in suum sacrificium." (*Hær.* XLIX. Migne XII. 1165.) It is just possible that the word "Cynicorum" should be "Scenicorum," or perhaps "Cyntillianorum," (i.e. Quintillianists.) Cf. "τῶν Κυντιλλιανῶν" in Epiphanius (XLVIII. 14).

the century. Augustin cautiously shields himself under "it is reported," but nevertheless furnishes us with an account how the child was pricked with needles, its blood mixed with flour, and made into bread, and so forth[1]. We will not even stop to point out the ridiculous contradiction between Cyril's summary "chopping up," and Augustin's "needle-pricking," upon which Wernsdorf grimly remarks: "*Uter ergo minus mentitur? utrumque enim mentiri, certum mihi est.*" That Isidor should join the chorus cannot surprise. ["*Ecce iterum Crispinus...monstrum scriptoris,*" exclaims Wernsdorf, "*cujus mendacia jam sæpe explosimus.*"] He perorates about "μαγγανείαις καὶ παιδοκτονίαις, μοιχείαις τε καὶ εἰδωλολατρείαις," and there is no doubt but that he believed what he said[2]. Jerome is undecided: "malo non credere, falsum sit omne, quod sanguinis est." Theodoret honestly admits the lack of any corroborating evidence. Of modern writers it is sufficient to say that they can be divided into two classes; those who indignantly repudiate the charge, and those who "*imitent de Conrart le prudent silence*[3]." What shall be our conclusion? We shall not be disposed to believe an unproved indictment, because a piece of original slander has been copied and enlarged; nor shall we suppose that a man like Augustin would have repeated it had it not taken deep root in the popular mind. It seems that all writers forget that this crime of slaying a child was laid to the charge of

[1] "Sacramenta *perhibentur* funesta habere. Nam de infantis anniculi sanguine, quæ de toto ejus corpore minutis punctionum vulneribus extorquent, quasi eucharistiam suam conficere *perhibentur,* miscentes cum farinæ, panemque inde facientes, qui puer si mortuus fuerit, habent apud eos pro martyre, si autem vixerit, pro magno sacerdote." (*Hæres.* xxvi.) Augustin attributes the same enormities ("*perhibentur*" again!) to the Pepuziani, whom he distinguishes from the Montanists proper.

[2] Lib. I. epist. 242. (*Patrol. Gr.* LXXVIII. 332.)

[3] Most Church of England historians shirk the dilemma. The author of the History (described supra, p. 24) thinks that "there were some particular rites, but kept very secret from the uninitiated." He expresses his conviction, however, that Montanus "*neither invented Transubstantiation, nor the Sacrifice of the Mass*"! (P. 163.)

BOOK II. all Christians, originally, by their heathen opponents. [Cf. *The Apologies*, Justin I. 26; Athenagoras, 3; Tertullian, 2, 4, and especially cap. 7.] Now this charge was simply made because the Christians had private meetings, and it was possible that unknown and terrible rites were celebrated. This easy weapon was grasped by the enemies of Montanism, but not until Montanism had lost its numbers, and, above all, its mighty champion. Had Tertullian lived to hear this cruel falsehood,—"gross as a mountain, open, palpable," he would have answered the worse than heathen slanderers: "Monsters of wickedness, we are accused of observing a holy rite in which we kill a little child and eat it.... This is what is constantly laid to our charge, and yet you take no pains to elicit the truth of what we have been so long accused. Either bring, then, the matter to the light of day, if you believe it, or give it no credit as having never enquired into it. On the ground of your double dealing, we are entitled to lay it down to you that there is no reality in the thing which you dare not examine!" [*Apol.* cap. VII.][1].

§ 10. Historical position of Montanism.

If we now know something of the Montanists,—what manner of men they were, and what they believed, it now behoves us to form an opinion as to the position which the party occupies in history, and, at first, as to the causes which brought them into existence. There is no small danger of being perplexed by the multitude of theories which the ingenuity of different writers has suggested, but a steady reliance upon our previously ascertained facts will serve as an antidote. Neander deduces all that is characteristic in Montanism from the features of heathenism as modified by the Phrygian nationality[2].

[1] Pascal shewed long ago that it is a waste of time to attempt to prove a negative against the unscrupulous assertions of enemies. "C'est ainsi qu'il faut faire toutes les fois que vous accusez les gens sans preuves. On n'a qu'à répondre à chacun de vous, *Mentiris impudentissime!*" (*L. Pr.* 15.)

[2] "In der alten phrygischen Naturreligion erkennen wir den Cha-

There is much that is attractive in this theory, more especially at a time when the historical influence of nationality is given perhaps an excessive share of attention. And if we believe the statement that Montanus was himself a convert from heathenism[1], and perhaps had been a priest of Cybele formerly, the notion gains no little in consistency. But when we attempt to account for *all* the phenomena of Montanism on this hypothesis alone, its insufficiency becomes apparent. Nor is it even clear that all the points of superficial similarity are connected radically. For instance, it is not accurate, with Schwegler, (p. 80), to trace the ascetic views of Montanism on the subject of marriage to this source. [" *Ueberhaupt haben die Ansichten der Montanisten von Ehe und Ehelosigkeit so Manches, was auf den Character der orientalischen Naturreligionen, auf ihr Bestreben die Geschlechtsdualität zu indifferenziren, zurückdeutet u. s. w.*"] It is rather, as we find in all later manifestations of cognate nature, the necessary corollary of the claim to higher and more spiritual knowledge. The objection is mentioned by Tertullian, and very fairly rejected[2], with regard to fasting. We have seen elsewhere[3] that there is a danger in comparing the Montanistic theory of ecstatic inspiration with the heathen μαντική, the argument being somewhat more destructive than some of its modern employers

---

racter dieses zur Schwärmerei und zum Aberglauben geneigten, leicht an Magie und Entzückungen glaubenden Gebirgsvolks, und es kann uns nicht wundern wenn wir die phrygische Gemüthsart, die sich in den Ekstasen der Priester der Cybele und des Bacchus zeigt, in den Ekstasen und Somnambulismen der Montanisten wieder finden." (*Kirchen-Gesch.* I. 3. 871.) The same view was taken by Münter, Baumgarten-Crusius, and Kirchner.

[1] The Anonymus (*ap. Euseb.*) declares him to have been τις τῶν νεοπίστων. (*H. E.* v. 16.)

[2] "Sed bene, quod in nostris xerophagiis blasphemias ingerens, Casto Isidis et Cybeles cas adæquas. *Admitto testimonialem comparationem.* Hinc divinam constabit, quam diabolus divinorum æmulator imitatur. Ex religione superstitio compingitur." (*De Jejuniis*, cap. 16.)

[3] Vide supra, pp. 65—68.

profess to think. At any rate the opinion was so clearly that of the majority of the Church, that an examination of the whole question would carry us much beyond our special subject.

Shall we then accept the view of Schwegler, who makes Montanism a simple after-growth of Ebionitism? Here again, while admiring the ingenuity of the writer, and freely admitting that many of the analogies he points out are correct, he yet does not solve the problem,—he does not account for the existence of Montanism in itself, he does not shew us how the marvellous mixture of prophecy, ectasy, ascetic severity, and chiliastic hope, came to be so moulded together[1]. But besides this shortcoming, his theory suffers necessarily from our very imperfect knowledge of the Ebionites themselves. We know, in fact, that at first all Christians were often called Nazareans or Ebionites. [καὶ πάντες δὲ Χριστιανοὶ Ναζωραῖοι τότε ὡσαύτως ἐκαλοῦντο. Epiphan. XXIX. 1.] The name (or nickname) was not bestowed on account of their accepting as Master so humble and poor a Christ, as Gieseler explained it, but rather as being themselves "poor," especially the case with the congregation at Jerusalem, where the name certainly originated.

§ 11. Montanism and Gnosticism.

Continuing the examination, we ask ourselves what relations existed between Montanism and Gnosticism. Tertullian's book against Marcion is a proof of the separations; what points of contact were there? Now both systems have at least this common ground, that they are based both upon a conception of the world's destiny. But the difference is that, while the Gnostics turned their

---

[1] "Diese Frage ist durch die Zusammenstellung des Montanismus mit dem Ebionitismus oder Judenchristenthum noch nicht beantwortet, man sieht ihm, je unpersönlicher er erscheint und je allgemeiner und abstrakter die Beziehungen sind, die man ihm giebt, noch nicht tief genug in den innern Mittelpunkt seines Ursprungs und concreten Daseins hinein." (Baur in *Theol. Jahrb.* 1851, p. 548.) In this article, Baur is certainly unfair in considering Ritschl's work as a mere contradiction of Schwegler's. See p. 553 ibid.

attention to the beginning of things, the absolute princi-ples whether of revelation or of the world's development, the Montanists on the other hand laid all stress upon the final catastrophe, from which they (as it were) reasoned back to the present and even to the past[1]. Neander seems to have expressed the nature of this great division very ably. There are two movements or forces acting in the Christian world in the first age after that of the Apostles: one idealistic, the other realistic; but both as well within as without the limits of the Church. The former attains its extreme in Gnosticism; the latter in Montanism. There does not seem any contradiction in the fact that the latter acknowledged a means of Revelation apart from, or rather explanatory of Holy Scripture; nor does a belief in the literal truth of the promises relating to the Paraclete involve in any way a "speculative direction," as Schwegler would infer. This writer is quite correct in describing the Montanistic doctrine of the three Stages as "modern ausgedrückt—die Annahme einer Perfectibilität des Christenthums," (p. 218), but surely the conclusion is quite gratuitous that, therefore, Montanism takes its place "*der Kirchenlehre gegenüber, auf eine und dieselbe Seite mit der Gnosis.*" And when he proceeds to find Gnostic elements in Tertullian's theory

[1] See Baur's *Christenthum der 3 ersten Jahrhunderte*, pp. 213—224. Möhler's comparison I can only regard as including every possible misconception of Montanistic doctrine:—" Fanden diese (sc. Gnostiker) im Christenthum nur göttliches, und in Christo lediglich die göttliche Vernunft, so dass sie dem Erlöser nur einen Scheinleib gaben, und ihn die Form eines Menschen nur vorspiegeln, nicht Mensch sein liessen, war ihnen überdiess die sichtbare Welt durch und durch böse: so entdeckten jene (sc. Montanisten) im Heilande nur einen, wenn auch von oben herab erleuchteten, Menschen, und läugneten die Sendung des göttlichen Geistes über die Apostel und die Kirche, die höhere übernatürliche Gnadenhilfe, der sie um so weniger bedurften, als sie in der menschlichen Natur kein eingedrungenes tiefes Verderben anerkannten." (*Symbolik*, ed. of 1871, p. 363.) One reason, at least, should have restrained Möhler from this astounding diagnosis; no lower authority than S. Epiphanius had solemnly declared:—Περὶ πατρὸς καὶ υἱοῦ καὶ ἁγίου πνεύματος ὁμοίως φρονοῦσι τῇ καθολικῇ ἐκκλησίᾳ." (*Hær.* XLVIII. 1.)

of the Trinity, and quotes the use of the term προβολή as evidence, one is almost driven to the conclusion that he had not read the 8th chapter of the *Adv. Praxeam*, in which the word occurs. For how is it employed? "If any man shall think," writes Tertullian, "that I am introducing some προβολή, that is, some prolation of one thing out of another[1], as Valentinus does when he sets forth Æon from Æon, one after another;—then this is my first reply to you: Truth must not therefore refrain from the use of such a term, and its reality and meaning, because heresy also employs it. The fact is, heresy has rather taken it from Truth, in order to mould it into its own counterfeit." And to argue that Tertullian must be in some way approximate to Gnosticism, because he was by no means "the worst thinker that the Church possessed" (p. 218), is surely a burlesque of serious argument, and a significant commentary upon the value of the "Ebionitic" theory[2].

In one singular analogy, not to be unduly pressed, but still not surely to be disregarded, Gnosticism and Montanism do approach one another. It is not in any theory or opinion, but in the persons of Tertullian and Marcion, who although bitter opponents, had not a few points of similarity. Both men, as Neander well said, "are alike in a stern one-sidedness, a fiery, passionate love, which embraced its object with all its forces, rejecting everything else....... The predominant element in both men was fulness and depth of feeling. All was the result of feeling, &c." [*Antignosticus*, p. 400.] Only in this similarity, Marcion shewed himself least a Gnostic,

---

[1] This technical term properly means anything which proceeds or is sent forth from the substance of another, as the fruit of a tree, or the rays of the sun. In Latin, it is translated by *prolatio, emissio*, or *editio*. In Tertullian's time, Valentinus had given the term a material signification. Tertullian, therefore, apologizes for its use, when writing against Praxeas. (Newman's *Arians*, II. 4.)

[2] "Die Wasserscheide des Gnosticismus und Montanismus ist die entgegengesetzte Stellung zum Juden- und Heidenthum." P. 219.

Tertullian most a Montanist. Both wished, and wished BOOK II.
sincerely, to restore Christianity, just as Savonarola and
Luther wished it. Both were hostile to the slowly en-
croaching inroads of hierarchical ambition and external
formalism. But Tertullian was content to restore by the
aid of the Spirit; Marcion with his own system.

We conclude then, as follows, as to the origin and § 12.
character of Montanism :— Summary.

I. That it was neither the individual theory pro-
pounded by a man, nor the reflection of any past manifestation, whether Jewish or Heathen; but a simple
reaction towards the primitive simplicity of Christianity,
with a claim to the fulfilment of distinct promises from
Christ to His Spiritual Church.

II. That a certain Montanus existed, and gave his
name to the party; and that he, together with certain
companions, claimed to have received revelations from
the Holy Spirit.

III. That these revelations contained nothing contrary to the Catholic Faith, as found in the Scriptures;
and that this fact is certified by Epiphanius and other
fathers of the Church.

IV. That the belief in the Paraclete, and in the
Persons and Work of the Father and the Son, was that
commonly held; and that the individual views of Tertullian may be regarded as substantially identical with
those of his party.

V. That the expectation of a speedy coming of the
Lord, to be followed by a physical Millennium, and the
reign of the Saints on earth, was common to the Montanists with many persons (like Justin Martyr) of un-
questioned piety and orthodoxy.

VI. That the Montanists received the Sacraments
of Baptism and of the Lord's Supper, with the same
belief in their nature and efficacy, and with the same
rites, as the Catholic Church.

VII. That the accusations which malignity or credulity brought against them of celebrating revolting mysteries are supported by no evidence, are totally contrary to known facts and the statements of the earliest witnesses, and only confer a stigma upon the writers who disgraced themselves by repeating them.

VIII. That, although women were admitted to prophesy and to communicate visions, they were allowed to exercise no ministerial function, nor was any innovation in ritual or in the form of Divine Service introduced[1].

IX. That the spiritual claims of the Montanists, and their belief in a speedy end of the world, encouraged a system of asceticism, not in harmony with the full liberty of the Gospel, as proclaimed by St Paul, but still in no way repugnant to the commands of Scripture, or the custom of the Church.

X. That certain fasts, either entire or partial, were enjoined; but that no supererogatory merit was believed to be gained thereby.

XI. That second marriage was condemned as contrary to the original dispensation of God, as well as to the injunctions of the Paraclete, but that (although celibacy was recommended to those able, as conducive to advantage) the rite of marriage in itself was never discredited.

XII. That while sin after baptism (and even a repeated lapse) was freely absolvable by God's boundless grace and mercy, it was inexpedient for the ministers of

[1] In the notice of unauthorized rites ascribed to the Montanists, should have been included the curious gesture which gave rise to the nickname Tascodrugitæ, i.e. raising the hand to the nose. Wernsdorf denies that it was the custom, but if it had been, "egregiò convenit in homines meditabundos."(!) Strauch (*Dissertatio de Montanistis*, § 17) also is of opinion that it was never practised. On the other side, see Epiphanius (*Hær.* XLVIII. 14); Nicetas (*Thesaur. orth. fid.* IV. § 20); and Baronius (anno 73). Tertullian declares:—"Atqui cum modestia et humilitate adorantes, magis commendabimus Deo preces nostras, *ne ipsis quidem manibus sublimius elatis*, ne vultu quidem in audaciam erecto." (*De Oratione*, cap. 13.)

the Church to declare absolution in the case of serious crimes, lest their repetition should follow.

XIII. That martyrdom was the highest privilege and glory to which a Christian could aspire: but yet that it did not confer merit unless proceeding from faith and a conviction that it was God's will.

XIV. That the Visible Church of Christ included all who, upon repentance and acceptance of the Rule of Faith, had been baptized; but that the Spiritual Church comprised those alone who accepted the higher teachings of the Paraclete, by the mouth of His prophets, and that each one of these belonged to the order of spiritual priesthood.

BOOK III.

THE INFLUENCE OF MONTANISM UPON THE CHURCH.

Book III.
§ 1.
Revolution and reaction.

WE see clearly now that Montanism is not to be regarded as a sect, growing from within, though virtually without the Church, but as the exaggerated statement of fundamental and original principles[1], which, in a period of transition, would excite as much antagonism as the most violent novelty. To use an illustration, it would be quite inaccurate to compare it to such a phenomenon as Swedenborgianism, the founder of which system made no appeal to antiquity, and though not forming a sect, prepared his followers to dispense with all ecclesiastical forms. We shall trace in a later chapter the remarkable series of manifestations in the Church which almost each century produced; all starting from the Montanistic standpoint; all erring by the same exaggeration of good intentions; all, or nearly all, falling at times into the glaring logical inconsistencies which we have sufficiently noted in their model; but all, without doubt, leaving an influence for good by stirring up the life and activity of

[1] Arnold has the credit of pointing this out first, although not very clearly. Wernsdorf overshot the mark in his endeavour to depict the Montanists in the light of amiable "Aufgeklärte" of the 18th century, transplanted back into the 2nd. Neander, in his *Church History* and *Antignostikus*, developed the theory with all his learning and moderation, e.g.: "Die Montanisten sagten nichts ganz Neues, sondern sie stellten eine schon vorhandene Denkweise über religiöse und sittliche Gegenstände nur auf die Spitze." (*K. G.* 1. 3. 1131.)

the Church. That at first the leading writers and thinkers were undecided what to say, fearful to approve extravagances of form, equally unwilling to censure principles which they cordially accepted, is clearly seen from the absolute silence of Justin, as well as the guarded utterances of Irenæus. I cannot myself agree with Schwegler (who is certainly wrong in quoting Neander on his side[1]), that the latter had any specially Montanistic leanings, other than as fighting the same battle against the Gnostics. Tertullian mentions him with praise, but does not add to his name, as with that of Proculus which follows, the significant "noster[2]." There are two passages in his great work which seem to refer to the Montanists, although only one of them can be declared strongly probable in that application. This occurs in the fourth book (cap. XXXIII. § 6) where he denounces "false prophets, who have not received from God the gift of prophecy nor fearing Him, but feigning for vain-glory's sake, &c.[3]" Now no reasonable explanation of this passage can refer it to any other party than the Montanists, although we fully recognise that in many respects, as on the Consummation of all things, on Marriage, and above all, on the nature of Prophecy, Irenæus was in perfect agreement with the sober element of Montanism[4]. But in another place, where he denounces certain persons who sought to

[1] He refers to *K. G.* I. 3. 1143, (*Montanismus*, p. 223, note,) where the statement is indeed "etwas limitirter."

[2] "Justinus philosophus et martyr, Miltiades ecclesiarum sophista, *Irenæus omnium doctrinarum curiosissimus explorator*, Proculus *noster*, christianæ eloquentiæ dignitas." (*Adv. Valent.* c. 5.)

[3] "Judicabit enim pseudoprophetas, qui non accepta a Deo prophetica gratia nec Deum timentes, sed aut propter vanam gloriam, aut ad quæstum aliquem aut aliter secundum operationem mali spiritus fingunt se prophetare, mentientes adversus Deum." See on this passage, Lipsius, *Quellen*, p. 217.

[4] Take for example this passage:—"Discipulus spiritalis vere recipiens spiritum dei, qui ab initio in universis dispositionibus dei adfuit hominibus, et futura annunciavit, et præsentia ostendit et præterita enarrat, judicat quidem omnes, ipse autem a nemine judicatur." (*c. Hær.* IV. 33. 1.)

BOOK III. diminish the πρόσωπα of the Deity, to reject the Gospel of St John, and above all, to "expel the gift of prophecy from the Church," he cannot possibly refer to the Montanists, but rather to their virulent opponents the Alogi[1]. In fact, with the exception of Bretschneider, no scholar of eminence has attempted to explain the passage as referring to the Montanists.

For a time then, in fact until the Church had entered into the new consciousness of a visible and secular organic unity, no measures were taken, and none in any case could have prevailed against so important a manifesto in favour of the Prophets as the letter of the Gallic martyrs. From the later turning-point of Praxeas' intervention at Rome, the course of separation was inevitable if slow. The gradual nature is well evidenced by an expression of Origen's, in whose time the absolute separation does not seem to have been fully accomplished[2].

§ 2. Points of cohesion.

It has been noted that one strange inconsistency pervaded the Montanistic system. While upon such subjects as prophecy, church-government, and the like, they adopted the Pauline liberty in its fullest extent; in matters of lesser moment, such as fasting, they seem to incline towards a Judaistic externalism, utterly foreign to their fundamental position. It is more easy to amass a number of examples of a similar intellectual "warp" in other times and parties, than to furnish any complete ex-

---

[1] (*Ibid.* III. 11. 9). Schwegler quotes it *in extenso*, p. 269.

[2] "Requisierunt sane quidam, utrum hæresin an schisma oporteat vocari eos, qui Cataphrygæ nominantur, observantes falsos prophetas." (*Pamphil. Apolog.* 2.) As to the original character of the opposition, it has been well remarked by Ritschl:—"Wenn also die nur auf wenige Punckte beschränkte Reaktion des Montanismus weder ein neues Princip aufstellt, noch auch so ganz antitraditionell ist, als sie zuerst erschien, so leuchtet ein, dass der Unterschied des Montanismus von dem übrigen Gebiete der christlichen Kirche, so weit wir ihn bisher kennen gelernt haben, nur als ein quantitativer anzusehen ist.... Nicht die neuen Propheten allein vertraten die strengere Grundsätze in der Kirche, u.s.w." (*Entstehung der A. K.* pp. 508, 9.)

planation of its cause. It is not sufficient to say that the separation of the Church into *Pneumatici* and *Psychici* involved an injunction (for the former) of a higher sanctity of life. Such an explanation is too obviously empirical, and is easily met by the fact that a precisely similar ethical differentiation followed in the Catholic Church from a totally opposite principle. The simpler solution, viz. that Montanists as well as Catholics succumbed to the same influence, the same tendency to "externalization" of religion, is at least in perfect harmony with the facts which we shall afterwards examine, and which certainly shew that the same Church which anathematized the form of Montanism, assimilated unconsciously no small portion of its substance. We may even assert that the principle of the later ascetic movements of monasticism, of the absurd over-estimation of virginity as found in Ambrose and Jerome, not to mention others,—all were developed out of the Montanistic germ, which itself was, in some part at least, a product of the Judaistic spirit.

It was not the ascetic spirit of Montanism which the Church expelled, but it was the claim to spiritual insight[1], and the consequent antagonism to the theory of finality.

§ 3. Reasons for rejection.

[1] Thomasius, in his quaint *Höchstnöthige Cautelen*, puts the matter inversely, but he was most certainly wrong. [I quote from the Latin translation:]—"Quodsi igitur in veram causam inquiramus, cur Montanistæ in classe Hæreticorum sint, nulla alia restat, quàm quod Montanus, *observans corruptam vitam Christianorum tam docentium quàm discentium*(!), in alterum extremum prolapsus fuerit atque ex bona quidem intentione et excusabili pro moribus illorum temporum, ignorantiâ genuinæ doctrinæ de moribus et natura humana, putaverit, jejuniis austera severitate.... *Sed talis vita planè non erat ad palatum Patrum orthodoxorum in Sec.* II *et* III. *Hinc illæ lacrimæ. Hinc opus est Montanum et Montanistas in catalogo hæreticorum collocare.*"(!!) (*Cautelæ Hist. Eccl.* XI. 37.) This writer is, even more than Wernsdorf, a specimen of what may be called the "philhæretic" school of theology, which flourished in Germany in the 18th century, and later. Even Wernsdorf admits: "Sed tentatam morum correctionem fuisse causam odii erga Montanum, planè non credo." (P. 119.)

[*quod semper*, &c.] which became the basis of the new ecclesiastical organization. Had Bishop Zephyrinus and his successors confined themselves to the simple exercise of authoritative separation employed against the Donatists, they would have been quite within their rights. No government is possible if the nominal sovereign is liable to the checks which the Montanistic prophecy would, if suffered to remain in the Church, have continually interposed. Accordingly one or other of the impulses had to succumb, and naturally the weaker. And we can hardly be surprised that, in order to account for the breach, it was deemed necessary to discredit the orthodoxy of the Montanists on other questions, where we now know that it was unimpeachable[1]. It does not involve any *mala fides* on the part of the accusers that they declared the prophets to be inspired by the evil spirit, and not by the Paraclete. Indeed, this is the ground for the final edict for their rebaptization as heretics, by the Synod of Constantinople[2]. Every phase of the prophetical claim became a mark for the hostility of the later generation. We have seen that, regardless of branding Justin and Athenagoras as heretics, the Church erected into a new dogma the assertion that a prophet must be conscious, and in command of his intellectual faculties[3]. The next step was to throw overboard Irenæus by repressing the exercise of that prophetic function in the Church to which

---

[1] Eusebius's authors are angry, but suggest no formal heresy; Hippolytus but doubtfully. Cyril begins.

[2] The *Lay-Gentleman* of 1709 puts this clearly enough. (P. 173 ff.)—"As the Spirit of the Montanists was not that of God, but another, therefore Exorcism was needed, which was given in the New Baptism," etc. etc.

[3] Vide supra, p. 65 ff. Perhaps the most distinct expression of the new doctrine is the following in Epiphanius: Ὅτε γὰρ ἦν χρεία, ἐν προφήταις, ἐν ἀληθινῷ πνεύματι, καὶ ἐῤῥωμένῃ διανοίᾳ καὶ παρακολουθοῦντι νῷ, οἱ αὐτοῦ ἅγιοι τὰ πάντα προφήτευσαν. (*Hæres*. II. 1. 3.) Which Jerome expresses thus:—"Non enim loquitur Propheta in ἐκστάσει, ut Montanus et Prisca Maximillaque delirant, sed quod prophetat, liber est visionis intelligentis universa quæ loquitur." (*Prol. in Nahum proph.*)

he had so clearly and consistently witnessed[1], and confining Book III.
the acknowledged manifestations of the Holy Spirit to the
miracles and visions wrought and seen by the orthodox.
Cyprian, however, the pupil of Tertullian, does not seem
to have departed from the ancient views of the Church.
He repeatedly bears witness to the very facts which
Montanists had asserted[2], and, on a very critical occasion
in his career, he accounted for his retirement from persecution by the statement that it had been enjoined in a
vision[3]. That a good deal of incredulity began to prevail
now with regard to the spiritual claims of those who did
not always seem to correspond in their lives, could be
reasonably conjectured, even if Cyprian did not expressly
deplore it[4]. And even Jerome speaks of his visions,
including that remarkable nocturnal scourging for reading
secular authors, which was so unceremoniously criticised
by Ruffinus. Now it was not to be expected that the
Catholic bishops should accept Tertullian's reasonings on
prescription, which now served to defend the really ancient
doctrines, now to excuse the new. Any statement of a

---

[1] In addition to the passages already quoted, (vide supra, p. 36,) may
be added the following: by Irenæus, (ap. Euseb. *H. E.* v. 7,) the famous
evidence for post-Apostolic miracles, including the statement that "οἱ δὲ
καὶ πρόγνωσιν ἔχουσιν τῶν μελλόντων, καὶ ὀπτασίας, καὶ ῥήσεις προφητικάς."
And again: (c. *Hær.* v. 6,) "καθὼς καὶ πολλῶν ἀκούομεν ἀδελφῶν ἐν τῇ
ἐκκλησίᾳ προφητικὰ χαρίσματα ἐχόντων καὶ παντοδαπαῖς λαλούντων διὰ τοῦ
πνεύματος γλώσσαις, καὶ τὰ κρύφια τῶν ἀνθρώπων εἰς φανερὸν ἀγόντων ἐπὶ
τῷ συμφέροντι καὶ τὰ μυστήρια τοῦ Θεοῦ ἐκδιηγουμένων."
[2] "Castigare nos itaque divina censura nec noctibus desinit nec
diebus. Præter nocturnas enim visiones, per dies quoque impletur apud
nos Spiritu sancto puerorum innocens ætas, *quæ in ecstasi videt*, et
audit, et loquitur ea, quibus nos Dominus monere et instruere dignatur."
(*Epist. ad Cler.* IX.)
[3] Dionysius of Alexandria claimed like Cyprian to have received
visions, and even swore to the fact. *Viro sanctissimo ne jurato quidem
credemus?* exclaims Dodwell. But much ponderous ridicule from Middleton.
[4] "Quanquam sciam somnia ridicula, et visiones ineptas quibusdam
videri; sed utique illis, qui malunt contra sacerdotes credere, quam
sacerdoti." (*Epist.* 68.)

Book III. new doctrine after the Synod of Nicæa was heretical *ipso facto*, as Athanasius says concerning the Council of Ariminum:—"They do not say: 'so we believe,' but 'so is the Catholic Faith now established,' thus disclosing how recently their faith is dated. For whosoever says... that his private way of thinking is Catholic, is guilty of the folly of the Montanists. For these equally declare that the Christian Faith began with them, &c." [Ap. Socrat. *H. E.* II. 36.]

Finally, the Chiliastic views, not introduced by Montanism (since so many Fathers, and according to Justin, the most orthodox Christians embraced it), but decidedly adopted by them, and in the third century probably identified with them, became another source of rejection. Useful indeed as an incentive to repentance and piety, this mysterious doctrine was attended with difficulties and objections which were clearly seen by the Fathers of the Third Century, and the first attack, made by the Presbyter Caius, seems to have received the assent of what we may style the "official" world.

So, one by one, the fundamental principles of Montanism, its links with the Apostolical Church, were regarded as heresies. How its less laudable elements were bequeathed to the victors, we have now to discover.

§ 4. Extent of influence.
As the Catholic Church proceeded in the course of re-assimilating the elements of Judaism, it was forced to adopt, one by one, all the ascetic opinions of Montanism which its short-sighted champions had so bitterly anathematized. In the third century we find even Origen condemning the absolution of grievous offenders[1], especially in the sins which Montanism so inexorably punished. Cyprian, who had not learnt in vain from his master, held the same stringent views, which he opposed to the more lenient principles of Stephen[2].

---

[1] "Οὐκ οἶδ' ὅπως ἑαυτοῖς . . . . . πορνείας ἀφιέναι." (*De Oratione*, § 17.)

[2] "Et quidem apud antecessores nostros quidam de episcopis istic in

In the matter of Fasting, the assimilation is even more startling, as Daillé proved in perhaps the most powerful and effective argument that the whole literature of controversy can boast. He failed to see, indeed, that, although Montanism was corrupt in its external rites, it was the type of true Protestantism in its fundamental theory, or he would not have claimed for his own friends the honour of being alone the true descendants of the "Psychici." He is perfectly right in asserting that the Church, from the fourth century onwards, out-Montanised Montanism in fasting; and, as Wernsdorf well put it, there was hardly a Council that met without adding some burthensome addition to the pile of ordinances[1]. The later phases of the question, the gradual introduction of luxury in reality, while preserving the outward form of maceration, have been sufficiently exposed to ridicule: it is probable, indeed, that the introduction of a fish-diet on fast-days was a relic of Manichæism,—a worthy addition to the mosaic of Judaism and Paganism[2]. Daillé, in the third chapter of the *De Jejuniis*, draws an effective parallel between the controversies of the second and sixteenth centuries, ending with the barbed arrow to which we alluded before[3].

provincia nostra dandam pacem mæchis non putaverunt, et in totum pœnitentiæ locum contra adulteria clauserunt: non tamen a co-episcoporum suorum collegio recesserunt aut catholicæ ecclesiæ unitatem vel duritiæ vel censuræ suæ obstinatione ruperunt, ut quia apud alios adulteris pax dabatur, qui non dabat, de ecclesia separaretur." (*Epist. ad Antonian.* No. 55, ed. Pearson.)

[1] "Jam Seculo IV. cuncta quasi ex præscripto Montani aut Tertulliani peragebantur inter ipsos Catholicos: nullum fere coibat concilium, quo non nova jejunia aut novi jejuniorum modi definirentur ac toti ecclesiæ imponerentur. Ex uno solemni annuo fiebant quatuor: quadraginta horæ antepaschales mutabantur in totidem dies; xerophagiæ infinitæ excogitabantur, cum superpositionibus multifariis." (*De Montanistis,* p. 75.)

[2] Beausobre, *Hist. du Manichéisme,* lib. IX. cap. 2. (II. 770.)

[3] "Ergo isti Montanistarum vera ac genuina proles: nisi, quod a parentibus, ut progenies origine deteriore esse solet, nonihil degenerârunt . . . . . Nos vero istos Psychicos libenter amplectimur: neque nos de eorum

BOOK III.   As to second marriages, we find the same inheritance as fully accepted. Jerome declaims against them far more bitterly than even Tertullian: he regards as "execrable" [*exsecrandam*] the act of a widow who had re-married; she is "*canem revertentem ad vomitum, aut suem lotam ad volutabrum luti,*" and he declares the twice-married as universally to be regarded as "*scortati*[1]." The Councils of Laodicea and Neo-Cæsarea subjected those who married a second time to public penance[2], while that of Eliberis imposed a five-years' excommunication upon a widow who had attempted to condone fornication by marriage[3].

Such was the influence which Montanism exercised upon the Roman Church in later times, precisely the reverse of that which it aimed at, but that which alone the historic conditions admitted. Its nobler influence was not transmitted, but it did not expire. We have now to trace the occasions on which, in later ages, that influence was permitted to exert itself.

§ 5. Later manifestations.

It would need a review of the whole course of ecclesiastical history were we to attempt to notice every occasion upon which some isolated note of Montanism has been manifested. The Novatianists and the Donatists, for example, are clearly linked by their severity of moral tone, and their rejection of an unlimited power of the keys. And in later times, each mystical writer might in some sense be claimed as occupying a Montanistic stand-point, especially when (as was so often the case in the Middle Ages) the aspiration to immediate union with the Giver

sanguine prognatos esse pudet ac poenitet. Nostri illi sunt, fatemur. Vos in tota hac causa Tertulliani clientes! Nos hanc vobis gloriam non invidemus!" (Dallæus *de Jejuniis*, lib. II. caps. 2, 3.)

[1] Hieron. *Epist. X. ad Furiam*, and *Contra Jovinian.* I. 8.

[2] *Conc. Laodic.* Can. I. Christophorus Justellus (*Not. ad codicem eccl. univ.* p. 84) tried to prove that this only referred to second marriages *after divorce*, but hardly with success.

[3] "Si qua vidua fuerit mæchata, et eundem postea maritum habuerit, post quinquennium tempus... placuit eam communioni reconciliari." (Conc. Elib. § 8. Ap. Harduin, I. 251.)

of all knowledge was coupled with an earnest desire to Book III.
reform the crying abuses of the Roman Church.

If the group of sects which are known by this generic 1. *Cathari.*
title really claimed the Paraclete as their Pope, if they
asserted themselves to be a Church within the Church,
and, above all, exaggerated the merit of martyrdom,
fasting, and virginity, there can be no question but that
they represent a revival of Montanism in its most striking
aspect[1]. But our records are not ample enough to justify
any exact conclusions, and more than one eminent authority has inclined to ascribe their origin as much to
Manichæan and Gnostic elements as to those of Montanism[2].

There are also considerable points of analogy with the 2. *Walden-*
Waldenses, more especially if the early date (and not the *ses.*
common derivation of their name from Pierre de Vaux) be
admitted. It is true that most authorities, both Catholic
and Protestant, now incline to the latter opinion, e. g.
Hurter, Füsslin, Guericke, Neander, Gieseler, and therefore would not date the sect before the year 1160. Hahn
holds to the other opinion, and quotes a not very con-
vincing explanation of the name from Bernard[3]. Be this

[1] The materials, such as they are, will be found in Flathe's *Vorläufer der Reformation*, and summarized in Gieseler. Among the utterances of (obviously hostile) witnesses, may be quoted the following:—"Dicunt apud se tantum ecclesiam esse, ... sibi datum esse, nosse mysterium regnum Dei; ... veros sacerdotes nusquam inveniri, nisi inter se. ... Dicunt quod omnis laicus bonus sit sacerdos, quod omnis laicus et etiam fœmina debent prædicare." Bonacursus attributes to them:—"quod Mosaica lex sit ad litteram observanda, et quod sabbatum et circumcisio et aliæ legales observantiæ adhuc habere statum debeant; ... vetus tes- tamentum observandum esse in ciborum perceptione," &c. (Ap. Schwe- gler, *Montanismus*, p. 308.) Guibertus de Novigento (Flathe, I. 308) declared that the Cathari "damnant conjugia, et fructificare coitibus."

[2] Gieseler, Neander, and Hahn (*Geschichte der Ketzer im Mittelalter*, I. 62 ff.) take this view, and support it with some evidence. Neander quotes the Abbot Ecbert of Schönau, who in his first sermon against the Cathari (*Bibl. patr. Lugd.* XXIII. 602) asserted that they celebrated the Manichæan festival Bema, and that they accused Augustin of having divulged their mysteries. (VIII. 370.)

[3] "Quidam autem, qui Vallenses se appellant, eo quod in Valle

as it may, there is no doubt but that the Waldenses held completely Montanistic views on the approaching end of the world, and against a plenary power of absolution. Of the former we quote an instance from the curious didactic poem, *La Nobla Leyczon*, published by Raynouard in his *Choix des poësies originales des troubadours* (Paris, 1817):—

> "Car nos veyen acquest mont de la fin apropriar,
> Ben ha mil e cent ancz compli enticrament,
> Que fo scripta l'ora car sen al derier temp."
> (*Modernized.*)
> Car nous voyons ce monde de la fin approcher,
> Bien à mille et cent ans accomplis entièrement,
> Que fut écrito l'heure que nous sommes au dernier temps.

The other passage differs from the utterance of Tertullian in the *De Pudicitia* only in language[1]. The question as to the orthodoxy of the Waldenses on all points could not be satisfactorily discussed except in a special monograph.

The fourteenth century was a deeply important era for Christianity. A long series of spiritually-minded men, Tauler, Ekhart, Amalric of Bena, David of Dinant, Gerard Groot, and many others, raised their voices against the combined tyrannies of scholasticism and the mediæval Papacy. But from the Franciscan order in particular a party arose, known from their origin as the "Fratres Spirituales," or Fraticelli, who proclaimed as a new revelation the approaching end of the world, and the conse-

lachrymarum maneant...... Dicti sunt Valdenses, nimirum a Valle densa, eo quod profundis et densis errorum tenebris involvuntur." (Bernardus Abbas ap. Hahn.)

[1] "Ma el sere enganna en aital asolvament,
E aquel que ho fay encreyre hi pecca mortalment.
Ma yo aus o dire, car se troba en ver,
Que tuit li cardinal, e tuit li vesque, e tuit li aba,
Tuit aquisti ensemp non han tan de potesta
Que ilh poissan perdonar un sol pecca mortal:
Solament Dio perdona, que autre no ho po far."
(RAYNOUARD, II. 73.)

quent necessity of an ascetic life[1]. Perhaps their most striking resemblance to the Montanists is in their adoption of the tri-periodic doctrine, i.e. that certain epochs in the world's history had been directed by each of the Persons of the Trinity in turn. We find an exposition of their views in the *Liber Sententiarum* of Petrus Johannes Olivus, which, it may be added, was condemned as heretical by Pope Clement V. at the Council of Vienne. Not only does Olivus develop this theory of the three periods[2], but he applies to the Church of Rome the very title that, more than a thousand years before, Tertullian had bestowed upon it[3]. We must admit, however, that no Montanist ever carried out the conclusions so far, the connection of the Papacy and "*Babylon magna meretrix*" being a far later discovery. As to ethical reform, it must be noted that some of those dangerous refinements of asceticism, certain to involve evil effects, are to be found in the same work[4].

Another section, almost at the same period, called at times Adamites, "Brothers of the Free Spirit," but more commonly "Homines Intelligentiæ," also adopted the Chiliastic and tri-periodic views of the Fraticelli, with an equally ascetic bent. ["*Ebenso sagten sie, die Zeit des alten Gesetzes sey die Zeit des Vaters gewesen, die Zeit des neuen Gesetzes die des Sohnes,*" u.s.w.[5]] But a

4. *Homines intelligentiæ.*

---

[1] The analogy between the Franciscan Mystics and the Montanists was pointed out in D. F. Strauss's *Dogmatik* (I. 257).

[2] " Tria tempora erant ecclesiæ, scilicet ab Adam usque ad Christum, quod tempus appropriatur Patri, quia fuit tempus potentiæ. Secundum tempus incepit a Christo, et durabit usque ad Antichristum, vel usque ad persecutionem vitæ evangelicæ, quod tempus est appropriatum Filio. Et tertium tempus erit usque ad finem mundi, quod erit tempus benignitatis, et est appropriatum ad Spiritum Sanctum." (Petri Joh. Olivi *Liber Sententiarum*, 308.)

[3] " Ecclesia Romana est pro nunc *ECCLESIA CARNALIS*...... Propter hoc ipsa reprobabitur et condemnabitur et destruetur per x cornua bestiæ, quæ etiam ecclesia carnalis est Babylon meretrix magna." (*Ibid.* fol. 302.)

[4] Cf. particularly *Lib. Sentent.* 382 ff.

[5] Hahn, *Geschichte der Ketzer im Mittelalter*. His authority is the

BOOK III. special antinomian doctrine, leading often to painful excesses, is also to be noted among their views: also an anticipation of the Swedenborgian theory that the Resurrection is not future but past, having taken place in Christ's person.

5. *Flagellants.*
6. *Joan of Arc.*

Passing over, with a bare mention, the singular manifestation of the Flagellants, the next Montanistic phenomenon is undoubtedly that of the Maid of Orleans, in the beginning of the fifteenth century[1]. No one with any pretension to historic perception thinks now of doubting the perfect (subjective) accuracy of her statements, which would alone be established by the singular consistency of her utterances during the course of the long interrogations[2].

7. *Savonarola.*

In the following Reformation-century, the claims to prophetic insight were many and striking. Savonarola, although his martyrdom took place in 1498, may fitly be deemed to inaugurate the grand period. Perhaps no character in modern history deserves so thoroughly to be placed in juxtaposition with Tertullian, although it was not permitted to the latter to seal with his blood his witness to the continuing work of the Holy Spirit. It is often forgotten that Savonarola, besides being the founder of the most remarkable of theocratic governments, and an orator

"*Errores sectæ Hominum Intelligentiæ,*" in the *Miscellanea* of Baluze (II. 277—297), which I have not been able to meet with.

[1] There is an admirable sketch of the Maid of Orleans in the late Karl Hase's *Neue Propheten*, worked out with all that lamented writer's learning and acumen. (2te Anfl. Leipz. 1861.)

[2] Even the partially drawn articles of indictment display this: (§ 1) "Primo quædam femina dicit et affirmat . . . ipsa suis oculis corporalibus vidit S. Michaelem, et quandoque Gabrielem, in effigie corporali apparentes. . . . . (§ 3) Propter quæ de S. Michaele sibi apparente credit, quod ipse est S. Michael, et dicta ejus M. et facta vera et bona æque firmiter, sicut ipsa credit quod Dominus noster Jesus passus fuit et mortuus pro nostra redemptione. . . . . Et frequenter dicit (§ 6) quod nihil fecit nisi per revelutionem et mandatum Dei." And her confessor deposed: "quod semper, usque ad finem vitæ suæ manutenuit et asseruit, quod voces, quas habuerat, *erant a Deo*." (See a full survey of the materials in Hase's *Anhang*, pp. 106—164.)

of unparalleled eloquence, left writings of considerable im- Book III.
portance, more especially on the subject of the prophetic
gift¹.

It was rather Möhler's controversial than his historical 8. *Ana-*
instinct which induced him to describe the Anabaptist *baptists.*
Sects of the Reformation as the logical development of
Montanism, regardless of the fact that, in every instance,
some phase of antinomianism, from the mild theories of
Schwenkfeld to the outrageous acts of the Zwickau and
Münster prophets, predominated. Now we have sufficiently
seen, in the former investigation, that the very opposite
principle was the note of Montanism, often carried to an
almost as dangerous extreme². In modern times we have
to note with shame and abhorrence not a few instances
(such as the Münster prophets, Eva von Buttlar, the sect
of Brüggler, the Königsberg "Mücker," &c.) where a pretended
claim to inspiration has merely been the cloak for
the most revolting vice. This, indeed, is the Proof of the
Spirits, whether they be of God; and this is our safeguard
in distinguishing between the vulgar imposture of Müntzer
and Bockelsohn, and the scriptural claims and teaching of
Tertullian³.

¹ For whole list see Quetif's collection of materials. The three works
to which I especially refer are (1) *Compendio di revelazioni.* (Fir. 1495.)
(2) *Tractatus de veritate prophetica.* (Flor. 1498.) (3) *Opera singolare
contra l'astrologia.* (Fir. 1497. Ven. 1513.) This last-mentioned, which
was published between the two others, completes them by exposing the
pretensions of the false prophecies of astrologers, still in vogue at many
European courts.

² "Nichts habe mehr Aehnlichkeit mit den Montanisten, als die zur
Zeit der Reformation hervorgetretenen protestantischen Secten." (*Symbolik*, p. 465.) And cf. Schwegler, p. 311. Möhler rested his case upon
detached passages in Luther's writings, such as—"Christianus intus a
Deo solo docetur. Christianum puto esse eum, qui Spiritum sanctum
habet, qui ut Christus ait, docebit eum omnia." (*De Inst. ministr. Eccl.*
Opp. II. 584. Quoted by Schwegler, p. 311.) As if Luther could be
fairly judged by such a method!

³ Vide supra, p. 60. Much as we may detest the conduct of the
leaders of the movement, it is impossible not to feel a wondering awe at
the records of the cruel persecutions, so marvellously endured, inflicted

Book III.
9. *Jac. Boehme.*

10. *Petersen, Lead, &c.*

11. *The Quakers.*

12. *Labadie.*

My knowledge of Boehme's theories only enables me to feel a strong impression that, although his general standpoint is similar to that of Montanism[1], and although he is in many senses the progenitor of thinkers who were representatives of a completely renovated Montanism, still, taken as a whole, he must be included rather among the number of theosophical enquirers, apart from any ecclesiastical system, than as the leader of a spiritual or moral reaction in any such body. One of his pupils, Petersen, will be found to have united all these deficient elements within the pale of German Protestantism, and to his work, as well as that of his English fellow-labourers, a special appendix is devoted[2].

Earlier than these, indeed, the labours of George Fox are almost in the same degree marked by the special notes of Montanism, as also those of Labadie (1610—1674), one of the most remarkable characters even in the seventeenth century. Passing from the Jesuits to their foes the Oratorians, then to the Jansenists, finally to the Reformed Evangelicals[3]. Nourished on the Bible and St Bernard,

on those who were persuaded that Christ ordered his followers to *teach*, and *then* baptize. There is something infinitely pathetic in the song of the martyr-maidens of Beckum (modernized by Hase):—

"Die Tyrannen thäten sie fragen
Ob sie wiedergetauft wär'n?
'Wir sind einmal getaufet
Und das nach Christi Lehr'.

Wie klärlich steht geschrieben
Marci am sechzehnten Ort,
Den Gläubigen soll man's geben,
So lehrt uns Christi Wort."

And this out of a hundred similar:—"In Salzburg wurden die W. T. gleich mit ihrem Versammlungshause verbrannt. Ein sechzehnjähriges hübsches Mädchen wollte man verschonen, sie war nicht zum Widerrufe zu bewegen. Die hat der Nachrichter auf den Arm genommen, und in der Rosstränke getragen, und sie unter das Wasser gedrückt bis sie ertrunken ist und nachmals den Körper verbrannt." (Ap. Hase, *Neue Propheten*, p. 34.)

[1] "Ich habe geschrieben, nicht von Menschenlehre, oder Wissenschaft aus Bücherlernen, sondern aus meinem eignen Buche, das in mir eröffnet ward." (*Theosoph. Sendschr.* XII. 14.)

[2] Vide infra, Appendix C, pp. 161 ff.

[3] At the town of Herford, his preaching was attended by the mani-

he passed through these stages of natural sequence, and finally, in the intimacy of such choice spirits as Anna von Schurmann, he ended his career in the utterance of ascetic views worthy of the pen of Tertullian[1].

Perhaps the most deeply interesting page in the religious history of the seventeenth century is the Quietistic movement, passing from Spain to Italy, and thence to France. The phenomenon was in many points a repetition of far earlier manifestations in mediæval mysticism, but it attained a far higher degree of historical importance, as much on account of the personages implicated in the movement as of being one of the main currents of reaction against the great Augustinian revival under Jansen and the Arnaulds. Madame Guyon derived the bulk of her opinions from Molinos, through her faithful but unfortunate friend the Abbé La Combe. In later life she enjoyed the intimacy of Poiret; but it is now proved upon good evidence that she obtained her first spiritual education from the learned mystic Bertôt. Her own doctrine of revelation added to that of the Montanists something of a theory of clairvoyance, which a quotation given below proves[2]. Her history is a strange one,—first patronised, then deserted by Archbishop Noailles and Mme de Maintenon; chivalrously defended by Fénelon at the risk of losing (as he did lose) the brightest prospects of political influence in the reformation of France; imprisoned, cruelly slandered, deprived of all spiritual privileges but those of which her gaolers could not deprive her,—at last, dismissed to lead a peaceful contemplative life, forgiving all her foes, and rejoicing in the society of her friends. Bossuet was

13. *Quietism.* [*Mme Guyon.*]

festations known technically as "Resurrectiones." (See Goebel, *Gesch. des christl. Lebens in der Rhein. Westph. evang. Kirche*, II. 181 ff.)

[1] Goebel declares that he went so far as to condemn even the first marriage of unbelievers as sin.

[2] "Mes véritables enfants ont une tendance à demeurer en silence auprès de moi. Je découvre leurs besoins, et leur communique en Dieu ce qui leur manque." (Quoted by Bossuet in the *Rel. sur le Quiétisme*, § 2.)

BOOK III. not wrong when he compared her to that Priscilla whom
Tertullian called "the holy prophetess[1]."

14. *Quir. Kühlmann.* Lastly, we conclude our summary of the seventeenth century by the mention of one whose claims were neither those of faith and purity, nor of immorality and imposture, but of sheer simple madness[2]. Quirinus Kühlmann

[1] "Si cette Priscille n'a pas trouvé son Montan (i. e. Fénelon) pour la défendre." (*Ibid.*) Fénelon bitterly resented this allusion, and hardly one of his pamphlets in the long controversy does not include a reproach on this score. Bossuet defended himself thus:—" Priscille était une fausse prophétesse: Montan l'appuyait. On n'a jamais soupçonné entre eux qu'un commerce d'illusions d'esprit. (? Isidor.) M. de Cambrai demeure d'accord que son commerce avec Mme Guyon était connu, et roulait sur sa spiritualité, que tout le monde a jugée mauvaise, ... ainsi je n'ai rien dit que de juste." (*Remarques sur la Réponse à la Rel. sur le Quiétisme*, XI. § 5.) Fénelon by no means was satisfied with this explanation.

[2] The assertion in the text need only be supported by very limited evidence. He describes his early life thus in the (now very rare) *Quinary of Sling-stones* (London, 1683):—"When yet a child the Holy Spirit sported with me in dreams: when I was 18 years of age, my glorious king Jesus revealed Himself twice visibly to me, in the company of so many prophets, patriarchs, apostles, martyrs, and saints; and poured forth into my heart His most secret treasures. .... In my 23rd year, I was very powerfully stirred up, driven, and compelled, until all of a sudden, the Paradisaic Light-World visibly in the Inward surrounded me with thousand thousand thousands of Powers, Colours, and Splendours, Glances, Changes, Wonders, and Aspects, being all inexpressibly surrounded with Light from the most Holy Triangle of the Lightest-Lightest-Light-Light-Light [*sic*]; and was now with my spiritual body in another element, wherein for these 5 years I have continued." .... "When now the Divine Light of the Eternal Wisdom had enlightened me, I pierced into the very inward heart of all Arts and Faculties, and apprehended a thousandfold more in all writers than they had apprehended themselves. In my person all hoped and expected another Opitz *or* new Homer and Virgil (!), Claudian and Statius, the very princes of poets; another Gryphius *or* new Sophocles, Seneca, Terence; another Taubmannus *or new Apollo;* another Thucydides, another Scaliger, &c. &c. &c." (P. 11.) Kühlmann's poetry is even more ambitious than his prose. He published (Amsterdam, 1684) a so-called *Kühlpsalter*, from which I detach one specimen:—

"Triumf! O Kühl-Triumf! Triumft zum Kühlpropheten;
Triumfftriumfftriumfft, ihr Himmel und ihr Erden!
In unserm Gott-Gott-Gott, der Götter ein'gem Gott:

wandered about Europe in the second half of the century, publishing works in German and English, each transcending the other in extravagance, but none the less (or, perhaps, on that account) attaching to himself a number of followers. The unfortunate man ended his career in Russia with a very unwilling martyrdom[1].

The eighteenth century once more affords a mirror of almost the same phenomena. While Zinzendorf and the Brethren of Herrnhut developed the simple primitive views and life of the first century, Eva von Buttlar and her friends revived the excesses of the Anabaptists; and, on the opposite side, Swedenborg, after exhausting the world of science as then known, proceeded to evolve an enormous scheme of theosophy upon the foundations of Origen, Richard of St Victor, and Boehme. How far Swedenborg really unites in himself and his system all or any of the notes of Montanism, we shall attempt briefly to examine in an appendix[2].

15. Zinzendorf. 16. E. von Buttlar. 17. Swedenborg.

What have we to say of the present century? The claims to supernatural revelation are frequent,—were their "proofs" in righteousness and truth? Surely not in Germany, where the exposure of certain painful episodes at Königsberg caused the profession of the truly pious to be viewed for a long time with a not unnatural suspicion[3].

18. Schönherr, Ebel.

Sein ist allein der Sieg: sein ist allein die Ehre,
Die Ehren-ehrenehr in Zeit und Ewigkeit!"
(*Triumflied ad fin.*)

[1] The history of Quirinus Kühlmann is very obscure, although one would have thought that so strange a career would have attracted somebody to write a monograph, as materials surely could be found.

[2] Vide infra, Appendix D, pp. 173—176.

[3] It is necessary to distinguish between the respective shares of Schönherr and Ebel, the former being in no way implicated in the practices which led to the judicial investigation of 1835—1841. Schönherr was an honest, pureminded, if not very acute, enthusiast. [As a youth he visited Kant, who dismissed him as an "unklarer Kopf."] At last he formed a small community at Königsberg, which met for prayer and meditation. Among these associates was Ebel, who from being a pupil became a rival, and finally seceded. (Cf. Art. *Schönherr* in Herzog.)

Book III.
19. Mormonism.

As discreditable, both from original imposture, and from the moral (or rather immoral) tendency which so soon became the leading principle, is the history of Mormonism. Perhaps there is no page of history which offers more capital to the pessimist than the narrative of Joseph Smith's career, utterly wanting even in the brute force and enthusiasm which made the Anabaptist Matthiessen rush alone upon the besiegers of Münster, to be immediately " hewn in pieces." Every feature is mean, vulgar, calculated to allure the basest of human passions, under the blasphemous guise of revealed authority. The so-called *Book of Mormon* is indeed a worthy " symbolical book," in its mixture of fustian, bad grammar, profanity and nonsense[1]. Happily the last chapter of the shameful history seems to have begun. The conviction of the " bishop" Lee on the charge of murder removed the last shreds of character that hung round Mormonism, while the death of Brigham Young (reported lately) deprives them of an able and unscrupulous leader. It would be almost a mockery to discuss the so-called "doctrines" of the party : but it may be noted that the belief in an approaching Millennium, and the rite of baptizing for the dead, were prevalent[2]. Happily we are

Schönherr died in the year 1826; while the sect of "Ebelianer" (or Mücker) did not come into existence until the years 1828—9.

[1] The MS. of the *Book of Mormon* was written as a romance by Solomon Spaulding, but failed to find a publisher. Joseph Smith secured it, and in the year 1830 he brought it before the world, asserting that "it was a translation from hieroglyphics on golden plates, delivered to him by angels." Here are a few specimens, taken from a copy of the first edition [Palmyra, U.S. 1830]:—

2nd *Book of Nephi*, ch. XII. "Thou fool, that shalt say,—'A Bible, we have got a Bible, and we need no more Bible.' Know ye not that there are more nations than one? Wherefore murmur ye because ye shall receive more of my word? . . . . . And because that I have spoken one word, ye need not suppose (sic) that I cannot speak another: for my work is not yet finished, &c." (P. 115.)

Book of Moroni, ch. x. "All these gifts of which I have spoken, which are spiritual, never will be done away, even as long as the world shall endure, only according to the unbelief of the children of men."

[2] The original articles of faith were modified in 1846 by the promul-

enabled to conclude this brief sketch by the mention of Book III. two still existing forms of "repristinized" Montanism, in neither of which are to be noted the elements of imposture and immorality, although neither, on the other hand, can display among its ranks a Tertullian or a Fénelon. Some 20. *Edw.* perhaps will deem this verdict unjust to the memory of *Irving.* Edward Irving. It may be so, and it would be wrong to demand of the orator the same lasting monuments as the writer: but still the eloquence which astounded Canning and drew all Mayfair to Hatton Garden does not seem to us of quite the same standard as the passionate denunciations of the Carthaginian presbyter, and the incomparable grace and pathos of the Archbishop of Cambrai.

Irving suffered the misfortune of being driven to defend deep opinions without the aid of a thorough theological education; and thus one who held and reverenced the Absolute Divinity of the Son, in the highest and fullest sense, was made to appear a heretic under the skilful cross-examinations of his inquisitors. If Neander's motto, " *Pectus facit theologum,*" were as true as it is suggestive, Irving would be the first of theologians, for none had a heart so true, so warmly-beating, and so sympathetic. None surpassed his humility when, in those last gloomy years, he became the mere subordinate in the system which his own individuality had called into existence. But when, in 1834, that noble soul was called away, it left nothing but a frigid eclecticism of ritual without rule, prophecy without inspiration, and a title (" *Catholic and Apostolic Church*") without a meaning! Still, if the visitor to an Irvingite Chapel finds some difficulty in reconciling the assumption of mediæval decoration and the claim of primitive doctrine, it must not be denied that the

gation of the *Doctrines and Covenants*, [apparently the Trinity modified into a Duality, cf. p. 47,] the simple presbyterian government now developes into a hierarchy. Baptism for the Dead enjoined §§ 105, 106, with allusion to 1 Cor. xv. 29. (Cf. Gunnison's *History of the Mormons*, Philadelphia, 1852.)

professed doctrines are very similar to those of Montanism. There is the strong belief in the Millennium, previous to which there is to be the reign of Antichrist, and the resurrection of the just. There is the claim to a continued revelation from the Holy Spirit, but limited by the nature of the hierarchy, as if in an attempt to harmonize Tertullian and Cyprian.

21. The Mennonites. Dating far back as to their origin (for their founder, Menno Simonis, belongs to the period of the Reformation), the Mennonites accomplished but four years ago an important step in their history, viz. their settlement in the territories of British North America. They do not claim prophetic revelations, but they profess to live after the model of the Gospel in refusing to take part in war, in declining all judicial oaths, and in practising a simple ecclesiastical discipline by banishing all committers of immorality from their societies. The first-named tenet caused them to leave their first settlements in Northern Germany, and to migrate to Russia under a pledge of exemption from military service. Notwithstanding their great services in civilising the vast plains north of the Black Sea, this pledge was broken by the Russian Government; and once more these primitive Christians have girded up their loins, have journeyed thousands of miles, and have settled in lands which can only profit by their presence. With this synopsis (which it would be only too easily possible to extend) we turn to the last and chiefest consideration which our work demands.

§ 6. Conclusion. What, then, shall we say upon the main question? What is to be the verdict justified by the impartial hearing of so vast a mass of evidence, and so numerous a body of counsellors? Are we to dismiss the Montanists to keep company with the dismal shadows of forgotten heresies, the inventions of foolish minds, the depravation of Scriptural truth? In one word, was the "Spirit" which

Tertullian preached, and for which Perpetua died, the Father of Lies, or was it the Spirit of God?

Some would tell us to answer the question by a simple reference to the "voice of the Church," always the same in every place and time. But we have already seen that, to unlearned and unskilful minds, this voice is only to be found in its discord, or (at best) unanimous when the event has been long decided. Surely in a question in which issues of fact as well as of doctrine were concerned, the defenders of the "*Quod semper, quod ubique*" cannot blame us for appealing to that voice as it spoke at or near the very time; and what have we found? Epiphanius declares that the Montanists "held concerning the Father, the Son, and Holy Ghost, the views of the Catholic Church." Cyril accuses Montanus of claiming to be the Holy Ghost *in propriâ personâ*. All the immorality that the contemporary Hippolytus can attest is "the eating of dry things and radishes, the introduction of new fasts and festivals:" but John of Damascus, in the eighth century, knows that they "made bread with the blood of murdered infants." Perhaps it will be said that these are the mere *obiter dicta*, and not the official utterances of the Fathers. I appeal then to the facts, that one successor of St Peter (viz. Soter) wrote against the Montanists, while another (be it Eleutherus or Victor) was prepared to acknowledge the prophets, and had formally so acknowledged them, but was persuaded into retractation by Praxeas the Patripassianist! Perhaps, like the monks in the "Epistolæ Obscurorum Virorum," the opponents on failing with the popes turn to Councils[1]; they must then have the goodness to instruct us which we are to select: for that of Iconium which commanded the rebaptization of

---

[1] I have not the reference at hand, but recollect some orthodox friend of Ortuinus Gratius saying (if I do not misrepresent his Latinity):—"Si Papa erit contra nos, tunc dicemus quod Consilium est supra Papam," and the converse also held good, in case of need. This excellent principle was often put in practice in the history of the Papacy.

Montanists is followed by that of Nicæa which imposed no such stigma.

Renouncing, then, our attempt to solve the problem in this way, let us adopt the test which Jeremy Taylor gave: "Whatsoever is either opposite to an article of creed, or teaches ill life, that is heresy: but all those propositions which are extrinsical to these two considerations, be they true or be they false, make not heresy, nor the man a heretic[1]. What, in the detached oracular utterances of the prophetesses, brought to us through a hostile witness, can be alleged as contrary to the *Regula Fidei*, as entertained by Justin, by Athenagoras, by Irenæus? Is it heretical for Maximilla to declare that "the end of the world was approaching," or that her followers were "to hear Christ, and not me"? Even in Tertullian's Montanistic writings, is there a sentiment, is there a statement about the Trinity, which is not to be found in almost the same form in other writers? And even if rash reasonings on mysterious subjects be found in the works, are we to stop here? Shall we not proclaim the heresy of Arnobius, Lactantius, and many others? In one word, have we not shewn, fairly and fully, that all the views of the Montanists on the work of the Spirit, the end of the world, the Millennium, are identical with those of Fathers whose orthodoxy no one questions? Our conclusion is that there was nothing opposite to an article of creed.

And now for Jeremy Taylor's second test:—"Or teaches ill life." The Montanists introduced some fasts, "deferring (says Tertullian) what we do not reject;" they condemned second marriages; they recommended the endurance of martyrdom rather than flight in persecution; they declared that only God should give absolution for certain awful sins. Is this "teaching ill life"? And which side do the charges of Infanticide discredit? Is there any need once more to refute them by their statement? We answer, that there was no "ill life" taught.

[1] *Liberty of Prophesying*, cap. 3.

If, indeed, other evidence shall in the future time be discovered, proving that any article of Creed was controverted by even an obscure follower of the Montanist Prophets, if any writer shall succeed in shewing that these Prophets taught immorality under the guise of asceticism, as some have done, we shall accept such a conclusion then as freely as we reject it now. But without it, there is but one guide, which tells us: " there are diversities of operations, but it is the same God which worketh all in all. And the manifestation of the Spirit is given to every man to profit withal....All these worketh that One and the Self-same Spirit, dividing to every man severally as He will." And again:—" The fruit of the Spirit is in all goodness and righteousness and truth;" it is " love, joy, peace, long-suffering, gentleness, goodness, faith, meekness, temperance: against such there is no law." And where this Spirit shews itself in these fruits, though Popes and Councils may anathematize, the Great Judge will one day reverse their judgment.

1 Cor. xii. 6 ff.

Eph. v. 9.
Gal. vi. 22 ff.

APPENDIX A.

KESTNER'S "AGAPÉ."

Appendix A.

This curious work, published by August Kestner at Jena in 1819, attempts to construct from existing historical materials a perfectly new theory as to the nature of the early Christian polity. According to him, we must regard the Christians of the first three centuries as forming a vast secret society, like the Carbonari of Italy, with distinct worldly ideals, and not without frequent alliances or understandings with the Roman Empire[1]. The foundation-stone of this theory, such as it is, seems to be the well-known passage in Orig. *adv. Celsum* (I. 1), in which the Christian Father replies to an accusation of the philosopher that the new faith involved "a secret, lawless association." This secret alliance, while denying the illegality, Origen seems to admit; and he points out to his adversary that such a proceeding was inevitable. He uses the well-known expression ΑΓΑΠΗ, usually identified with the love-feast, but to which, in this case, a more extended meaning may be given. From Ignatius's Epistle to the Romans, Kestner ventures to base the assertion that :—" Die Römische Gemeinde wird vom Ignatius 'Vorsteherin der Agape' genannt[2]," and, from another early source, the statement that Clement of Rome "gave great pains to bring Christians, Jews, and Heathen into the Agape[3]." It is not necessary to quote all the passages[4] in which he finds

---

[1] He starts from Pliny's mention of the "sacramentum," Irenæus's assertion that Marcus Aurelius subsidized some Christians, (c. *Hær.* IV. 50,) and, above all, "die unbegreifliche Erscheinung, dass im Gefolge der siegenden Christusreligion ein völlig organisirtes jüdischheidnisches Priesterthum zugleich mit auftaucht." (p. 3.)

[2] I have not verified Kestner's quotations. He refers to Ignatii *Ep. ad Rom.* ed. Usserii, p. 81.

[3] "Martyr. Clement. nach dem Pariser MS. No. 814."

[4] He quotes Ignat. *Epp.* pp. 68, 103; and many passages from Clement's Epistle *Ad Cor.* including the well-known imitation of the inimi-

and explains the use of the same term ; it will be sufficient to summarize briefly his alleged history of the society until the appearance of Montanism.   APPENDIX A.

Clement of Rome was its founder, and the date of founda- [p. 25 *et*
tion may be fixed immediately after the destruction of Jeru- *seq*.]
salem, while the rapid rise of the society in numbers may be
attributed to the disgust evinced by the civilized world at
Domitian's tyranny. The first action taken was to circulate a
large number of writings, falsely ascribed to Apostles, with the
purpose of reconciling the fiercely discordant factions of
Paulinists, Petrinists, and Judaizers, not to mention that of
the Johanneans, still possessing their leader[1]. After having,
by this admirable means, attained his end, Clement next dis-
seminated some "newly fabricated or interpolated works of
Jewish or Heathen Prophecy," and crowned his diplomatic per-
formances by "purloining from the Evangelist John the secret
archives of his own 'Mysterien Gesellschaft,' the so-called
'Society of Theologians,' and with this and other ingredients
(heathen and Jewish chiefly) compounding an esoteric system
of ritual and mysteries, together with a priesthood."

Domitian had suspected and attempted to reach the society,
but in vain : he probably owed his assassination to its machinations[2]. Trajan pursued its traces with severity, and caused
many of the leaders to be slain. Under Hadrian, the leaders
succeeded in gaining the Emperor's favour by assuming the
disguise of Building Societies [Bau-Gesellschaften], and thus
forming the origin of Masonic Lodges (!). Under Antoninus
Pius, the society worked quietly by means of published

table xiiith chapter of another's epistle to the same Church. On this
(Clement's) Kestner has the *naïveté* to remark: "Einige Züge dieses
Panegyrikus der "Agape" *passen besser auf die christliche Liebe, als auf
den Bund.*" (P. 15.) Who would have thought so, but for this candid
admission!! Here is another exegetical gem:—"Iu einigen Stellen in
den Briefen des Ignaz und Polycarp, '*Agapè*' *kann ebensogut Liebe
als Liebesbund bedeuten; wir aber haben gewiss ein Recht, die letzte Bedeutung der erstern vorzuziehen.*" (Risum teneatis amici?)

[1] "Im Namen des Paulus, dessen Tod in entfernten Weltgegenden
noch nicht sogleich bekannt seyn konnte, schickte er an viele Brüder-
Gemeinden *erdichtete Briefe*, welche zu den nachfolgenden Einladungen
zur Agape einstweilen vorbereiten sollten. . . . . . Mehrere solche Pseudo-
Paulinische Briefe, welche ohne Zweifel auch aus der vielproducirenden
Klementinischen Schriftenfabrik herrührten, sind uns verloren." (P. 53.)
Semler, it will be recollected, also introduces this 'manufactory.'

[2] "Eine Stelle des Origenes scheint nicht undeutlich zu verrathen,
dass die klementische Gesellschaft an dem Tode des Tyrannen Antheil
gehabt habe." (P. 101.) [The passage is in *adv. Cels.* 1. 1.]

APPENDIX A.

apologies, and enjoyed the assistance of Lucian in combating the heathen-gnostic element, while under Aurelius the fullest success was reached. The Emperor allowed himself to be initiated into the mysteries of the Agapé, "behaved himself throughout as the protector of Christianity" (*sic*), and obviously proposed to erect it into the state-religion of the Empire, had he not been hindered by a strong anti-Christian reaction, and, above all, by his premature death. During his reign the "Rebellion" of Montanism broke out. Its author, a daring ambitious character, entertained the notion of effecting, at one stroke, the long-planned reforms of the Agapé, viz. of reorganizing society under the rule of the secret priesthood; and he was encouraged in his attempt by the manifest change in public opinion that the last generation had witnessed. He began by circulating a species of manifesto (called the Προφητεία), which announced the speedy end of the world and the glory prepared for the faithful. In this document many of the Agapetic mysteries were revealed, a proceeding which caused the bitterest resentment against Montanus on the part of his former colleagues. The former, however, gained numerous adherents and wealth, and was even contemplating, if necessary, armed resistance to the Roman power. He enforced upon his followers a system of life calculated not only to nourish visionary and enthusiastic feelings, but to detach them from the ties of family and society. Above all, they were to give their lives in every case when persecution came.

The leaders of the Agapé were filled with consternation at this outbreak, which not only imperilled their recently acquired amnesty, but fatally shattered their hopes of further peaceful progress in the Empire. Montanus had been successful in gaining the Overseer of the Society at Rome; but in Asia Minor active steps were taken at once. Even at Rome the skilful diplomacy of Praxeas was able finally to restore the supremacy. Seeing himself gradually forsaken by his followers, officially condemned in Asia, deserted at Rome, Montanus ended his career by suicide. Kestner points out the remarkable *rôle* played by the Roman power, which took no steps to crush the rising, and inflicted no penalty on even an open rebel (of the Montanistic party) at Rome. The Emperor was satisfied with the prompt and loyal action of the main body of Christians, which amply sufficed to crush the dangerous insurrection. Among the special anti-Montanistic manifestos should be mentioned Lucian's *Philopatris*.

THUS FAR KESTNER: and the reader will ask perhaps, "Why have you taken the trouble to quote so much of a rather tedious paradox?" Paradox indeed, to those who accept history honestly and critically; but is there not a large party to whom this romance of the Agapé ought to be a godsend? The writers who profess to believe that the whole ecclesiastical system, as we find it in the fifth century, was revealed to the Apostles in the "forty days,"—what can they believe but that there was a "doctrina arcani" (they admit the "disciplina"), and what real difference is there between such a theory and that of Kestner, except in a few artistic details? [*E.g.* the late Mr Chambers wrote in *Essays on Eccles. Reform*, 1873: "The sayings of S. Paul (sc. on virginity, etc.) are chapters from the great body of ecclesiastical jurisprudence, as the result of the great forty days' communing with Jesus Christ." I am not clear whether it is from the same source that, according to this learned writer, "S. James legislates concerning auricular confession and extreme unction" (p. 111).] Now, as this view is by no means confined to the members of the section to which this writer belonged, would it not be reasonable to furnish some explanation of this strange concealment? And would not the romance of August Kestner answer the purpose as well as any other?

APPENDIX B.

PASSIO SS. PERPETUÆ ET FELICITATIS CUM SOCIIS EARUM.

APPENDIX B.

1. Editions.

This monument of Christian piety and fortitude was first brought to light in modern times by Lucas Holstenius, the librarian at the Vatican, from a MS. in the convent of Monte Cassino, after long search. It was well known in the Early Church, and Augustin records that it was so highly reverenced as to be read aloud in the Church in his time[1]. After the death of Holstenius, it was again edited by Valesius (Parisiis, 1664), and subsequently by Peter Possinus, a learned Jesuit, for Ruinart's collection (Veronæ, 1731). It is to be found, moreover, in Cardinal Orsi's *Dissertatio Apologetica* (Florent. 1728), and in Muenter's *Primordia ecclesiæ Africanæ* (Hafniæ, 1829), as well as in the recent edition by Hurter of the *Opuscula Selecta SS. Patrum* (Œniponti, 1871).

2. Chronology, &c.

The time and place of the martyrdom cannot be settled with complete precision. All that can be fairly inferred has been stated by Uhlhorn in his dissertation upon the chronology of Tertullian's life[2]. We are told in the Acta that Geta was Cæsar. This limits the period within four years, from A.D. 199 to 203. Of these years 203 seems preferable, as being that of Geta's consulship (together with Septimius Plautianus), when he celebrated some gladiatorial games on his birthday[3]. But,

---

[1] "Exhortationes earum (sc. Perpetuæ et Felicitatis) in divinis revelationibus triumphosque passionum cum legerentur audivimus; eaque omnia verborum digesta et illustrata luminibus aure percepimus, mente spectavimus, religione honoravimus, caritate laudavimus." [Quoted by Hurter in his notes to the *Opuscula Selecta*, XIII. 115.]

[2] *Fundamenta chronologiæ Tertullianeæ*, (Gotting. 1852,) p. 5 et seq.

[3] "Arctat nos ab accuratissimis chronologis anno Christi 202 alligata epocha persecutionis ab eo imperatore in Christianos motæ, qua posteriorem SS. P. et F. fuisse passionem hæc ipsarum Acta demonstrant." (Possinus ap. Uhlhorn, p. 9.)

on the other hand, there is reason to doubt the certainty of these dates, and Uhlhorn himself considers that Geta officiated as Consul in the years 205 and 207[1]. Morcelli supports the same year, chiefly on the authority of Julius Capitolinus, who relates that Severus celebrated games in Thrace on the birthday of Geta[2]. But it is wisest to refrain from an attempted accuracy which the evidence does not justify, and to be satisfied with the knowledge that the martyrdom must have occurred in the first decade of the third century. The place of the martyrdom is equally uncertain, but the better opinion seems to be in favour of Carthage rather than Tuburbium. The supposition of the latter rested on a passage in one of the sermons attributed (but not unanimously) to Augustin[3]. But as we have a statement that Augustin had written three sermons in commemoration of Perpetua and Felicitas, and all three are extant, this must refer to some other martyrs. And the constant reference in the Acta to the camp, fortress, amphitheatre, &c., could hardly have reference to so unimportant a city.

Appendix B.

Naturally the most important and interesting question remains: whether we have been justified in the course of the preceding essay in including Perpetua and Felicitas among the number of the Montanists. It must be recollected that the Acta proceed from two writers: an anonymous secretary, who writes the beginning and end, and about whose Montanistic sentiment not a few Roman Catholic writers are confident, and the narrations of the martyrs themselves[4]. Uhlhorn very rightly dismisses as irrelevant the arguments employed, whether by Basnage on the one side (who wished to prove the Montanism of Perpetua from the praises of Tertullian and the opinions of the Redactor), and those of Orsi, who also laid almost exclusive stress upon the external argument. A far better criterion must be found in the utterances and visions of the martyrs themselves: and these we propose briefly to examine[5].

3. Orthodoxy of the Martyrs.

[1] He quotes Eckhel, (*Doctr. numm. vett.* VII. 230.)

[2] In vita Maximinorum, cap. 2, apud Morcelli, (*Africa Christiana*, II. 58.)

[3] "Sed dura est, inquis, via: quis per istam illum sequatur? Erubesce barbare, erubesce; a virtute vir diceris. Feminæ secutæ sunt, quarum hodie natalitia celebramus. Feminarum martyrum *Tuburbitanarum* solemnitatem celebramus." (August. *Opp.* ed. Bened. v. 933, Serm. 345, § 6.)

[4] Cardinal Orsi himself admitted that the orthodoxy of the "Redactor" could hardly be maintained. And see Uhlhorn, p. 14 ff.

[5] Some doubt has been cast upon the authenticity of the Acta from the frequent untranslated Greek words and idioms in the text, which caused some to suppose that the whole was a mere translation from the Greek. [Cf. "turbarum *beneficio*," χάριν· cap. 3; "bene venisti, *teg-*

APPENDIX B.

Let it first be noted that the Redactor's language is precisely that of the Montanists, whose cardinal passage of Scripture he puts forth, as it were, as his text (viz. Joel ii. 28), adding:—" Itaque et nos qui sicut prophetias, ita et visiones novas pariter repromissas et agnoscimus et honoramus, ceterasque virtutes Spiritus Sancti, ad instrumentum ecclesiae deputamus, etc." Perpetua's brother says to her : " Domina soror, jam in magna dignitate es ; et tanta, ut postules visionem et ostendatur tibi, an passio sit, an commeatus[1]." As Milman admits, this is indeed " the language of Montanism ;" and we question whether there was any higher grade among the Pneumatici than those who might " postulate a vision." " Et ego (continues Perpetua), QUÆ ME SCIEBAM FABULARI CUM DOMINO,...fidenter repromisi, ei dicens : Crastina die tibi renunciabo." She asks, and is answered by the following vision. A great part of this it would be impossible to claim as evincing any specially Montanistic trains of thought : that appears from what came before. But the last part, the appearance of the man with white hair, milking his flock, who gives to her a morsel of cheese : " et ego accepi junctis manibus, et manducavi : et universi circumstantes dixerunt Amen. Et ad sonum vocis expergecta sum, etc.," is important (whether we admit or reject the conclusions already mooted as to the use of cheese), and especially the proof that this vision, like all those of Montanistic prophecy, was received in a state of ecstasy.

The vision of Saturus is even more important, (*a*) as testifying to the Montanistic views of the martyrs ; (*b*) as confirming our previously expressed view that the absolute separation of the party from the Church was of far later date than most writers imagine, since the martyrs not only speak of the Bishop with respect and love, but are welcomed by him. We transcribe part of the text :—

cap. 13.

"Et exivimus, et vidimus ante fores Optatum episcopum ad dexteram, et Aspasium presbyterum doctorem ad sinistram, separatos et tristes, et miserunt se ad pedes nobis, et dixerunt nobis : Componite inter nos, quia existis et sic nos relinquitis. Et diximus illis : Non 'tu es papa noster, et tu presbyter, ut quid vos ad pedes nostros mittatis ? Et misimus nos, et complexi illos sumus. Et cœpit Perpetua cum illis loqui, et segregavimus eos in viridario. Et dum loquimur cum eis, dixerunt illis angeli : Sinite illos, refrigerent ; et si quas habetis inter vos dissensiones, dimittite vobis invicem et conturbaverunt eos. Et dixerunt Optato : Corrige plebem tuam, quia sic ad te

non," τέκνον· cap. 4; " in oramate," ὁράματι· "diastema"=διάστημα; "agios, agios, agios," etc.]

[1] I quote from Hurter's edition. The above is p. 120, cap. IV.

conveniunt quasi de circo redeuntes, et de factionibus certantes. Et sic nobis visum est, quasi vellent claudere portas."

I agree fully with Morcelli and Münter that Optatus must have been Bishop of Carthage, and Aspasius (called "doctor") the special instructor of catechumens. The divine admonition is obviously in the sense of a Montanistic asceticism; the Bishop having allowed the reins of discipline to become lax, and not having duly condemned participation in the amusements of the pagan world [vide supra, pp. 44, 45, also p. 99]. But Uhlhorn's conclusion, viz. that the Montanists, though alienated in spirit from the Bishop, had neither renounced their obedience, nor received his excommunication as yet, is quite justified. The object of the vision was to suggest a pacific solution on the basis of a certain concession to Montanistic scruples.

The apostrophe of the Redactor (after relating the end, with the inimitably beautiful description of Perpetua's guiding the sword herself,—"fortasse tanta femina aliter non potuisset occidi,...nisi voluisset,") is another outburst of Montanism:—

"O fortissimi ac beatissimi martyres! O vere vocati et electi in gloriam Domini nostri Jesu Christi, quam qui magnificat, et honorificat, et adorat, utique et hæc non minus veteribus exempla in ædificationem ecclesiæ legere debet, *ut novæ quoque virtutes unum et eundem Spiritum Sanctum usque adhuc operari testificentur.*"

That so staunch an anti-Montanist as Hurter should pass this over can only be accounted for by his satisfaction in pointing out the passage (cap. 8) in favour of purgatory, and release from it through the prayers of saints.

APPENDIX C.

JANE LEAD, PETERSEN, AND THE PHILADELPHIAN SOCIETY.

APPENDIX C.

In the comparative study of later manifestations of a Montanistic nature, great care has to be taken not to confuse together with these the results of widely different influences. This mistake is specially liable to be made with regard to the various theosophical writers who have claimed a special insight not only into the truths of Scripture, but into the mysteries of Nature, and who may far more fitly be styled the Modern Gnostics. In this class, Paracelsus, Cornelius Agrippa, and perhaps even Jacob Boehme, have to be placed, and in later times, the "unknown philosopher," Saint-Martin, and, perhaps strictly, Swedenborg. It is necessary, then, once more to remind ourselves of the special notes of Montanism.
 I. Belief in continued, immediate revelations.
 II. Attachment to the simplest forms of Christianity.
 III. Theory of a Spiritual Church within a Natural Church.
 IV. Stringent ascetic life incumbent on the Spiritual man.

To these might be added, what is indeed the strict converse of No. 1., a distrust or even contempt for mere human speculations on the mysteries of salvation, and thus it is impossible to include the mediæval and modern thinkers who ignored the primitive doctrines, and ran riot in the regions of astrology and alchemy. Nor would it be accurate, upon these data, to include those excellent men who, like Gerson and Richard de St Victor, found the bonds of scholastic theology too narrow, and strove towards a more spiritual insight. As we pointed out in a former chapter, Theresa appears almost alone as the fitting successor of Maximilla and Priscilla. But, for the purposes of illustrating the Montanistic principles in modern application, there are even better examples to be found in that remarkable period, the seventeenth century, when the immense renovation caused by Catholic zeal was evoking a sort of afterglow of the Reformation in Protestant Europe.   APPENDIX C.

Although later in date than his English co-religionists, it will be well to consider the career of Johann Wilhelm Petersen first, as better displaying the first stages of the modern Montanistic movement.   Petersen (1649—1727.)

Born at Osnabrück in 1649, where his father, a lawyer of eminence, had been sent by his native city of Lübeck as its envoy at the Congress, the son enjoyed an excellent education, and in 1669 was sent as a theological student to the University of Giessen, where he obtained the degree of Magister. He afterwards studied at Rostock and the Saxon Universities, and upon his return to Giessen delivered philosophical lectures. About 1675 he made the acquaintance of Spener, whose subsequent influence upon his writings was considerable. He received the appointment of Preacher at the church of Lübeck, but was forced to leave the city owing to the machinations of the Jesuits, whom he had offended by a satire, and who petitioned the Emperor for his punishment. He finally settled at Hanover, but after a short residence was compelled to leave, owing to the increasing attacks from the Catholic party. At last a haven appeared in the neighbourhood of his native city, and here he laboured for the next ten years (1678—1688). He married a lady, Johanna Eleonora von Merlau, of great piety, and soon after formed the acquaintance of the Frl. von Asseburg, whose visions and prophecies were beginning to excite attention. This remarkable person first opened his mind to wider views on the subject of God's present revelations to His Church. In the account of her which he published[1], he writes:—"As therefore we as yet knew not anything of these Heavenly Testimonies, or of the manner in which the Lord gave and dictated them, He was pleased to comfort and lift us up, who were wearied, and despised before the world for having believed and witnessed to His Kingdom. On the 20th day of October of the year MDCXC. we received this Testimony by this Blessed Maid, which here follows: 'I the Spirit of Love, I the Truth of Jesus Christ, do in the Spirit witness and declare, that ye my dear friends do stand in the truth....I have witnessed this in the Spirit from the abundance of the love which I bear towards you. Amen.' Reading from this Divine ex-

---

[1] "*A Letter to some Divines, concerning the Question, Whether God since Christ's ascension doth any more reveal Himself to Mankind by means of Divine Apparitions? With an exact account of what God hath bestowed upon a Noble Maid.*" (Written originally in High-Dutch, and now set forth in English by the Editor of the Laws of Paradise. London, 1695.) This editor was Dr Francis Lee, a physician of note, and one of Lead's supporters in the Philadelphian Society.

APPENDIX C.

hortation and encouragement (continues Petersen), of which we had no manner of doubt, we fell upon our knees, giving thanks for it, and directing our vows to God the Father of our Lord Jesus Christ, of sacrificing up to him our whole life, of placing our confidence in him preferably to all Men, and of declaring abroad his holy truth" (p. 43 ff.).

On these matters becoming public, Petersen was subjected to new attacks, which resulted in his suspension from his post of Superintendent at Lüneburg, to which he had been promoted in 1688, and in 1692 he was compelled once more to depart, and for ever to relinquish the work of public ministrations. Supported by friends, he was enabled to live in peace on a little estate near Magdeburg, which he exchanged subsequently for one in the neighbourhood of Zerbst, occupying the remainder of his life by writing in defence of the new Revelations, and later in organizing the German branch of the Philadelphian Society. He died on the 31st of January, 1727. The genesis of opinions in Petersen's case is precisely what we have found in Montanism, viz. :

1. Chiliastic views (leading to—)
2. Expectation of Divine aid in preparing the True Church for its future glory.
3. Joyful reception of prophetic claims.

A full statement of his theology will be found in the Articles of the Philadelphian Society (vide infra, p. 15 ff.), in which, if he took no part in their drawing up, he expressed his full agreement. It remains to be observed of Petersen that he had no insignificant claims to notice as a scholar and poet, apart from his theology. Leibnitz edited his *Uranias de operibus Dei magnis*, and his *Stimmen aus Zion* (Halle, 1698—1701) contain passages of real poetic value.

Before passing to the more important English branch, it is necessary to note the appearance in Germany, during Petersen's career, of a far less laudable character. Eva von Buttlar, a woman of birth and position, was attracted by the almost universal pietistic movement in the North of Germany in the last years of the seventeenth century, and joined a community of separatists, in which she soon gained the predominant influence. The opinions of this " Christliche u. Philadelphische Gemeinde" (of course not to be confounded with the real Philadelphian Society), were simply Millennarianism and opposition to outward forms, and involved at first no claim to new revelations. A stringent asceticism was proclaimed, and marriage between unbelievers was declared sinful. But the same degrading obscenities connected with a supposed purification of sexual intercourse were introduced (as by the Brüggler in 1750, and the Königsberg "Mücker" in 1835—40), which ended in whole-

E. von Buttlar. (1670— 1721.)

sale prostitution. Eva claimed to be the "Heavenly Sophia," and the "Gate of Paradise," and at last, with her companions Winter and Appenfeller, actually the incarnate Trinity! In 1704 the first rumours became public; discovery and arrest followed; the culprits escaped to Cologne and embraced Catholicism in order to avoid legal pursuit. But in 1706 they were once more seized and condemned to imprisonment, after which this disgraceful sect disappears from history[1]. {APPENDIX C.}

Having fairly noticed an instance where fraud and obscenity assumed the covering of spiritual elevation, we now turn to the events in England which accompanied the labours of Petersen. Jane Lead was born in Norfolk in 1623. Early in life she relinquished worldly pleasures, although not moving in Puritan circles, and in her 19th year she began to claim revelations from the Holy Spirit. She married in the year 1644, and had four daughters, one of whom was subsequently married to Dr Francis Lee, the secretary and editor-general to the Society. Jane Lead was a woman not only of deep religious convictions, but of considerable mental power. Her numerous works, whether we accept their spiritual claims or not, cannot be condemned as the ravings of a visionary, although their literary form (when Dr Lee's hand is not employed) is certainly open to criticism. Her views were identical with those of Petersen, and are found expressed clearly and tersely in the subjoined Articles. The inmost and highest tenets (for there was undoubtedly an esoteric creed even within the spiritual code), are to be found in *The Laws of Paradise*[2], first published in 1695, but circulated in MS. many years before. Lead's powers shone to special advantage as an organizer, and to her talent and diplomatic tact is due the formation of the Philadelphian Society and the affiliation of the kindred communities in different parts of Europe. Even those who condemn in other respects, will admire the wisdom which inspired the Constitutions. Her chief assistant in the work was John Pordage, a clergyman who had also imbibed his theosophic principles from Boehme's works, although he claimed the authority of individual revelation. He relates that near midnight on the third of January, 1651, he had three visions, which were repeated constantly for three weeks, and shared by other members of the {Pordage. (1608—1686.)}

[1] See Keller's *Die Buttlarische Rotte*, in Niedner's *Zeitschrift*, 1845, and especially Goebel's *Geschichte des christl. Lebens in der rhein-Westphal. evang. Kirche*, II. 778 ff. Since writing the above, I learn that a monograph by L. Christiany, (Stuttgart, 1870), which I have not seen, throws new light upon this rather unpleasant chapter of history.

[2] *The Laws of Paradise, given forth by Wisdom to a Translated Spirit.* (London, 1695.) The "Spirit" is Jane Lead, and the editor was Dr Francis Lee mentioned above.

APPENDIX C. Society who had been collected together. The accounts of these manifestations led to Pordage's deprivation in 1654, after an investigation before the magistrates of Berkshire[1]. The Philadelphians now moved to London, and held regular meetings, continued until the Plague drove many of the members, including Jane Lead, into the country. The Society did not return to London until the year 1670, and in fact from this year alone its public existence and complete organization may be dated. Pordage procured a house for its meetings, and the number of members rose to more than a hundred, Thomas Bromley, Edward Hooker, and Sabberton, being the most important. He continued however to be its leader until his death in the year 1686[2].

We have few records of the Society during the next ten years, but in 1697 a monthly magazine was established, entitled the *Theosophical Transactions*, in which general articles, letters, and poetry appeared.

Finally, it remains to notice the connection between the English and foreign Philadelphians. Before 1694, a German, Loth Fischer, living at Utrecht, engaged in the translation of Lead's writings and their circulation on the continent. Petersen and his wife warmly welcomed the new allies, and a correspondence ensued which cemented the alliance. An inspector for Germany was appointed, Johann Dittmar von Salzungen, and provided with due credentials and instructions, being specially charged to promulgate the Fundamental Articles of Faith, the twelve Rules of outward conduct (vide infra), and also the 44 Constitutions[3]. A common seal was introduced, with a mystical figure upon it, and the inscription "*Non est vol. nec curr. sed Dei miseric.*" The idea of a fixed contribution to a common fund did not find favour with the Germans. Notwithstanding

[1] The proceedings are minutely, although rather malevolently, recounted in Fowler's *Dæmonium Meridianum. Satan at noon, or Antichristian blasphemies, anti-scriptural divisions . . . . . evidenced in the light of truth, and punished by the hand of justice.* (London, 1655.) Pordage replied with *Innocency revealed* (1655), and, at the close of the same year, by another pamphlet, entitled *Truth appearing through the clouds of undeserved scandal and aspersion: or a brief and true account, &c. &c.*

[2] Pordage's works are very scarce, the British Museum only containing the two above-mentioned. Others, which I have not seen, are mentioned by Poiret in his *Bibliotheca mysticorum selecta*, p. 174; and the whole subject is well treated by Hochhuth in some articles in Niedner's *Zeitschrift*, the same writer contributing a valuable article in Herzog's *Real-Encyclopädie*.

[3] These are in MS. in the library of Gotha. A German translation is in Niedner's *Zeitschr.* xxxv. 228 ff.

differences between Dittmar and Gichtel, the Society continued to flourish until the year 1703, when some secessions took place, including that of Dittmar, it is said on Spener's advice. In the following year Lead met with an accident, her death following on the 19th of August, 1704. She was buried in Bunhill Fields, the gravestone bearing the following inscription:

A. Ω.

Exuvias carnis hic deposuit Venerabilis Ancilla Domini Jane Lead, anno Peregr^{is}. suæ LXXXI.

After her death the London Society soon lost its importance, and gradually was dissolved. Although traces of her influence are found in England in the eighteenth century, it is in Germany that her legitimate successors appeared.

Jane Lead's Works[1].

1. The Heavenly Cloud. (1682.)
2. Revelation of Revelations. (1683.)
3. Enochian Walks with God. (1694.)
4. The Fountain of Gardens. (1696—1700.)
5. Laws of Paradise, Wonders of God's Creation. (1695.)
6. The Ark of Faith. (1696.)
7. The Tree of Faith. (1696.)
8. Messages to Philad. Soc. (1696.)
9. Revel. of everlasting Gospel. (1697.)
10. Messenger of Universal Peace. (1698.)
11. Ascent to Mount of Vision. (1699.)

Petersen's Works.

1. Die Oeffnungen des Geistes. (?1690.)
2. Der Schlüssel z. heil Offenbarung. (1691.)
3. Die offene Thür der heil. Offenb. (1692.)
4. Das Geheimniss des in der letzten Zeit gebährenden apokalyptischen Weibes. (1693.)
5. Wahrheit des herrlichen Reiches, J. C. (? 1693.)
6. Geheimniss der Wiederbringung aller Dinge. (1701-1710.)
7. Erklärung der Psalmen und Propheten. (1719—1723.)

The Fundamental Propositions of the Society are as follows:—

I. The Church, or Bride of Christ, is to be made conformable to Christ throughout. (Rom. viii. 29 ff.; Phil. iii. 10—21; 1 John iii. 1—3.)

II. This conformity is the adornment of the Lamb's Bride, who is now called to make herself ready. (Is. lxi. 10; Rev. xxi. 2.)

III. This preparation and adornment cannot be otherwise, but by the Holy Spirit of God. (John iv. 24; Rom. viii. 11; Gal. iv. 6.; Is. xliv. 3; Joel ii. 28; Zech. iv. 6.)

IV. This Spirit is one: and thence the Church must be also but one. Herein consists the true undivided Unity, and

---

[1] All published in London.

perfect Uniformity. (Cant. vi. 9 ; Eph. iv. 3, 4 ; 1 Cor. vi. 17 ; Phil. i. 27.)

V. This Spirit is Holy : and thence the Church must be also Holy. Herein consists the virgin sanctity of all the members of this Church, that is to be redeemed out of the Earth. (Cant. iv. 1 ; Rom. xi. 16 ; Eph. i. 4 and v. 2 ; Col. i. 22 ; 1 Pet. ii. 5 ; Rev. xiv. 4—xx. 6.)

VI. This Spirit is Catholic : and thence the Church must be also Catholic, according to the most strict sense of the Word, in an universal latitude of love, without any narrowness, partiality, or particularity of spirit. (Gen. i. 2, vi. 3 ; Joel ii. 28 ; John iv. 21 ; Luke x. 30—38 ; Acts x. 11—16 ; 1 Cor. ii. 10.)

VII. This One, Holy, and Catholic Church is not barely assisted by an Irradiation from the Spirit of Christ, but is actually and vitally informed by it, as the body is by the soul. (Rom. viii. 6—10 ; 2 Cor. iii. 6—iv. 10, 11 ; Gal. ii. 20 ; Col. iii. 3, 4 ; Eph. iv. 18 ; Heb. vii. 16.)

VIII. This vital operation and information being at present but in a very languid and faint degree, there must be a resuscitation and resurrection of the same, in order to the glorious kingdom of Christ. (Ezek. xxxvii. 1—15 ; Luke xviii. 8 ; Acts xv. 16, 17 ; Rev. xx. 5.)

IX. The resuscitation of this spirit is to be waited for. (Is. xl. 31 ; Mark xiii. 33 ; Rom. ii. 3 ; 1 Cor. xii. 31 ; Eph. vi. 18.)

X. It is to be waited for not only separately, but also jointly. (Acts i. 14—ii. 1—46.)

XI. Such a waiting is in obedience to our dear Lord and Master's command. (Matt. xxv. 13 ; Mark xiii. 37 ; John xiv. 16.)

XII. It must be with these qualifications : (1) Humility, (2) Resignation, (3) Perseverance. (James iv. 10 ; Rev. iii. 17, 18 ; Rom. viii. 27 ; Col. i. 9 ; Matt. x. 22—24 ; Heb. vi. 14 ; Rev. ii. 26.)

XIII. It must be for these ends : (1) Power from on High (Luke xxiv. 49 ; 1 Cor. v. 4 ; 2 Tim. i. 7) ; (2) Wisdom from Above (Luke xxi. 15 ; 1 Cor. xii. 8 ; Col. ii. 3) ; and (3) Divine Learning and Theosophy (Eph. iii. 4 ; Phil. iii. 8 ; 2 Pet. iii. 18).

XIV. It is lawful to wait upon God for power from on high, or the return of the miraculous deeds, by which His kingdom, that has hitherto been withheld, may come to be witnessed and proclaimed. (Luke xxiv. 49.)

XV. It is lawful to wait and pray for the spirit of wisdom and revelation, descending from the throne of God. (Col. i. 9 —iii. 16.)

XVI. This is necessarily required in order to a right APPENDIX government in all spiritual affairs. (Is. xxviii. 26 ff.; Acts vi. C. 3; 2 Tim. iii. 15.)

XVII. It is lawful to wait and pray for divine learning, and to prefer it above that which is human. (Is. xxviii. 9; Hab. ii. 14; Phil. i. 9.)

XVIII. This secret learning vastly exceeds the wit and industry of the most sagacious enquirers. (Job xxviii. 7; Ps. xxv. 12.)

XIX. It shall be given of the Lord to all the members of this church. (Is. iv. 5; Jer. xxxi. 34; Eph. iv. 13; Heb. viii. 11.)

XX. God is stirring up some persons in several countries, to wait in faith and prayer until such a pure church may arise.

XXI. To which a prospect of the present state of Christendom has very much conduced. (Dan. vii. 8; Matt. xxiv.; Mark xiii.; Luke xvii.; John v. 16, 17.)

XXII. The many divisions and sects of Christianity, all pretending to be the true church, cannot be otherwise cured but by the effusion of the Spirit. (Jer. xxx. 17 ff.; Ez. xi. 19; Zeph. iii. 9.)

XXIII. The insufficiency of all other means and methods have been hitherto experimentally proved: (1) Of Human Learning, (2) Of Policy, (3) Of Power.

XXIV. Neither of which, separately or conjointly, is able to heal the divisions, supply the imperfections, or remove the corruptions of any one body of Christians. As (1) In the Church of Rome, (2) In the Lutheran Church, (3) In the Calvinistic or Reformed Church, (4) In the Church of England.

XXV. The consideration of the insufficiency of all human means, with a deep sense that Charity is waxen cold, and that Faith is hardly to be found, must needs excite us to wait upon those means which are sufficient. (Dan. ii. 34; Zech. ii. 13 ff.)

XXVI. These means are not confined to a party, but are extended to all; even as far as the Holy Catholic Spirit reacheth, which passeth and goeth through all things: and by the effusion of this Spirit, all shall be taught OF GOD. (Is. liv. 3; John vi. 45.)

XXVII. The Oneness, the Holiness, and the Catholicity or Universality of this Spirit, will not suffer us to appropriate it to any, and therefore not to our own Society, both with respect to ordinary and extraordinary operations of the same. (Rom. x. 12; 1 Cor. xii. 13; Gal. iii. 26 ff.; Col. iii. 11.)

XXVIII. The design of our assembling is not to divide, but to unite; not to set up for a new religion, or Church, but to keep warm the spirit of love towards those of all religions and churches, and to endeavour after the only method of reconciling them into a perfect and lasting unity, by the power of the Holy Ghost. (Is. lviii. 12.)

[**** In pursuance of this proposition, it has been our custom to advise persons, when interrogated, to keep still the bond of peace in the visible unity of the Church. And even our assemblies have been very far from being grounded on sectarian principles, as we are able to demonstrate.]

XXIX. Catholic Love, and Apostolic Faith, are the two grand pillars of our Society, and the main objects for which we labour and pray, both separately by ourselves, and jointly in our assemblies. (Gal. v. 6; Eph. vi. 23; 1 Thess. v. 8; 1 Tim. i. 14.)

XXX. The primary object of the Apostolical Faith is the revelation of the kingdom of God within the soul. (Luke xvii. 21; 1 Cor. iv. 20; Col. i. 13.)

XXXI. This internal revelation is by Christ, the sovereign Head of the Church. (1 Cor. xii. 5 ff; Heb. i. 2.)

XXXII. Which, as it is diligently to be waited upon, so is it to be held fast, so far as it shall be received; a loss herein, or a relapse, being extremely dangerous. (Heb. iii. 6, iv. 14, x. 23; Rev. ii. 4, 5.)

XXXIII. Such a Revelation of the kingdom of God will constitute a Virgin Church, representative of its Head in (1) Holiness, (2) Truth, and (3) Power. (Lev. xi. 44; Joel iii. 17; Obad. 17; Acts viii. 10; 1 Cor. i. 24; Phil. iv. 8; 2 Thess. i. 17.)

XXXIV. The members of this Church are to be anointed with Christ, and consecrated into (1) the Priestly Order, (2) the Prophetical, (3) the Royal and Davidical Order. (Zech. xii. 8; 1 Cor. iv. 8, and xiv. 31; 1 Pet. ii. 9; Rev. i. 6, v. 10, xx. 6.)

XXXV. The model thereof we do press after as attainable, and do not therefore rest in what we have attained. (Phil. iii. 12.)

XXXVI. The perfection of this model must be gradual, and the beginnings therefore of it consistent with a state of weakness and imperfection. (Acts xx. 32; Heb. vi. 1, 2; Jude 20.)

XXXVII. The Personal Appearance of Christ from Heaven is not to be, till after there be such a Philadelphian Church on Earth to receive him. (Rev. iii. 11; compare with xxii. 7, 17.)

XXXVIII. Our design is Apostolical; abating only from what was of a temporary constitution, or fitted to such a particular Church. (Acts i. 26, iv. 34, 35, xv. 13—30; 1 Cor. vii. 25.)

XXXIX. The Will of God must be done in Earth as in

Heaven, by the Inspiration of His Spirit. (Matt. vi. 10; Heb. x. 7.)

XL. The Kingdom of God must come on Earth, as it is in Heaven, by Virtue of the same Inspiration. (Dan. ii. 44, vii. 27.)

XLI. We receive the Holy Scriptures of the Old and New Testament as the foundation of our Hope and Faith. (2 Tim. iii. 16; 2 Pet. i. 19.)

XLII. There are some promises and prophecies which have not had yet their full completion. (Luke xxii. 16; Rev. xvii. 17.)

XLIII. The Civil Government is an Ordinance of God, as He is the Supreme Governor of the World, and is accordingly to be submitted to. (Rom. xiii. 1; 1 Tim. ii. 2.)

APPENDIX C.

[It is curious to note that the "Short Project of the Manner of Education of Youth," published in the same number of the *Transactions*, embodies all the main ideas which J. J. Rousseau and Basedow afterwards made into a system.]

IN THE NAME OF HIM WHO HAS THE KEY OF DAVID!

(We design not to set up any Form, or to lay any Burthen either upon ourselves, or upon others; but to maintain the Evangelical Liberty of Prophesying to all those that are, or shall be, anointed with the Spirit of Christ. However, it seems good to us, after having waited for the counsel of the Holy Spirit hereupon, to propose some certain Orders and Constitutions both to ourselves, and others whom they may concern, that may be either desirous to be admitted into our Society, or else inquisitive to hear a reason of our Faith or Hope.)

Philadelphian Constitutions. *Transactions*, p. 221.

I. Let one of the Society open the Assembly with reading some portion of the Holy Scriptures. Upon which he, or any other, may have leave to prophesy, and to unveil the Mysteries of the Kingdom of God therein contained.

II. Let every one that prays or prophesies first wait in silence to be filled with the sweet internal breathings of the Divine Spirit upon their soul, before they presume to break into words.

III. Let none confine this spirit to any, or go about to restrain the various manifestations of it in such as are sanctified and taught by it.

IV. Let none erect to themselves hereby such a superiority as we esteem inconsistent with the Philadelphian purity of brethren and sisters.

Appendix C.

V. Let there be a free liberty granted for any one of the strangers, if touched in their hearts by the Holy Ghost, to take up the Scriptures and read some portion in them (according to the custom admitted in the Jewish Synagogue, and then in the Apostolical Church), and to expound the same experimentally, or any otherwise to declare the movings and teachings of God upon their souls.

VI. But that abuses and disorders may be herein prevented, let there be no disputative or controversial way of propounding anything admitted, neither let there be asking of questions, which may engender strife; but let all be done and spoken for the promotion of Peace and Love.

VII. However, if there be any doubts upon the hearts of any who truly love the Lord Jesus, and desire to be obedient to His Gospel, they may after the hours of our solemn worship propose the same, either by word or writing, but rather by the last, to be considered of by the Society, in presenting before the Lord what shall be so proposed. And, if they desire it, let a private hearing be appointed for them by some of the members of the same.

VIII. Let also, for the same end, all they who prophesy be so far subject to the spirit of the Prophets, as united and combined together; that none of an irregular conversation be permitted to take up the Name of the Lord, or to speak as from His Spirit, till after a sufficient satisfaction be given.

IX. Let even the true spirit of Prophecy, wherever it shall be found, be under regulation; as anciently, in the schools of the Prophets: therefore let those who prophesy learn how and when to obey the conduct thereof; for (1) Imitation, (2) Exhortation, (3) Comfort.

X. If a woman pray or prophesy, let it be with all sobriety and modesty, to speak forth her own experience, sensation, or manifestation in the Divine matters.

XI. Let the various operations of the Spirit of Prophecy be encouraged and excited, for the ends proposed in the Reasons for the Foundation of our Society; what is not according to these, let it be rejected.

XII. Let not the manifestations of the Spirit be hindered in exercise, though attended with weakness: but rather let it be encouraged in the inferior degrees, so that all shall finally come to speak as the very Oracles of God, without the alloy of their own natural imperfections.

APPENDIX D.

SWEDENBORG.

SCHWEGLER, in his final chapter upon the later echos of Mon- tanism, declares summarily that Swedenborgianism is "a renovation of the Montanistic system[1]." What grounds are there for this statement? Their examination, in any case, must throw light upon the subject, regarded from the stand-point of this essay.

Swedenborg claimed to have received direct revelations.— He relates that from his earliest childhood he had seen flames, heard admonitions, and had remarkable dreams. But the year 1745 (when he had attained the age of 57), was the beginning of his Seership. From that time he noted all visions in his Dream-Book, and regarded them as the materials for the most careful investigation. His theory of seership is that every man possesses, while in the body, spiritual senses, which may be, and in many cases have been, opened; contrary to the usual notion that angels and spirits render themselves visible by a temporary assumption of a material form, dissipated as soon as the purpose of the vision is accomplished. [He naturally referred to Numbers xxiv. 3, 4, and 2 Kings vi. 16, 17, in confirmation of his opinion.] Swedenborg claimed to have enjoyed the privilege of seership for twenty-seven years; and that he was thus enabled to live consciously in both the natural and spiritual worlds, to converse with the inhabitants, and to have cognizance of the affairs of both. He erects a distinction between prophets and seers. Some seers were prophets, but all the prophets were not seers. Indeed, it by no means follows that "seers" must necessarily be good men or women. Seer-

[1] "Endlich ist noch kurz darauf aufmerksam zu machen, dass die Kirche des Neuen Jerusalems so viele grossentheils frappant-ähnliche montanistische Züge an sich aufweist, dass man den Swedenborgianismus ohne Bedenken eine Repristination des Montanismus nennen kann." (p. 312.)

APPENDIX D.

ship is the normal condition of all, and, according to Swedenborg, will become the actual condition in the future. It does not involve a sixth sense, but the twofold range of each of the five senses, with the addition only of an internal consciousness of the truth [1]. It does not concern us to enquire here into the substance of these alleged revelations, except as regards the doctrines which he educed, and upon which we shall treat later. The second question is as to the object for which these revelations were afforded. Swedenborg answers it thus:—

Its object.

I. "To learn the true doctrines of the Christian religion, by entering intellectually into the things of faith, that thus I might teach them authoritatively to mankind."

II. "To learn the true and internal signification of the Word of God, and show that therein consists the genuine inspiration of the Scriptures [2]."

III. "To learn the true relationship between the natural and spiritual worlds, and, in the 'science of correspondences,' supply at once a key to this relationship, and also to that which subsists between the spiritual and natural senses of the Scriptures."

IV. "To learn concerning the states of man in the other life, the nature of heaven and hell, the character of heavenly

[1] See *Four Leading Doctrines*, § 4; *True Christian Religion*, § 192; *Heaven and Hell*, p. 41.

[2] There can be no doubt but that Swedenborg, probably through ignorance, ascribed to his own revelation a theory of Inspiration which very many earlier writers had already adopted. Möhler, who devoted a considerable portion of the *Symbolik* to an examination of his tenets, has a good passage on the subject:—"But what is Swedenborg's distinction between the various senses of Holy Writ other than the Sod, Derusch, and Phaseuth, of the Cabbala,—senses which themselves respond to the σῶμα, ψυχή, and πνεῦμα of Philo? And wherein do the Swedenborgian correspondences differ so essentially from the celestial and terrestrial Jerusalem (the ἄνω and the κάτω 'Ιερουσαλήμ), the carnal and the spiritual Israel (the 'Ισραὴλ σαρκικός and πνευματικός) with which the same Philo had made us acquainted? And what shall we say to the astounding assertion, that in the first centuries of the Church the allegorico-mystical exegesis was unknown? Just as if Basilides, Valentinus, and Origen had lived in the sixth century! That Swedenborg should have possessed any acquaintance with the writings of Gregory the Great, of Alcuin, of Richard of St Victor, or with the description of the three senses given by Thomas Aquinas and others, it would be too much to require of him, &c. &c." (*Engl. Transl.* II. 304.)

Mr Clissold, the learned and able champion of the New Church, wisely thinks "that it is not desirable to divert the attention from the main subject, by entering into the questions here raised by Möhler, and which after all are very superficial." (*Spir. Exp. of the Apoc.* I. 28.)

joys, employments, habitations, and scenery, and of infernal miseries; the relationship between life in this world and the next, and to solve the problem of the fate of the heathen."

V. "Learn from angels concerning creation, preservation, and Providence, the origin of evil, and the ultimate triumph of goodness, and make known such angelic wisdom to man."

VI. "Learn concerning the sanctity and perpetuity of the marriage relationship, and make known to the world the real nature of the spiritual difference between the sexes; the true character of conjugal love, and its heavenly blessedness; and, contrarily, of the real character of adulterous love, and its infernal pleasures."

VII. "Be the witness of the great event in the spiritual world, which is so frequently referred to in the Word as the 'Last Judgment,' and thus be the forewarner of mankind of the vast spiritual, mental, and political issues which should result therefrom."

VIII. "That I might thus be an instrument in the Divine hands of aiding in the inauguration of a new age for the Christian Church, an age of clearer light, more fervent love, more intelligent faith, and more devout charity; which new state of the Church, I assert, was predicted in the Apocalypse of John, under the symbol of the descent of the New Jerusalem."

In these articles of belief (all of which find their fulfilment in Swedenborg's works, according to his adherents,) we trace several notes of similarity to Montanism, and also some striking differences. In both the doctrine of the non-finality of the Gospel dispensation appears, and in both the possibility of the direct intercourse of man with the Divine Spirit; but the mode of revelation is widely diverse. The Montanist prophet falls into a trance or ecstasy, and there receives the higher instruction, which he sometimes communicates in a fragmentary, oracular form. The Swedenborgian is armed with the two theories, viz. of the three senses of Scripture, literal, spiritual, and Divine, and of correspondences, and with these he operates upon the Bible, in the coolest and most matter-of-fact mental condition. There is a remarkable similarity between the ideas of Swedenborg and Tertullian on the subject of marriage. It is true that the special polemical discussions of the latter are wanting in the former, but there is the same lofty ideal of the spiritual as well as carnal union of the Christian man and wife. Finally, it was neither intended by Montanus, nor by Swedenborg, to found a sect, or separate Church. In the Church of the future, Swedenborg declared that there would be slight doctrinal differences, but a far broader charity: at

APPENDIX D.

present his doctrines are fitted to be the esoteric creed within the worship of any religious community[1].

But the great gulf is in the region of pure dogma. The Swedenborgian conception of the Trinity can only be described as Sabellian, and Tertullian would certainly not have welcomed into the ranks of the Pneumatici one who asserted: "that Jehovah Himself, and not a Son born from eternity, became incarnate in the world; that the Divine Trinity is a Trinity of Essentials in the One Person of the Lord Jesus Christ; that He, as to the Divinity, is the Father, as to the Humanity is the Son, and as to the Divine proceeding, operative energy, or outflowing Spirit, is the Holy Ghost; that during His sojourn in the world, He made His humanity Divine from the Divinity which was in Him, and which thus became one with the Father, &c." This doctrine was developed by Swedenborg in his treatise published in 1763 [*Doctrine of the N. J. respecting the Lord*], and sufficiently prevents any complete approximation with the original Montanists, although possibly there may be analogies with the Æschinist sect. The obvious reaction against the vulgar rationalism of the eighteenth century (as also in Lavater and St Martin) must not be disregarded.

[1] The Swedenborgianism of the present day has degenerated into mere sectarianism, nor are there any signs in England or Germany of future vitality. The only two men of note since Swedenborg's time were Dr Tafel of Tübingen, who wrote an able reply to Möhler; and Mr Clowes of Manchester, a clergyman of the Church of England. The latter was denounced as a heretic to the excellent Bishop Porteus of Chester, who sent for him, heard his views, and dismissed him with the assurance that he found nothing repugnant to Scripture or the Anglican formularies. Fortunately there was no Praxeas here to force "litteras pacis revocare emissas." (See Compton's *Life of Clowes*, London, 1874, p. 27.)

APPENDIX E.

CHRONOLOGICAL TABLES, A.D. 130—250.

Anno.	Emperor.	Bp. of Rome.	Political and Ecclesiastical Events.	Ecclesiastical Writers.	Events connected with Montanism.	Anno.
130	Hadrian.	Telesphorus.	Hadrian arrives in Egypt in the Autumn (Clinton, *F. R.* 118), passes in next year to Syria. Founds Ælia Capitolina.	Aristo of Pella.	Montanus begins to teach at Pepuza in Phrygia: is joined after a time by Maximilla and Priscilla: they attract no especial notice for some years, or none beyond a limited area.	130
1						1
2			The Jewish War (revolt of Bar Cochba).			2
3			Jewish War still continues: the rebels torture the Christians for not joining them. (Hieron. *Chron.* Ann. 2149.) War ends.	Eusebius places Basilides in this year. Agrippa Castor flourished. Eus. *H. E.* iv. 7; Jer. *Vir. Ill.* 21; Theod. *Hær. fab.* i. 4.		3
4						4
5						5
6		Hyginus.	"Telesphorus, 11 Jahre, Märtyrer, † frühestens 135, spätestens 137." (Lipsius. Pearson gave 122. Cf. *M. Theol. W.* ii. 497.)	Hermas. Cf. Mosheim, *de rebus ante C. M.*—p. 164.	Opposition on the part of some bishops.	6
7						7
8	Antoninus.		"Valentinus et Cerdo sectæ Marcionitarum antistes Romam venerunt."			8
9						9

158 CHRONOLOGICAL TABLES, A.D. 130—250.

Emperor.	Bp. of Rome.	Political and Ecclesiastical Events.	Ecclesiastical Writers.	Events connected with Montanism.	Anno.
Antoninus.	*Hyginus.*	Hieron. Anno 2156. "Hyginus, 4 Jahre. † frühestens 139, spätestens 141." (Lipsius.)			140
	Pius.				1
					2
		"Valentinus ab hoc tempore usque ad Anicetum permanebat." (Euseb. *Chron.* Anno 2159.)			3
					4
		Birth of Severus.			5
			Justin Martyr: *Apology* (1). [2nd Apol. & Dialogue in 146—7. (Hort ap. Westcott.)] Justin Martyr. †		6
					7
				The Asiatic bishops determine upon more active measures: Apollinaris, bishop of Hierapolis, convenes a Synod in his city. It is attended by twenty-six bishops, and it promulgates a condemnation of the Prophets.	8
					9
			Marcion taught. (He was still living when Clemens Alex. wrote the *Stromata*.) Ἡγήσιππος. Eusebius makes him remain at Rome μέχρι τῆς ἐπισκοπῆς Ἐλευθέρου. Bardesanes born.	Second Synod held at Anchialus by Sotas, bishop of that city, with twelve others: here also a condemnation is pronounced. (II. § 5.) Phrygian sympathisers with Montanism begin to settle in countries beyond Asia: some in Gaul, but not yet in Africa, nor are there any signs at Rome.	150
					1
					2
					3
				Montanus †.	4
	Anicetus.	"Pius, Bischof im engeren Sinn, 15-16 Jahre, † frühestens 154, spätestens 156." (Lipsius.)		Maximilla still survives: Themiso and Alcibiades are the official leaders under her.	5
					6
					7
					8
					9
M. Aurelius.	Anicetus.	Verus associated in the Empire. *Parthian War.* "Imminebat Britanicum bellum, et Cattu in Germaniam ac Rhoetiam irruperant." (Capitolin. c. 8.) Death of Peregrinus. (Lucian.)		Montanism begins to make way at Rome: Proculus arrives between 160—170. Many join him.	160
					1
					2
					3
					4
					5

CHRONOLOGICAL TABLES, A.D. 130—250.

Bishop	Year	Event	Literature/Notes
Soter.	6		
	7	Martyrdom of Polycarp. (Al. A.D. 169.) "Anicetus, 11 oder 12 Jahre, † 166–167." (Lipsius.) Death of Verus.	Thomiso writes a "catholic epistle" in defence of Montanism. [Euseb. v. 18].
	8		
	9		
	170		First official manifestation at Rome against the Montanists: "Scripsit contra Montanistas Soter papa urbis." *Pred.Her.* xxvi.
	1		Athenagoras περὶ Χριστιανῶν. [So Clinton, but Pagi prefers 166; Mosheim 177; Baronius 179.]
	2		Theophilus, Br. of Antioch, flourished. (Hieron. *Cat.* 25.) Melito. Eus. *H. E.* iv. 26, & Hieron. *Vir. Ill.* 24.
	3	"Soter, 8-9 Jahre, † 174 oder 175." (Lipsius.) *The Miraculous Rain.* (Related by Dio, Capitolinus, Claudian, Themistius, among secular writers, and by Tertullian, Eusebius, Orosius, Greg. Nyssen &c.)	
Eleutherus.	4	The Emperor at Athens. *Persecution of the Christians in Gaul* (p. 39 in the Essay). Martyrdom of Pothinus.	Eleutherus strongly against the Montanists.
	5		
	6		
	7		Letter of the Gallic Martyrs.
	8		Ἰρηναῖος ἐπιστολὴ περὶ σχίσματος, written (in answer?) to Blastus. (? *Montanist.*)
	9		Theophili ad Autolycum libri tres.
	180		Irenæus adv. *Hæreses.*
	1	Roman successes in Britain.	Miltiades "Scripsit M. contra gentes volumen egregium."
	2		
	3		Origen born.
	4		The epistle from the Gallic Confessors to the Asiatic Churches and to Eleutherus: this results in a virtual amnesty during the life of that bishop.
	5	"Eleutherus, 15 Jahre, † 189, Commodi x." (Lipsius.)	Death of Maximilla.
Victor.	6		
	7		Serapion writes against Montanism. "S. undecimo Comm. imp."
	8		Miltiades writes against the Montanists: "scripsit contra eosdem volumen præcipuum." (Hieron. *Cutal.* 39).
	9		
	190		Great efforts on both sides: Victor, preparing to crush the Quartodecimans, is inclined
	1		

160 CHRONOLOGICAL TABLES, A.D. 130—250.

Anno.	Emperor.	Bp. of Rome.	Political and Ecclesiastical Events.	Ecclesiastical Writers.	Events connected with Montanism.	Anno.
192	Commodus.	Victor.	Commodus slain, ἐν τῇ τελευταίᾳ τοῦ ἔτους ἡμέρᾳ. (Dio. 72.)	anno, scripsit Epist.... de hær. Montani". (Hier. Catal. 41.)	to make allies of the Montanists.	2
3	Pertinax. Julianus.		Purchase of the Empire by Julianus.	Clement of Alexandria.	Victor determines to acknowledge the Prophets: the "letters of peace" are already signed, when Praxeas arrives,	3
4	Severus.		Severus besieges Byzantium.—Praxeas at Rome.	Pantænus flourished.	and succeeds in rescinding them. Asterius Urbanus(?ap. Euseb.) writes against the	4
5			Excommunication of Theodotus the tanner.	Clemens Alexandriæ presbr. & Pantænus philosophus stoicus nostri dogmatis illustres erant.	M^{us}. "14 years after the death of Maximilla."	5
6			Byzantium taken after a three years' siege.	[Hieron. Anno 2210.] Rhodon. (H. E. v. 22.)	Victor's Letter to the Asiatic Bishops.	6
7			Beginning of the (renewed) Easter-dispute: [see Eus. H. E. v. 23 ff.] This date given by Jerome.			7
8			Asiatic Bishops resist.	Tertullian:—Apology. Ad Nationes. De Pænitentia; De Oratione; De Baptismo, Ad Martyres; Ad Uxorem; De Patientia; De Præscr. Hær.; De testimonio Animæ.	Spread of Montanism in Africa.	8
9			"Victor, 9—10 Jahre. † 198 oder 199." (Lipsius.)			9
200		Zephyrinus.				200
1			Persecution under Severus. Martyrdom of Perpetua and Felicitas at Carthage.	Clement's Stromata. Irenæus †. Origen (æt. 18) teaches at Alexandria.	Tertullian becomes a Montanist: writes his—De Corona Militis; De fuga in persec.; De cult. fœminarum; De virg. velandis; De exhort. castitatis; De Monogamia; De Paradiso; De Jejuniis; De Ecstasi; De Pudicitia; De censu Animæ; De Anima; De Carne Christi; De Res. Carnis; De Spectaculis; Adv. Marcionem (Pame-	1
2						2
3						3
4						4
5						5
6						6
7			Severus goes to Britain.	"Tertullianus celebratur." (Hieron. Chron.)		7
8						8
9						9
210						210
1	Caracalla.					1

CHRONOLOGICAL TABLES, A.D. 130—250.

Macrinus.				
Elagabalus.				
	Callistus.	The massacre at Alexandria.	Origen at Cæsarea. (*H. E.* vi. 19.)	lius gives 208); *Adv. Praxeam; Scorpiace; De Pallio; Adv. Valentinianos; Adv. Apelliacos; De Vestibus Aaron; Adv. Hermogenem; De Idololatria; De spe Fidelium; Ad Scapulam; Adv. Judæos* (continuation of treatise *Adv. Marcionem†); Ad amicum philosophum; De Animæ Submissione.* [*.*.*]
		"Zephyrinus 18—19 Jahre. †217, 26 August." (Lipsius.)		Caius writes against the Montanists: (Πρόκλῳ τῆς κατὰ Φρύγας προϊσταμένῳ αἱρέσεως ἐγγράφως διαλεχθείς.) *H. E.* vi. 20.
Alex. Severus.	Urbanus.	"Callistus, 5 Jahre, †14 Octob. 222." (Lipsius.)	Tertullian †. Hipolytus writes the "Ἐλεγχος κατὰ πασῶν αἱρέσεων." The best authorities do not venture to fix more nearly than A.D. 210—230.	*Proculus* † But his name adheres to the completely orthodox majority, while a section under Æschines adopts Noëtian or Sabellian views.
			Origen at Antioch. (Eus. *H. E.* vi. 21.)	The Procleian Montanists diminish in numbers at Rome: in Africa a separate sect of Tertullianists is formed. [Cf. Augustin. *Hær.* 86: "Tertullianistæ .... usque ad nostrum tempus paulatim deficientes."]
			Origen ordained a presbyter. (*H. E.* vi. 23.)	
	Pontianus.	"Urbanus, 8 Jahre, †230." (Lipsius.) Persian War. (*Lamprid. Alex.* c. 50 *ff.*)	"Origines hoc tempore in scholâ versabatur Alexandriæ." (Hieron. Anno 2245.)	
			Origen at Cæsarea. (Eus. *H. E.* vi. 26, 27.)	

. As has been remarked before, this list only attempts to make an approximate *order*, and does not propose to fix the *extent* of the period.

CHRONOLOGICAL TABLES, A.D. 130—250.

Anno.	Emperor.	Bp. of Rome.	Political and Ecclesiastical Events.	Ecclesiastical Writers.	Events connected with Montanism.	Anno.
233	Alex. Severus.	Pontianus.	"Pontianus, 5 Jahre 2 Monate, 7 Tage; dankt ab 28 Sept. 235; Severo et Quintino Coss., deponirt 13 Aug. 236." (Lipsius.)	Porphyry born.	The Synod at Iconium determines to reject *all* heretical baptism, including that of the Montanists.	3
4						4
5	Maximin.	Anteros.	Persecution of Christians, chiefly in Asia Minor.	Origen *De Martyrio*.	A Montanistic Prophetess appears in Cappadocia, obtains many followers. [Recorded by Firmilian in his Epistle to Cyprian. See lib. I. § 11, note.]	5
6		Fabianus.	"Μαξιμῖνος . . διωγμὸν ἐγείρει etc." (Eus. *H. E.* vi. 28.)			6
7			"Anteros, 1 Monat 12 Tage, † 3 Jan. 236." (Lipsius.)			7
8	The Gordians. Pupienus and Balbinus. Gordian.					8
9				Origen writes τὰ εἰς τὸν Ἠσαΐαν, ... καὶ τὰ εἰς τὸν Ἰεζεκιήλ." (Eus. *H. E.* vi. 32.)		9
240						240
1						1
2						2
3	Philip.		Persecution entirely ceases. (Cf. Eus. *H. E.* vi. 34, 36.)			3
4						4
5				Cyprian appointed Bp. of Carthage.		5
6						6
7						7
8	Decius.		Great Persecution. "Fabianus, 14 Jahre 10 Tage, Märt. in der Dec. Verfolgung. 20 Jan. 250." (Lipsius.)	Origen imprisoned and tortured. (Eus. *H. E.* vi. 39.)		8
9		Interregnum.	"Sedisvacanz vom 21 Januar, 250, bis Anf. März 251." (Ibid.)		The remaining Montanists coalesce in the schisms of Novatian and Felicissimus.	9
250			Schism of Novatian commences.			250
1	Gallus.	Cornelius.		Epistle of Cornelius to Fabius.		1

2	3	4	5	6
—	Lucius. Stephen.	Council at Carthage. "Cornelius, 2 J. 3 M. 10 T. † Mitte Juni 253 zu Civita Vecchia in Verbannung." (Lipsius.) "Lucius, 8 M. 10 T. † 5 März 254." (Ibid.) Synods on subject of Heretical Baptism.	Origen †. Firmilian's Letter to Cyprian.	Synods at Carthage. Bishop Stephen declares the Montanistic Baptism valid. A proof that some were returning to the Catholic Church.
—	Valerian.			

INDEX.

A.

Absolution, 86 et seq.
Acta Perp. et Felic. 44, 99, and App. B.
Adamites, 121
Æschines, 35, 54
African Church (Progress of Montanism in), 44
Alcibiades, 35, 62, note 3
Alexander, 35, 94
Alogi, 49 et seq.
Alombrados, 3
Amalric of Bena, 120
Ambrose, 10
Ambrosiaster, 13
Anabaptists, 2, 123
Anchialus (Synod at), 37, 158
Anicetus, 41, notes 2 and 3, 158
Apollinaris, 6, note 2
Apollonius, 6, 80
Arnold, 15, 16, 110
Artotyriti, 30, note 2
Asceticism, 79 et seq., 112, 113, 117
Asterius Urbanus, 6, note 2
Athanasius, 9, 30
Athenagoras (theory of inspiration), 66, 67
Asia Minor (Progress of Montanism in), 36
Augustin, 10, 13, 53 and note 1, 138, 139
Authorities, list of, 22 et seq.

B.

Baptism, 98
Baronius, 15, 39, 41, 62
Basil, 70
Baumgarten-Crusius, 55, 56
Baur, 1, 5, 7
Beausobre, 117, note 2
Bertôt, 125
Blastus, 36
Boehme, 2, 124
Bonacursus, 119
Browne (bp. of Winchester), 4, 89
Buttlar (E. von), 123, 144, 145

C.

Caius, 48
Cataphrygians, 29, 30
Cathari, 119
Cerinthus, 50
Chiliastic doctrine, 77, 116
Chladenius, 82
Church (Montanistic doctrine of), 91
Clemens Alexandr., 9
Confessors of Lyons, 38 et seq.
Councils which dealt with Montanism, 36, 37, 51
Cyprian, 7, 8, 115
Cyril Hieros., 9, 71, 77, 100, 101

D.

Daillé, 11 and note 1, 117 and note 3
David of Dinant, 120
Didymus Alexandrinus, 10, 115
Dionysius   ,,   , 49
Dodwell, 26, 41, 115
Döllinger, 23, 73
Donatists, 118

E.

Ebionites, 33, note 3, 101
Eckert of Schönau, 119
Ecstasy, 62, 63 et seq., 114
Ekhart, 120
Eleutherus, 39, 41 and notes 2, 3
Epiphanius, 8, 10, 25 et seq.
Eschatology (Montanistic), 77 et seq.
Eusebius, 6, 8, 25 et seq.
Exomologesis, 87, 88

F.

Fasting (cf. Asceticism)
Fénelon, 3, 125
Firmilian, 7, 54, 69
Flathe, 23, 119, 120
Fox (George), 3, 124
Fraticelli, 2, 120

G.

Gervaise, 16, 17
Gieseler, 54, 119
Gnostics, 104, 105

Gregory of Nazianzum, 9, 10, 54
Groot (Gerard), 120
Guibertus de Novigento, 119
Guyon (Madame), 3, 125

H.

Hagenbach, 23, 73
Hahn, 23, 119
Harnack, 21, 49
Hase, 122, 124
Hauber, 58
Hebrews (Epistle to the), 48
Hefele, 8, 21, 26, 37, 51, 52
Hegesippus, 38
Heinichen, 19, 49
Hermas, 38, 82, 86
Herzog's *R. E.*, 21
Hesselberg, 22, 47, 71
Hierapolis, 36
Hilary, 10
Hilgenfeld, 20
Hippolytus, 7, 69, 80, 131
Historic methods, 1 *seq.*
Homines Intelligentiæ, 2, 121
Hug, 49
Hurter, 138, 141

I.

Illuminaten Orden, 3
Infanticide (charged against the Montanists), 99 et seq.
Inspiration (Montanistic doctrine of), 62 et seq., 103, 114
Irenæus, 1, 6, 7, 111
Irving, 9, 129
Isidor of Pelusium, 12, 75, 101
Ittig, 15

J.

Jerome, 6, 13, 70, 80, 118
Jerusalem (the New), 3, 77, App. D.
John of Damascus, 14, 131
John the Evangelist, St, 49, 50
Justin Martyr, 65, 72, 78

K.

Kallistus, 7, 100
Kaye, 46, 59, 78
Kestner's "*Agape*," Appendix A.
Kirchner, 19
Königsberg "*Mücker*," 127, 128
Kühlmann, 126, 127

L.

Labadie, 3, 124
Laodicea (council of), 37, 52
"Laws of Paradise," 115

"Lay-gentleman" (hist. of Montanism by), 24, 101, 114
Lead (Jane), 124, Append. C.
Lee (Archdeacon), 67, 68
Lee (Dr Francis), 24, 143, 145
Leucius (or Lucius), 35, 36
Libellus Synodicus, 37
Lipsius, 8, 20, 21, 75, 157 *et seq.*
Longuerue, 18, 32
Lucian, 136
Luther, 124

M.

Macarius, 67
Manichæanism, 119
Marcion, 91, 106, 158
Marius Mercator, 13, 14
Marriage, 83
Martyrdom, 93 *et seq.*
Maximilla, 25, 27, 28, 34 *et seq.*
Melito, 159
Merkel, 19, 49
Merlau (Frl. von), 143
Mennonites, 130
Middleton, 16, 17
Miltiades, 47, 48, 62, 111, 159
Möhler, 19, 105, 123, 154
Molinos, 3, 125
Möller, 21
Monarchianism, 73 *et seq.*
Montanus, 3, 4, 27, 28, 30, 31 *et seq*, 34, 36, 40
Morcelli, 22, 45, 139
Mormons, 128
Mosheim, 16 *et seq.*, 25, 59, 62
"*Mücker*," 123, 127, 128
Münter, 22, 138
Muratorian Fragment, 48
Mysteries, 99, 100

N.

Neander, 12, 19, 20, 41, 42, 45, 46
Noble Leyczon, la, 120
Nösselt, 120
Novatianists, 118

O.

Olivus, 121
Optatus Milev., 12
Origen, 7, 9
Orsi, 23, 35, 44, 138

P.

Pacian, 8
Papias, 78
Paraclete (the), 40, 58 *et seq.*, 71, 79
Patripassianism, 73

INDEX.

Pelagius, 11
Penance, 87
Pepuza, 30
Pepuziani, 30
Perpetua, 44, 99, 131, Append. B.
Petersen, 65, 124, Append. C.
Philadelphian Society, Append. C.
—————— Constitutions, 151
—————— Articles, 147
Philaster, 10, 11, 59
Philo, 154
Phrygian Religions, 9, 19, 102 *et seq.*
Pietism, 124
Pneumatici, 91 *et seq.*
Poiret, 16, 23, 125
Polycarp, 38
Pordage, 145, 146
Prædestinatus, 14, 29, 42
Praxeas, 8, 38, 40 *et seq.*, 70, 71
Priesthood, 93
Priscilla, 34
Proclus (or Proculus), 35, 43, 53
Prophetic gifts, 31, 58 *et seq.*, 114
Pseudo-Tertullian, 24, 35, 69
Psychici, 91

Q.

Quakers, 3, 124
Quintilla, 34

R.

Reformation, 122, 123
Réville, 18, 20
Rhodon, 6
Ribovius, 11
Rigaltius, 56
Ritschl, 20 *et passim*
Rome (progress of Montanism at), 37
Rothe, 6
Routh, 15, 41
Ruel, 18

S.

Sabellianism, 69 *et seq.*
Saint Cyran, 3
Saturus, 140
Savonarola, 122, 123
Schönherr, 127
Schroeckh, 19
Schwegler, 20 *et passim*
Semisch, 66, 79, 86

Serapion, 6
Sibylline Oracles, 32
Socrates, 42, 75
Sotas, 36
Soter, 29, 41
Sozomen, 42
Spirituales, 31, 120
Stationes, 82
Strauch, 18
Ströhlin, 21
Sulp. Severus, 40
Swedenborg, 3, Appendix D.

T.

Tauler, 120
Tertullian, 5, 22, 45 *et seq.*, Book II.
    passim, 111, 115, 131
Tertullianists, 53
Themison, 35
Theodoret, 14, 69
Theodotus, 35
Thiersch, 1
Thomasius, 23, 113
Tillemont, 6, 15, 95
Trinity (Montanistic doctrine of the), 68

U.

Uhlhorn, 6, 22, 47, 138, 139

V.

Valois, 6
Vater, 41
Victor, 7, 41, 42
Volkmar, 21, 48

W.

Walch, 19, 39
Waldenses, 2, 119
Wernsdorf, 18, 30, 44, 62, 75, 82
Westcott, 3, 68

X.

Xerophagiæ, 81 *et seq.*

Z.

Zephyrinus, 41, 88
Zinzendorf, 127
Zoticus, 47

York Street, Covent Garden,
September 1876.

THEOLOGICAL WORKS

PUBLISHED BY

GEORGE BELL & SONS.

BARRETT (A. C.) Companion to the Greek Testament. For the use of Theological Students and the Upper Forms in Schools. By A. C. Barrett, M.A., Caius College. *Third edition, enlarged and improved.* Fcap. 8vo. 5s.

This volume gives in a condensed form a large amount of information on the Text, Language, Geography, and Archæology; it discusses the alleged contradictions of the New Testament and the disputed quotations from the old, and contains introductions to the separate books.

BARRY (Dr.) Notes on the Catechism. For the Use of Schools. By the Rev. Alfred Barry, D.D., Principal of King's College, London. *Fifth edition, revised.* Fcap. 2s.

BLEEK (F.) An Introduction to the Old Testament. By F. Bleek. Edited by J. Bleek and A. Kamphausen. Translated from the second edition of the German by G. H. Venables, under the supervision of Rev. E. Venables, Canon of Lincoln. *New edition.* In 2 vols. Post 8vo. 10s.

BLENCOWE (E.) Plain Sermons by the Rev. E. Blencowe. Vol. I. *Sixth edition.* Fcap. 8vo. 6s.

BLUNT (J. S.) Readings on the Morning and Evening Prayer and the Litany. By J. S. Blunt. *Third edition.* Fcap. 8vo. 3s. 6d.

—— Life after Confirmation. 18mo. 1s.

BOYCE (E. J.) Examination Papers on Religious Instruction. By Rev. E. J. Boyce, M.A. Sewed. 1s. 6d.

—— Catechetical Hints and Helps. A Manual for Parents and Teachers on giving Instruction in the Catechism of the Church of England. *Third edition, revised and enlarged.* Fcap. 2s. 6d.

> 'Perhaps the most thoroughly *practical* little book on its subject we have ever seen. Its explanations, its paraphrases, its questions, and the mass of information contained in its appendices, are not merely invaluable in themselves, but they are *the* information actually wanted for the purpose of the teaching contemplated. We do not wonder at its being in its third edition.'—*Literary Churchman.*

BUTLER (Bp.) Sermons and Remains. With Memoir by the Rev. E. Steere, LL.D., Missionary Bishop in Central Africa. 6s.

*** This volume contains some additional remains, which are copyright, and render it the most complete edition extant.

CARTER (T. T.) The Devout Christian's Help to Meditation on the Life of Our Lord Jesus Christ. Containing Meditations and Prayers for every day in the year. Edited by the Rev. T. T. Carter, Rector of Clewer. 2 vols. Fcap. 8vo. 12s. Or in five parts, three at 2s. 6d., and two at 2s. each.

DAVIES (T. L. O.) Bible-English. Chapters on Words and Phrases in the Authorized Version of the Holy Scriptures and the Book of Common Prayer, no longer in common use; illustrated from contemporaneous writers. By the Rev. T. Lewis O. Davies, M.A., Vicar of St. Mary-extra, Southampton. Small crown 8vo. 5s.

> 'We can heartily commend this book.'—*Saturday Review.*
> 'Every one who takes an interest in the history of the English language, and indeed every one who is not absolutely inattentive to the words spoken around him, may turn to Mr. Davies's little book with the certainty of finding both useful information and agreeable entertainment in its pages.'—*Pall Mall Gazette.*

DENTON (W.) A Commentary on the Gospels for the Sundays and other Holy Days of the Christian Year. By the Rev. W. Denton, A.M., Worcester College, Oxford, and Incumbent of St. Bartholomew's, Cripplegate. Vol. I. Advent to Easter. *Third edition.* 18s. Vol. II. Easter to the Sixteenth Sunday after Trinity. *Second edition.* 18s. Vol. III. Seventeenth Sunday after Trinity to Advent; and Holy Days. *Second edition.* 18s.

DENTON (W.) Commentary on the Epistles for the Sundays and other Holy Days of the Christian Year. By the Rev. W. Denton. Vol. I. Advent to Trinity. 8vo. *Second edition*. 18*s*. Vol. II. completing the work, 18*s*.

These Commentaries originated in Notes collected by the compiler to aid in the composition of expository sermons. They are derived from all available sources, and especially from the wide but little-known field of theological comment found in the 'Schoolmen' of the Middle Ages. The special nature of the sources from which they have been derived ought to make them indispensable to all who wish to expound the Holy Scriptures with as much understanding as may be obtained by extraneous help.

—— A Commentary on the Acts of the Apostles. Vol. I. 18*s*. Vol. II. completing the work, 14*s*.

GOODWIN (Bp.) Confirmation Day. Being a Book of Instruction for Young Persons how they ought to spend that solemn day. By the Right Rev. Harvey Goodwin, D.D., Bishop of Carlisle. Eighth thousand. 2*d*., or 25 for 3*s*. 6*d*.

—— Plain Sermons on Ordination and the Ministry of the Church. Preached on divers occasions by Harvey Goodwin, D.D. Crown 8vo. 6*s*.

'The suggestions offered in these pages are all in good taste, and inspired by a true regard for the interests of the Church.'—*English Churchman.*

'Very simple in their teaching, direct, unadorned, and not doctrinal.'— *Literary Churchman.*

—— Parish Sermons. By Harvey Goodwin, D.D. First Series. *Third edition.* 12mo. 6*s*. Second Series (*Out of print*). Third Series. Third edition. 12mo. 7*s*. Fourth Series, 12mo. 7*s*. With Preface on Sermons and Sermon Writing. 7*s*.

—— A Guide to the Parish Church. By Harvey Goodwin, D.D. 1*s*. sewed; 1*s*. 6*d*. cloth.

—— Lectures upon the Church Catechism. By Harvey Goodwin, D.D. 12mo. 4*s*.

—— Sermons Preached before the Universities of Oxford and Cambridge. By Harvey Goodwin, D.D. Crown 8vo 6*s*.

—— Plain Thoughts concerning the Meaning of Holy Baptism. By Harvey Goodwin, D.D. *Second edition*. 2*d*., or 25 for 3*s*. 6*d*.

GOODWIN (Bp.) The Worthy Communicant; or, 'Who may come to the Supper of the Lord?' By Harvey Goodwin, D.D. *Second edition.* 2*d.*, or 25 for 3*s.* 6*d.*

HARDWICK (C. H.) History of the Articles of Religion. To which is added a Series of Documents from A.D. 1536 to A.D. 1615. Together with illustrations from contemporary sources. By the late Charles Hardwick, B.D., Archdeacon of Ely. *Third and cheaper edition.* Post 8vo. [*In the press.*

HAWKINS (Canon). Family Prayers :—Containing Psalms, Lessons, and Prayers, for every Morning and Evening in the Week. By the late Rev. Ernest Hawkins, B.D., Prebendary of St. Paul's. *Fifteenth edition.* Fcap. 8vo. 1*s.*

HOOK (W. F.) Short Meditations for Every Day in the Year. Edited by the late Very Rev. W. F. Hook, D.D., Dean of Chichester. *New edition, carefully revised.* 2 vols. Fcap. 8vo. Large type. 14*s.* Also 2 vols. 32mo. Cloth, 5*s.*; calf, gilt edges, 9*s.*

—— The Christian Taught by the Church's Services. *A new edition, revised and altered to accord with the New Lectionary.* 1 vol. Fcap. 8vo. Large type. 6*s.* 6*d.* Also 1 vol. Royal 32mo. Cloth, 2*s.* 6*d.*; calf, gilt edges, 4*s.* 6*d.*

—— Holy Thoughts and Prayers, arranged for Daily Use on each Day of the Week, according to the stated Hours of Prayer. *Fifth edition, with additions.* 16mo. Cloth, red edges, 2*s.*; calf, gilt edges, 3*s.*

—— Verses for Holy Seasons. By C. F. Alexander. Edited by the late Very Rev. W. F. Hook, D.D. *Fifth edition.* Fcap. 3*s.* 6*d.*

HUMPHRY (W. G.) An Historical and Explanatory Treatise on the Book of Common Prayer. By W. G. Humphry, B.D., late Fellow of Trinity College, Cambridge, Prebendary of St. Paul's and Vicar of St. Martin-in-the-Fields. *Fifth edition, revised and enlarged.* Fcap. 8vo. 4*s.* 6*d.*

—— The New Table of Lessons Explained, with the Table of Lessons and a Tabular Comparison of the Old and New Proper Lessons for Sundays and Holy Days. By W. G Humphry, B.D. Fcap. 1*s.* 6*d.*

LEWIN (T.) The Life and Epistles of St. Paul. By Thomas Lewin, Esq., M.A., F.S.A, Trinity College, Oxford, Barrister-at-Law, Author of 'Fasti Sacri,' 'Siege of Jerusalem,' 'Cæsar's Invasion,' 'Treatise on Trusts,' &c. With upwards of 350 Illustrations finely engraved on Wood; Maps, Plans, &c. In 2 vols. *Third edition, revised.* Demy 4to. 2*l.* 2*s.*

―― Fasti Sacri; or, a Key to the Chronology of the New Testament. 4to. 21*s.*

LIAS (J. J.) The Doctrinal System of St. John, considered as evidence for the date of his Gospel. By the Rev. J. J. Lias, M.A., Professor of Modern Literature and Lecturer on Hebrew at St. David's College, Lampeter, sometime Scholar of Emmanuel College, Cambridge. Crown 8vo. 6*s.*

LUMBY (J. R.) History of the Creeds. By J. Rawson Lumby, M.A., Tyrwhitt's Hebrew Scholar, Crosse Divinity Scholar, Classical Lecturer of Queens', and late Fellow of Magdalene College, Cambridge. Crown 8vo. 7*s.* 6*d.*

MILL (Dr.) Lectures on the Catechism. Delivered in the Parish Church of Brasted, in the Diocese of Canterbury. By W. H. Mill, D.D., formerly Regius Professor of Hebrew in the University of Cambridge. Edited by the Rev. B. Webb, M.A. Fcap. 8vo. 6*s.* 6*d.*

―― Observations on the attempted Application of Pantheistic Principles to the Theory and Historic Criticism of the Gospels. By W. H. Mill, D.D. *Second edition, with the Author's latest notes and additions.* Edited by his Son-in-law, the Rev. B. Webb, M.A. 8vo. 14*s.*

―― Five Sermons on the Temptation of Christ our Lord in the Wilderness. Preached before the University of Cambridge in Lent, 1844. By W. H. Mill, D.D. *New edition.* 8vo. 6*s.*

MONSELL (Dr.) Simon the Cyrenian, and other Poems. By the late Rev. J. S. B. Monsell, LL.D., Vicar of St. Nicholas, Guildford. *Second thousand.* 32mo. 5*s.*

―― Watches by the Cross. Short Meditations, Hymns, and Litanies on the Last Seven Words of our Lord. *Third edition.* Cloth, red edges, 1*s.*

―― Near Home at Last. A Posthumous Poem. *Fifth thousand.* Cloth, red edges. Imp. 32mo. 2*s.* 6*d.*

MONSELL (Dr.) Hymns of Love and Praise for the Church's Year. By the late Rev. J. S. B. Monsell, LL.D., Vicar of St. Nicholas, Guildford. *Second edition*. Fcap. 8vo. 3s. 6d.

—— The Parish Hymnal; after the Order of the Book of Common Prayer. Cloth, 32mo. 1s. 4d.

—— Our New Vicar; or, Plain Words about Ritual and Parish Work. Fcap. 8vo. *Seventh edition*. 5s.

—— The Winton Church Catechist. Questions and Answers on the Teaching of the Church Catechism. 32mo. cloth, 3s. Also in Four Parts, 6d. or 9d. each.

PAPERS on Preaching and Public Speaking. By a Wykehamist. *Second thousand*. Fcap. 8vo. 5s.

PARISH PRIEST'S (The) Book of Offices and Instructions for the Sick. Compiled by a Priest of the Diocese of Sarum. Post 8vo. 3s. 6d.

PEARSON (Bp.) on the Creed. Carefully printed from an Early Edition. With Analysis and Index. Edited by E. Walford, M.A. Post 8vo. 5s.

PEROWNE (Canon). The Book of Psalms; a New Translation, with Introductions and Notes, Critical and Explanatory. By the Rev. J. J. Stewart Perowne, D.D., Canon Residentiary of Llandaff and Hulsean Professor of Divinity, Cambridge. 8vo. *Third edition*. Vol. I. 18s. Vol. II. 16s.

—— The Book of Psalms. An abridged Edition for Schools and Private Students. Crown 8vo. *Second edition in the press.*

SADLER (M. F.) The Church Teacher's Manual of Christian Instruction. Being the Church Catechism expanded and explained in Question and Answer, for the use of Clergymen, Parents, and Teachers. By the Rev. M. F. Sadler, Author of 'Church Doctrine—Bible Truth,' 'The Sacrament of Responsibility,' &c. *Thirteenth thousand*. Fcap. 8vo. 2s. 6d.

'It is impossible to overrate the service to religious instruction achieved by this compact and yet pregnant volume. . . . . We owe many boons to Mr. Sadler, whose sermons and theological lectures and treatises have wrought much good in matters of faith. This Catechetical Manual is second to none of such.'—*English Churchman.*

—— The Lost Gospel and its Contents; or, the Author of 'Supernatural Religion' refuted by himself. Demy 8vo. 7s. 6d.

SADLER (M. F.) The One Offering. A Treatise on the Sacrificial Nature of the Eucharist. Fcap. *Third edition.* 2s. 6d.

―― The Second Adam and the New Birth; or, the Doctrine of Baptism as contained in Holy Scripture. *Seventh edition, greatly enlarged.* Fcap. 8vo. 4s. 6d.

'The most striking peculiarity of this useful little work is that its author argues almost exclusively from the Bible. We commend it most earnestly to clergy and laity, as containing in a small compass, and at a trifling cost, a body of sound and Scriptural doctrine respecting the New Birth, which cannot be too widely circulated.'—*Guardian.*

―― The Sacrament of Responsibility; or, Testimony of the Scripture to the Teaching of the Church on Holy Baptism, with especial reference to the Cases of Infants; and Answers to Objections. *Sixth edition.* 6d.

―― The Sacrament of Responsibility. With the addition of an Introduction, in which the religious speculations of the last twenty years are considered in their bearings on the Church doctrine of Holy Baptism, and an Appendix giving the testimony of writers of all ages and schools of thought in the Church. On fine paper, and neatly bound in cloth. 2s. 6d.

―― Church Doctrine—Bible Truth. *Seventeenth thousand.* Fcap. 8vo. 3s. 6d.

This work contains a full discussion of the so-called Damnatory Clauses of the Athanasian Creed. The new edition has additional Notes on Transubstantiation and Apostolical Succession.

'Some writers have the gift of speaking the right word at the right time, and the Rev. M. F. Sadler is pre-eminently one of them. 'Church Doctrine —Bible Truth,' is full of wholesome truths fit for these times. . . . . . He has the power of putting his meaning in a forcible and intelligible way, which will, we trust, enable his valuable work to effect that which it is well calculated to effect, viz. to meet with an appropriate and crushing reply one of the most dangerous misbeliefs of the time.'—*Guardian.*

―― Parish Sermons. Trinity to Advent. *Second edition.* 6s.

―― Plain Speaking on Deep Truths. *Third edition.* 6s.

―― Abundant Life, and other Sermons. 6s.

―― Scripture Truths. A Series of Ten Tracts on Holy Baptism, The Holy Communion, Ordination, &c. 9d. per set. Sold separately.

SADLER (M. F.) The Communicant's Manual; being a Book of Self-examination, Prayer, Praise, and Thanksgiving. By the Rev. M. F. Sadler. Royal 32mo. *Seventh thousand.* Roan, 2s.; cloth, 1s. 6d. Also in best morocco, 7s.

⁎⁎ A Cheap Edition in limp cloth. *Nineteenth thousand.* 8d.

—— A Larger Edition on fine paper, red rubrics. Fcap. 8vo. 2s. 6d. ; best morocco, 8s. 6d.

SCRIVENER (Dr.) Novum Testamentum Græcum, Textus Stephanici, 1550. Accedunt variæ lectiones editionum Bezæ, Elzeviri, Lachmanni, Tischendorfii, et Tregellesii. Curante F. H. Scrivener, M.A., LL.D. 16mo. 4s. 6d.

This Edition embodies all the readings of Tregelles, and of Tischendorf's Eighth or latest Editions.
An Edition with wide Margin for Notes. 7s. 6d.

—— Codex Bezæ Cantabrigiensis. Edited, with Prolegomena, Notes. and Facsimiles, by F. H. Scrivener, M.A., LL.D., Prebendary of Exeter. 4to. 26s.

—— A Full Collation of the Codex Sinaiticus with the Received Text of the New Testament; to which is prefixed a Critical Introduction. *Second edition, revised.* Fcap. 8vo. 5s.

—— A Plain Introduction to the Criticism of the New Testament. With Forty Facsimiles from Ancient Manuscripts. Containing also an Account of the Egyptian Versions by Canon Lightfoot, D.D. For the Use of Biblical Students. *New edition.* Demy 8vo. 16s.

—— Six Lectures on the Text of the New Testament and the ancient Manuscripts which contain it. Chiefly addressed to those who do not read Greek. With facsimiles from MSS. &c. Crown 8vo. 6s.

THOMAS À KEMPIS. On the Imitation of Christ. A New Translation. By H. Goodwin, D.D. *Third edition.* With fine Steel Engraving after Guido, 5s.; without the Engraving, 3s. 6d. Cheap edition, 1s. cloth ; 6d. sewed.

YOUNG (Rev. P.) Daily Readings for a Year, on the Life of Our Lord and Saviour Jesus Christ. By the Rev. Peter Young, M.A. *Third edition, revised.* 2 vols. 8vo. 1l. 1s.

www.ingramcontent.com/pod-product-compliance
Lightning Source LLC
Chambersburg PA
CBHW032148160426
43197CB00008B/812